FROM TRAPPERS
TO TOURISTS

FREMONT COUNTY, COLORADO, 1830-1950

by

ROSEMAE WELLS CAMPBELL

CENTURY ONE PRESS
A DIVISION OF GRAPHIC SERVICES, Inc.

2325 East Platte Avenue
Colorado Springs, Colorado 80909

ISBN 910584-29-x

Printed in the United States of America

First printing, May 1972, is limited to 1000 copies
of which 600 are numbered and signed by the author.

To

The Fremont-Custer Historical Society

ACKNOWLEDGMENTS

I very much appreciate the kindness of those who loaned unpublished and other materials and the graciousness of those who granted interviews, brief or extensive. In addition to persons listed on the bibliography, I want to express my gratitude to others who assisted in furnishing information. These include Mrs. Grace Bennett of the Ramapo Catskill Library System, Middletown, N.Y., and past and present members of the staffs of the Canon City Public Library, the Canon City Municipal Museum, the Florence Public Library, the Florence Pioneer Museum, the Western History Room of the Penrose Public Library in Colorado Springs, the Colorado Room of The Colorado College Library, the Western History Collection of the Denver Public Library, the Library of the State Historical Society, and the Colorado State Archives and Record Center.

Thanks also go to those who corresponded with me on various points and to the many who kindly offered to reminisce but were not interviewed because of the necessity of keeping the length of the book within reasonable bounds.

Especial thanks go to Riley M. Simrall of Canon City who initially proposed such a book and who enthusiastically aided in gathering information during the six years of research. And to Lydia Simrall for her constructive comments on the manuscript. Without their persistent interest the book might never have been.

And, as always, thanks to my husband, William Tod Campbell, for his patience and proofreading.

R.W.C.

FOREWORD

While a good deal of history has been fitted into this small frame, much necessarily has been omitted. It is impossible to mention everyone whose existence was important to the growth of Fremont County in an account such as this. In order to sketch the entire canvas of the county's picture, I have had to choose representative examples from the many who gave direction to its development and from those whose lives were typical of their times. These, peopling the basic framework of business development in the county over 120 years, give hint of the social background of life in this place in those years. Many others, unsung, gave substance to each community as they made their places in history.

To keep footnotes to a reasonable minimum, I have limited them to sources that are not obvious from scanning the appended bibliography, or to references that call for some comment.

The sketch maps make no claim of utter accuracy. They are provided merely to assist the reader in realizing the relationship of localities.

Together, I hope that these parts provide a story of the continuity of the development of Fremont County, the longest settled in all Colorado.
Colorado Springs, February 1972.

Rosemae Wells Campbell

PUBLISHER'S NOTE

Except where used as part of a name or proper noun, the English spelling canyon is used. The Spanish tilde (~) was used in the name of the city, then dropped for a number of years, and recently resumed. Therefore in this book it is spelled Cañon City or Canon City as the period of usage dictated, or as it was used permanently in corporate or place names.

MAPS

CONTENTS

Part I Early Days

Part II Routing the Rails

Part III Royal Gorge and Westward

ILLUSTRATIONS

PART I

EARLY DAYS

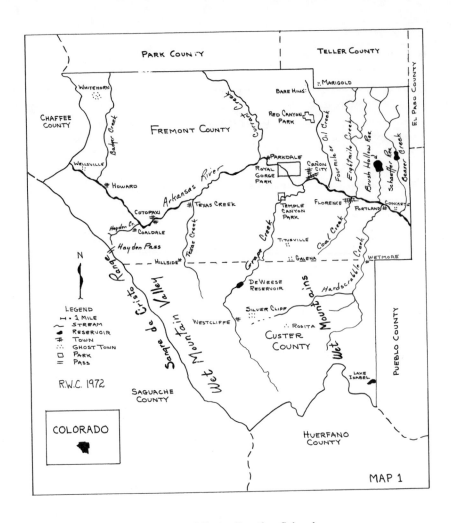

Fremont and Custer Counties, Colorado

The original boundaries of Fremont County, in the south central part of the State of Colorado, as surveyed by Anson Rudd, J. B. Cooper, and Lewis Conley in 1862 encompassed all of Fremont and Custer Counties indicated above, and more. The perimeter was eroded with the creation of adjacent new counties. The major deletion was Custer County's formation from the lower portion of Fremont County in 1877. The last loss of territory was the rectangle in the northeast corner that became part of newly organized Teller County in 1899.

CHAPTER I

THE GRAND CANYON OF THE ARKANSAS

Although the now renowned Royal Gorge received its name in rather recent times, the unique Grand Canyon of the Arkansas in present Colorado was millions of years in the making. The Arkansas River, with few tributaries, is one of the longest rivers in the United States. It drains an extensive area as it flows from its mountain source to the Mississippi. For thirty-four miles it winds through a canyon of unusual interest where the banding of granite and many dikes and veins reveal a variety of colors.

After the great inland sea that once covered the entire West was disturbed by violent upheavals, the Arkansas River began to flow to the east, finding a course on the sandstone, shale, and limestone of the exposed sea bed that lay above the Pre-Cambrian or granite formation. While the river wore a channel, a gentle upthrust continued as the mountain masses of the Rockies rose to their present heights. Thus the river, dropping some five thousand feet in the first one hundred twenty-five miles, cut through the rock as it rose until it severed the center of Fremont's Peak now a thousand feet above the surrounding countryside.

The rate of erosion by the Arkansas has been calculated to be approximately one foot every twenty-five hundred years. The persistent saw-like action of the sand and water on the granite river bed cut a gorge as narrow as fifty feet in some places and more than a thousand feet deep. A close look at the rock walls of the deep pass shows that this spectacular crack in the earth was not the result of an earthquake as geologists once suggested. The canyon follows the course of a meandering stream rather than a straight fissure. Scientists now agree that the Grand Canyon of the Arkansas is the result of erosion alone, a remarkable accomplishment for a young river.

This natural wonder probably looked much as it does today when the first human inhabitants arrived on the scene. The Utes, mountain Indians, frequently wintered in the area, and various Plains tribes, such as the Sioux, the Cheyenne, the Kiowa, the Blackfeet, and the Comanche, followed buffalo herds as they moved to mountain meadows in the spring and summer.

For years after the discovery of our continent, Spain held a large share of western North America as New Spain. Vast and remote, this colony slumbered undisturbed for a long time. Eventually, the Spanish missionaries of the seventeenth century learned of the Grand Canyon of the Arkansas when they journeyed north from their settlements in what is now the State of New Mexico. Some trappers also probably passed that way during the following century, but the few native residents knew nothing of the confusing political switches of sovereignity over the land they considered theirs.

In 1762, La Salle claimed for France all the land drained by the Mississippi River and her tributaries. Spain threatened war, but by 1801 Napoleon had forced her to cede the disputed territory to him. The new French-Spanish boundary was as vague as the guesswork map on which it was drawn.

The line was no firmer when France sold her Louisiana Territory to the United States in 1803. The geography of the region was still hazy when Zebulon Montgomery Pike continued up the Arkansas with a party of government explorers after an unsuccessful attempt to conquer the Grand Peak to the north that later bore his name.

Lt. Pike's party camped at the east entrance of the Grand Canyon of the Arkansas on the fifth of December, 1806. Three days later, while searching for a way through the narrow gorge, he discovered the hot springs on the south side of the river. Unable to proceed upstream, Pike and his men headed northwest to South Park, most probably following the well-defined Ute trail along present Fourmile, or Oil, Creek. What is now called Trout Creek led them to a larger river that they mistook for the long-sought Red, legendary boundary of the Territory. After a dangerous trip downstream, they were much embarrassed and disappointed to find themselves back at their camp of a month earlier.

They raised what was probably the first structure built by whites in present Fremont County, Colorado. Here, near the canyon mouth, they left part of the baggage with the weary horses in charge of the interpreter and another man. The rest of the party ventured on foot up Grape Creek into the Wet Mountain Valley and across the Sangre de Cristos into the San Luis Valley where the Spanish captured Pike, accusing him of trespassing. He was; perhaps not unwittingly.

When the boundary was clearly defined by treaty with Spain in 1819, the Arkansas River, plus a line due north from its source, wherever that might prove to be, became the fixed international boundary through present Colorado. Thus, all the present State to the west and south of the river was acknowledged Spanish territory.

Soon after this boundary was set on a still uncertain map, the United States Government sent out Major Stephen Harriman Long with instructions to explore the upper Arkansas. On July 18, 1820, Dr. Edwin James, Capt. J. R. Bell, and two men, left Long's camp near the junction of the Arkansas with La Fontaine qui Bouille (Fountain Creek) and proceeded up the river. They seem to have found no trace of Pike's structure. Like Pike, they were unable to discover a way through the gorge. Early maps indicate that Bell gave his name to several mineral springs which he found on the north bank.

The Arkansas marked the Spanish frontier only until 1821 when Mexico gained her independence. In 1836, Texas rebelled against Mexican dictatorship. The new Republic of Texas then claimed as her western border the Rio Grande plus a line due north from *its* source, wherever *that* was. Thus Texas was the third foreign country, until the United States annexed her in 1845, to occupy present Fremont County south and west of the Arkansas. Mexico disputed the Texas claim and continued to consider the region hers. This dispute was resolved by treaty in February, 1848, when Mexico ceded her territory north of the Rio Grande following the Mexican War.

Later, jurisdiction of the land on the north bank also changed a number of times before the present state and county governments were established. But the Grand Canyon of the Arkansas itself, rather than any government, was the obstacle that kept men from being attracted to that part of the country. The first settlers in present Fremont County, who came not from the East but from the South, ignored. the Canyon in favor of the well-watered valley of a small tributary some miles to the east.

For years these first attempts at settlement in the present State of Colorado have been forgotten or ignored. Recognition of the prior lures of farming and commerce perhaps tends to tarnish the glamor of the gold rush period. However, the adventure and profit of smuggling more than matched the early prospectors' experiences.

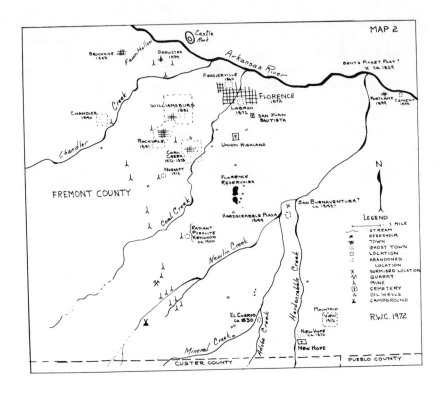

Earliest Settlements

The well-watered slope between the Wet Mountains and the Arkansas River attracted the earliest ranchers and farmers. Coal, oil, and the materials for cement were the magnets that attracted later arrivals.

CHAPTER II

HAMLETS ON THE HARDSCRABBLE

The lush valley of the Rio Peñasco Amarillo (now Hardscrabble Creek) was watered then by a stream as pure and purling as those that supplied Don Fernando de Taos,[1] the nearest settlement several days' journey to the south. East of the Peñasco, beyond the bounds of present Fremont County, the Trapper's Trail continued from the mouth of the Fontaine qui Bouille along the edge of the mountains south to Santa Fe, with a branch off to Don Fernando, then but a drab collection of adobe huts.

Samuel Chambers and his party attempted one of the earliest trading trips from the United States to the long inhospitable Spanish colony. Although these traders were clapped into jail for their trouble, Chambers elected to settle in Don Fernando de Taos when he was liberated nine years later. He was already at home in the little mud village when Matt Kinkead[2] arrived.

Kinkead had left Boone's Lick, Missouri, at the east end of the Santa Fe Trail with a group of traders headed for Santa Fe in 1824 when he was twenty-nine. He made another trip the following year, arriving in Taos with three mule loads of goods on which he paid duty. Matt may have been skilled in the art of making Missouri moonshine for, instead of returning to the States, he made plans with William Workman, a young Englishman, to start a distillery financed by Samuel Chambers. William Workman wrote to his brother, David, of Franklin, Missouri, close to Boone's Lick, to order two eighty-gallon stills and other articles to be sent out with Abraham Barnes. He explained that he and Kinkead would pay half the cost and Chambers would pay the rest.

While Kinkead was in Taos the winter of 1826-27, he harbored sixteen year old Kit Carson, also of Boone's Lick, who was then but a runaway apprentice from David Workman's saddle shop. Kit, the eleventh of his father's fifteen children, had probably lived at Fort Kinkead, built by Matt's father, while Kit's father and two elder brothers served there with the militia during the War of 1812. Kit spent the winter with Kinkead, then took off on his own. Kinkead became a Mexican citizen and was seen around the village the next several winters. He was no doubt running the stillhouse in Ranchos de Taos for John Rowland and Workman by the time the Bent boys, later to be founders of Bent's Fort, came to town.

Twenty year old William Bent very likely built the first trading post[3] in what was to become Fremont County, Colorado. If he did, it was probably in the winter of 1829 after he had been in Taos with his older brother, Charles. He is thought to have joined a group of independent trappers, including Charles Autobees, instead of returning east with the wagons. They took trade goods and went northeast to the Arkansas.

Historians fail to agree on the location of William Bent's picket outpost where he is known to have saved the lives of two trading Cheyennes by concealing them from a Comanche horse raiding party. Some suggest that it was on the north bank of the Arkansas near the mouth of the Rio Peñasco Amarillo just west of present Portland. This legendary post, wherever it was, can claim distinction as the first commercial establishment in the present State of Colorado.

Captain John Gantt[4] may have been in the area, too, for in that year he was dismissed from the Army after being accused, perhaps wrongly, of falsifying pay accounts. In 1831, he and his partner, Jefferson Blackwell, did take out a license that allowed them 180 gallons of whiskey to trade during a three year period. This was a niggardly amount compared to 2666 gallons allowed the American Fur Company for half that time.

Gantt and Blackwell traded at various locations. Later they had a fort on the Trapper's Trail near where it forded the Arkansas. To liven trade, Gantt is supposed to have sugared whiskey to make it palatable to the Cheyennes. This too could be a false accusation made by a rival trader since one, Tom "Broken Hand" Fitzpatrick, did seek to put him out of business by spreading rumors that Gantt was bankrupt and unable to buy any furs. Fitzpatrick then bought them himself and left none to go to Gantt. Whatever whetted the tribe's taste for whiskey, they were drunkards in a few years and the whites were more than happy to supply their demand.

The rewards of trapping diminished. More and more trappers turned to trading as the market for beaver began to break. Many a pack animal plodded along the Arkansas and its few tributaries.

Maurice LeDuc[5] was with William LeBlanc and some other French trappers working out of Taos when they established a post on the bluff at the confluence of Mineral and Adobe Creeks, tributaries of the Peñasco, to take advantage of the Ute traffic from the plains to the Wet Mountain Valley. The Indian trail led over Mosca Pass to the San Luis Valley then down to Taos. This post was known to Americans as the Crows' Nest or Buzzards' Roost and to Mexicans as El Cuervo because of the number of turkey buzzards that nested near the mouth of Mineral Creek.

Blond, blue-eyed, stocky Maurice LeDuc had left LaCrosse as a boy. By the time he was seventeen, in 1825, he had penetrated a large part of the far west wilderness with Tom (later Peg Leg) Smith. Young LeDuc's peregrinations are difficult to trace because there was another, older, Maurice LeDuc, possibly his father. Both men appear in records under a variety of bastardized spellings. It seems clear, however, that the younger was in and out of Taos from time to time. In the 1830's, he settled down

FORT MAURICE LEDOUX

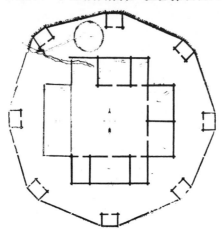

El Cuervo

This plan of the trading post was drawn by James McFall from measurements made by Fred Walters many years after it had been abandoned. *Courtesy of John R. McFall.*

El Cuervo

Harry Chalfont, using McFall's plan, fashioned this diorama of the trading post built in the 1830's. *Photo by the author.*

for a spell across the creek from El Cuervo. When he wasn't trapping, he cultivated the fields below his cabins. one a *jacal,* the other an adobe of several rooms.

By the time Gantt built near present Pueblo, William Bent was at Big Timbers near the mouth of the Purgatoire. He also had a small stockade about eight miles below Fountain Creek to tempt trade away from Gantt. Gantt countered by moving his post to within three miles of that spot and built his Fort Cass of adobe. Kit Carson worked for him there. William Bent soon put a black blot on his name by attacking a trading party of Gantt's Shoshone customers, killing three and carting off two women and thirty-seven horses. Although he allegedly did this in retaliation for Shoshone raids on Bent mules, it successfully served to drive away Gantt's customers.

Bent and his brothers soon began to build their impressive Fort William, later to be niched in history as Bent's Fort, near present La Junta. While these walls were going up, the United States Government, at the request of the big traders, outlawed liquor at trading posts on American soil with the idea that this might put the growing number of little traders out of business. Perversely, it had the reverse effect. Enforcement of the law sharply reduced the supply of spirits from the East. Although most of the large fur companies respected the restriction, at least while the authorities were looking, less law abiding individuals set up their own operations to fill the gap, some by supplying *aguardiente,* the fiery liquor known as Taos Lightning, distilled from wheat grown in Taos Valley.

Each year a varying number of Mexicans raised crops in the low valley of the Peñasco and returned to their villages in the winter. They began to remain in the area once there was a fortified post to protect them from the Indians. When Henry Dodge of the First Regiment of United States Dragoons, with Gantt as his guide, reached the Arkansas near the Peñasco on July 20, 1835, he noted that there were some sixty lodges of Arapahoes in camp there.

Matt Kinkead could well have spent his summers disposing of the product of the Rowland and Workman distillery at the various trading posts. He may have supplied El Cuervo. Later, Charles Autobees[6] possibly was there on a similar errand. After his contract with Wyeth expired in 1836 he had gone to Arroyo Hondo to work for Simeon Turley, another early distiller of the notoriously potent Taos Lightning. Autobees, a teetotaler, was Turley's head salesman for eleven years. He lead trains of mules packed with whiskey up San Luis Valley and over Sangre de Cristo Pass to the trading posts.

By the time Autobees began to peddle whiskey, Matt Kinkead had obtained a grant of land on the mountain branch of the Santa Fe Trail near the later town of Mora, New Mexico. His neighbors there included

Manuel Suaso, his wife, Maria Teresa Sandoval Suaso, and their four children. Sometime in the next few years, Manuel's "pretty as a peach"[7] Teresita either was widowed or left her husband to live with her bachelor neighbor and become the mother of Kinkead's children, Rafaela and Andres.

Rowland and Workman sold out in 1841 to head for California with other Americans made nervous by the increasing violence of the anti-foreign demonstrations and enraged at the unjust taxes heaped on foreigners and naturalized residents. By this time, Kinkead and his family had moved up to ranch on the Arkansas opposite the mouth of Fountain Creek. The hundred or so inhabitants of Fort William downstream provided a good market for meat and milk.

Kinkead hired young Richens Wootton,[8] who years later had a toll road over Raton Pass, to drive a flock of sheep to Westport, sell them, and buy forty milch cows. When Dick returned with these, he built a corral, caught forty-four newborn buffalo calves, and turned them in with the cows. Three years later, Wootton drove the calves back to Westport to sell them to a dealer supplying zoos and curiosity shows. In the meantime, Kinkead built a *jacal* hut below the Cañon del Rio Peñasco Amarillo where he ran cattle on the plentiful grass there in conjunction with his ranch to the east.

Some years earlier, George Semmes Simpson,[9] the well-educated, adventurous, black-sheep son of a St. Louis doctor, had determined to head West through the wilderness to Oregon instead of following his father's profession. In 1838, he was camping in barren Pah-Ute country with Calvin Briggs and other mountain men when Maurice LeDuc, his Shoshone squaw, Ka-Wat, and a couple of others who had lost their traps and most of their horses to the Indians, came into camp. The following June, Simpson met the trappers, Henry Fraeb and John Burroughs, who was a particular friend of Calvin Briggs.

Young Simpson evidently went back to St. Louis then to return again as a member of the California-bound Bidwell-Bartleson party in 1841. However, at Ft. Laramie, he decided to leave the party and go to Bent, St. Vrain and Company's Fort William. Simpson wrote to his family asking for a wagon load of trade goods. When it arrived, he set himself up as a trader in a room at the fort. While he was there, he met two of Bent's employees with whom he later became closely associated, Alexander Barclay, an Englishman, and Joseph Bainbridge Doyle,[10] an educated Virginian. In 1842, he joined the men who built an unauthorized trading post where the Trapper's Trail crossed the Arkansas near Fountain Creek, not far from Gantt's earlier post. They called this Nepesta, an early name for the Arkansas, but because of its adobe architecture, it soon became known as El Pueblo.

11

Matt Kinkead, who still ranched nearby, and Simeon Turley are among those who allegedly had an interest in this endeavor. There they traded in Taos Lightning brought in by pack mules over the then less commonly used route through the San Luis Valley. From the beginning, however, stock raising and farming were as important as trading at El Pueblo.

Busy as he was with the new trading post, Simpson had time for more romantic matters. On November 30, 1842, he married Teresita Kinkead's daughter, Juana. A notary at Fort William performed the ceremony despite the fact that, in the eyes of the Catholic Church, no civil officer had the right to do so.

Kinkead continued his bison business for a couple of years. Each spring he and Teresita drove cows out on the plains to persuade newborn buffalo calves to suck and follow their source of sustenance back to the ranch. When they were old enough to travel, the buffalo were driven east for sale, much to the annoyance of the Indians who felt that far too many buffalo were being appropriated, dead or alive, by the white men.

Although the eastern market for baby bison soon became saturated, the whiskey business boomed. Turley had to send to Missouri for a new still to supply the needs of all the little traders who were willing to sell whiskey and whatever wherever a customer could be found. Surely El Cuervo was one source of such illicit goods since it was located close to the mountain route to Taos, an official trading post since 1723 and the northernmost customs office in Mexico.

Avoiding customs while conveying contraband in and out of Mexico kept many a man busy, especially after Governor Manuel Armijo imposed an arbitrary duty of five hundred dollars flat on each wagon entering Santa Fe regardless of the value of its contents. Not only the small posts were guilty. Dick Wootton and John Hawkins, son of the maker of the famous Hawken rifle, once testified that they smuggled goods for Fort William in December, 1842. Neither bullion nor beaver could legally leave Mexico, but they packed $60,000 in specie, quite a fortune then, and a thousand pounds of beaver pelts on ten mules and sneaked them over Sangre de Cristo Pass to the fort.[11] No doubt many a trader on the return trip managed to carry forbidden sugar, tobacco, and coffee into Mexico disguised as approved commodities.

El Pueblo became the collecting spot for good men and bad when the hunters came in from the hills for the winter. Maurice LeDuc may have been in Kinkead's employ then since Lt. John Charles Fremont reported that Maurice was camped on Fountain Creek catching buffalo calves when he passed that way.

Bent and St. Vrain wrote an angry letter from Fort William on January 1, 1843,[12] complaining about the renegade Americans who had built houses near El Pueblo, a harbor for all Mexican whiskey traders. They were piously silent about their own trade in this beverage and suggested that establishment of a military post would put a stop to the liquor trade from Mexico. Possibly even then Simpson, Doyle, and Barclay were building yet another post on the American bank of the Arkansas opposite the mouth of the Peñasco, to be operated in conjunction with El Pueblo. This post, visited by Kit Carson, by then Charles Bent's brother-in-law, seems to have existed but briefly.

About this time, Simpson's father-in-law, Matt Kinkead, moved west to his ranch on the Peñasco where he built a house of upright logs for his family and *jacal* cabins for his hired hands. Calvin Briggs and his friend, John Burroughs, married to Shoshone sisters; LeDuc; Tom Whittlesey; Rube Herring; Gagnez; Six Hommes; LaFontaine; and others, retired trappers all, lived along the stream. They may have worked for Kinkead or at El Cuervo.[13]

That post was then a square of eight dirt-floored rooms whose doorways opened on an inner court. There was a large thick-walled adobe room, and smaller rooms built of wood except for their crude adobe fireplaces. A reservoir, twenty-four feet in diameter, served by a ditch, was within an outer picket enclosure that encircled the complex of rooms. In addition, evidence indicates outbuildings to the west, south, and east but none on the north where the land slopes down to the Arkansas in the distance.

In the early 1840's, Mexico made an effort to colonize her frontier south of the Arkansas to keep out the no longer welcome immigrants from America and to defy the new Republic of Texas. Several of her leading citizens, especially those not native born, were eager to establish interests away from distrustful Padre Martínez of Taos and suspicious Mexican officials.

Charles Beaubien,[14] a prominent naturalized Mexican of French blood, was among those who petitioned for property as the anti-foreign sentiment rose. In January, 1841, he and Don Guadalupe Miranda, a native, requested a grant of land east of the Sangre de Cristo Mountains. The nationalistic fervor that followed an aggressive expedition from Texas delayed his formal possession of this two million acre tract for two years. In the meantime, Beaubien went ahead with plans for peopling his property.

Governor Armijo in 1843 awarded Ceran St. Vrain,[15] another naturalized Mexican, and his co-petitioner, Cornelio Vigil, a grant comprising the four million acres that lay between Bent's Fort and the Beaubien and Miranda grant. Charles Bent soon had a substantial interest in both grants. That may account for the fact that Beaubien, St. Vrain, Bent, and Beaubien's son-in-law, Lucien Maxwell, are sometimes credited with establishing a colony near the confluence of Adobe and Newlin Creeks, southwest of the iron bridge on the old Hardscrabble Road out of present Florence, about six miles north of Kinkead's ranch.[16] These settlers were

13

possibly Taos farmers rounded up by Beaubien to settle on his grant. Impatient of Armijo's delay in the matter, they may have headed over the range to choose a likely spot for themselves on what they thought was part of Beaubien's expected property. This could have been an honest error since it was some years before there was an accurate map of the area. This group may have been the ones to call the location San Buenaventura de los Tres Arroyos in typical Spanish style. The settlement didn't last long although it had the advantage of relatively low altitude compared to Taos, broad bottc.n lands for raising corn, and water from three sparkling streams.

Utes of the mountains and Sioux and Arapahoes of the plains had long disputed claim to the area. Plains Indians, increasingly hostile since the independence of Texas, probably threatened the newcomers. Then Texan attacks on the Nueva Mexico border towns during the spring and summer of 1843 resulted in the ouster of all foreigners from Taos and a suspension of commerce between that supply point and the settlements to the north. Dictator Santa Anna's edict of August, 1843, officially closed the customs houses at Taos and Santa Fe and decreed that all trade between Mexico and the United States must stop. This state of affairs no doubt sent the Taoseños scurrying home.

There was evidently no one left at San Buenaventura when ex-trapper Andrew Drips, then a U. S. agent charged with preventing the importation of liquor into Indian country, reported in December that there were two towns of whiskey traders, one on a fork of the Arkansas and the other lately built in Spanish territory, the principal person in which was Kinkead.[17] This implies that Kinkead's cattle ranch was more than it appeared to be.

Since by this time Kinkead seems to have had an interest in El Cuervo, it is possible that, with his experience as a distiller, he actually made moonshine there to relieve the drought caused by the trade ban. One of the evidences that remained long after the buildings had disappeared from the site was the large cistern dug to hold water for those forted up there during Indian attacks. It could easily have been used by a distiller, too. In addition to ample water, El Cuervo was close to wooded slopes that could supply the necessary fuel.

Interestingly, Santa Anna had excepted from his edict foreigners who lived on Mexican soil with their families. When George Simpson heard this, he crossed the river and early in 1844 moved to the deserted San Buenaventura. With Joe Doyle and Alec Barclay, he built a trading post about one and one quarter miles above the junction of Newlin Creek on the west side of the Peñasco.

In a letter begun at El Pueblo in March and finished at San Buenaventura in April, 1844, Simpson reported to his cousin, George

Sibley, in Missouri, that he had located the settlement and persuaded seventy souls to join him there within the past six weeks. He also indicated that there was much fruit in the vicinity and asked his cousin to send apple seeds and whatever other seeds he had. Although Simpson was then but twenty-six, he confessed to a fondness for idleness and drink, but expressed hope that he'd make something someday.

The partners built a high adobe wall around their plaza to protect the motley mixture of whites and half-breeds. The good fortune implied in the Spanish name must soon have deserted the place for the inhabitants usually called it the Plaza del Rio Peñasco Amarillo, or simply La Placita. When the going got tough, it became Hardscrabble Plaza to the Americans.

As early as 1845, a St. Louis paper described Hardscrabble as an agricultural settlement of twenty-five families. It seems to have been the center of activity for the area, although there was a fandango now and then at El Cuervo or LeDuc's Buzzard Ranch.

The description of the Plaza as an agricultural settlement evokes a pastoral scene much more peaceful than the fragmentary records indicate. Other references to the settlement reveal that a reckless band of desperadoes there was responsible for illicit and destructive trade with the Indians. The residents cultivated corn which they traded to the tribes for robes and skins that in turn they bartered in Santa Fe or Taos for whiskey and flour for trading to the Indians at a high markup. They also obliged travelers by trading one sound head of cattle for two lame ones. In addition, they drove cattle to St. Louis for sale. The peons who did most of the work received from eight to twelve dollars a month in goods from the post.

When Isabel Simpson, the first white child born in present Colorado, arrived behind the high adobe walls in June, 1844, her birth was the occasion for a huge feast attended by Indians who came from miles around to see the paleface papoose. Simpson must have prospered there, for he entertained the idea of a church wedding in Taos, a luxury denied those who couldn't afford the outrageous fees charged by Padre Martínez in addition to the tithes expected by the church. The peons and poor, superstitious and ignorant, had to be satisfied with common-law marriages and to devise their own wedding celebrations, if any, since there was no provision for civil ceremonies under Mexican law.

That fall, when the Simpsons went to Taos to be properly married and baptised on November 14, 1844, Mrs. Simpson's thirteen-year-old sister, Maria de la Cruz Suaso, called Crusita, went along to marry Simpson's partner, Joe Doyle. The third partner was soon solaced by Teresita herself. She left her son with middle-aged Matt Kinkead and moved down to the Plaza to live with the Englishman. Barclay, then, became an in-law without the law, of both his partners.

15

The next winter left four feet of snow along the base of the mountains with more in the high mountain parks. It wiped out the upland buffalo and greatly reduced the herds of other large game. The settlements and Indians alike faced hard times. The natives grew less hospitable and begrudged having to share their reduced meat supply with a growing number of settlers. But the Indians weren't alone in causing trouble.

Albert C. Boone, grandson of the famous Daniel, is said to have had charge of the trading post at the Plaza during this time and was probably still there when Tom Whittlesey butchered his mistress, Candelaria Sena of Taos, and killed LaFontaine, with whom he accused Candelaria of having an affair. Tom fled to El Pueblo after he dismembered his erstwhile sweetheart.[18] Ever after called *Tomas el Matador,* he escaped with the aid of friends. LeDuc could have been one. He was at El Pueblo that year, temporarily without a woman. Agent Drips by this time considered the residents of both El Pueblo and Hardscrabble no better than outlaws. Stephen Watts Kearny also recognized Hardscrabble as a source of smuggled whiskey.

Unfortunately, accounts become confused because visitors sometimes referred to El Pueblo as Hardscrabble and to Hardscrabble as the upper Pueblo. Barclay noted on New Year's Day, 1846, that "all Hardscrabble is feasting at Maurice LeDuc's today".[19] Hardscrabble Plaza had reached its peak by the time Simpson's second child, Joseph Robert, was born on March 19, 1846. Dwellings along the creek housed Kinkead's hands and employees of the trading post. The dozen or so adobe rooms around the central plaza also were cozily crowded. Shortly after Marcelino Baca's daughter was born in his house on the rise one-eighth of a mile southwest of the Plaza,[20] the settlement dwindled even more rapidly than it had grown.

Word of the war with Mexico drove many back from the border. Baca took his wife and three children to Taos for the proper sacraments of marriage and baptism. They then returned to the more protected settlement that had grown up at Greenhorn where the Taos Trail crossed Greenhorn Creek.

Simpson and Doyle left to build a new place two miles up the Arkansas from El Pueblo. Barclay stayed on the Hardscrabble until fall. Before leaving on October 14, 1846, he recorded that he went up to cuckolded Kinkead's and met "the old man" face to face for the first time in two years. In December, after Boone had left with his large family, West Point graduate Lancaster P. Lupton opened a store in a building that he rented from Barclay.

Simpson, with his wife and children, then left for Taos. En route, because they learned of the brutal death of Governor Charles Bent during the attempted revolt of the Pueblo Indians and Mexicans on January 17,

1847, they turned back to winter at Greenhorn.

Simpson returned to the Plaza in March to put in a crop of corn. Lupton's account books to May, 1847, show him, Kinkead, and some ten other customers trading at the store but business was anything but brisk. In September, Tom Fitzpatrick, then an Indian agent, reported from Bent's Fort that the villages of Pueblo and Hardscrabble were resorts of idlers and loafers and were depots for the smugglers of liquor from New Mexico into the United States.

On October 10, 1847, when a band of hostile Arapahoes and Mexicans arrived, the few at El Cuervo sought refuge in the stockaded post. The Indians demanded LeDuc's wife as a pledge of peace. Maurice, who over the years had had a long succession of squaws and Mexican wives, spoke most of the local Indian languages as well as a mixture of French, Spanish, and English, usually all in one sentence. This linguistic peculiarity often affected the clarity of his accounts. In this instance, he seems to have claimed that he craftily parlayed with the braves until a courier could leave secretly to alert the Ute camp in the Wet Mountain Valley. There was a fierce battle after these allies arrived.

Luz Metcalf, whose husband, Archibald, had traded whiskey with the Cheyennes for Lupton until Fort Lancaster went out of business in 1844, was visiting at the Plaza at the time.[21] She reported that she and Teresita Barclay, Juanita Simpson, and Crusita Doyle could hear the guns six miles away. Since they thought that the men at El Cuervo were simply having another whiskey inspired shoot-out, the ladies weren't concerned until the victorious Utes went down to the Plaza and forced them to prepare a victory feast of buffalo meat boiled with corn. The Indians ate seated on the ground within the walls.

This hostile attack may have caused Kinkead to decide to leave the area. Later that month, he took his son Andres to Barclay and Doyle's new trading house above El Pueblo.[22] There Andres visited his mother while Matt arranged to leave some pigs for Barclay to sell for him. Then Kinkead drove several hundred head of cattle north and by July was trading them with emigrants on the Oregon Trail.

After the Taos uprising and the destruction of Turley's Mill and the murder of its owner, there was little Taos Lightning to trade to the tribes for awhile. Furthermore, the United States Government started to *give* goods to the Indians. The red men lost interest in trading when they could get what they wanted without the trouble. After Mexico ceded the vast domain south of the Arkansas to the United States in February, 1848, there was no reason to smuggle goods across the river. Swindling the government then became the popular profitable ploy. There was money to be made in building forts, freighting government goods, carrying mail, and scouting for the U. S. troops.

When Fremont on his ill-fated expedition stopped by the Plaza that fall to obtain corn for his horses, he found Lupton with little company other than the few hunters who had summered at Hardscrabble. Lupton, who had accompanied him on his first trip to California, was glad for Fremont's trade. What is now Colorado was suffering from its first business depression. El Pueblo and the log houses near there where the Mormons had wintered were deserted.

The Simpsons returned to the Plaza briefly, then joined the Barclays and Doyles at Fort Barclay which Barclay and Doyle had built at a cost of $28,000 where the Taos branch left the Santa Fe trail near present Watrous, New Mexico. There they expected to take advantage of the army trade and perhaps sell the post to the United States Government. However, the Government upset their plans by building Fort Union only seven miles away on Doyle and Barclay land. Teresita seems to have been reunited with her daughter Rafaela at this time. The child had apparently been left with friends or family when the Kinkeads moved to the Arkansas.

Both the Plaza and El Cuervo, no longer useful, were deserted after Lupton finally left the Hardscrabble. Maurice LeDuc went to San Geronimo, a tiny village west of Las Vegas, New Mexico, with his Sioux wife and their two children. There he met the love of his life, Elena Mendoza. He was so smitten with the thirteen-year-old girl that, at forty, he married her in church on August 15, 1848. When Marguerita, the Sioux, got wind of this, she took his children, his horses, and all she could haul, then returned to her people.

Burroughs and Briggs and, later, Kinkead headed for California where they each grew well-to-do in ranching and shipping. Hardscrabble was deserted until 1852 when many of the Mexican families, and probably the LeDucs, returned. They had their crops garnered when a band of hostile Plains Indians appeared. When the men couldn't engage the savages in an open encounter, they once again packed up their families to steal south under the cover of darkness.

Maurice and his beloved Elena with their two children, Amada and Augustin, were back on the Arkansas the following year with Joe Doyle. None stayed long on the Hardscrabble. Doyle, who had a variety of partners in his multiple trading activities, had as early as 1851 joined Dick Wootton on the Huerfano where they built houses about a hundred yards apart not far from Charley Autobees. Simpson rejoined Doyle after trying his luck in California for a couple of years.

LeDuc worked on the ranch for Wootton who later claimed that Maurice was an idle, drunken, worthless fellow but that Elena was a good worker. Wootton and LeDuc had several scraps. Wootton finally shot LeDuc in the right elbow "in corn shelling time." The LeDucs left after that for Mora, by then one of the larger settlements.

18

The development of ranches along the Huerfano affected Hardscrabble history. Such signs of settlement irked the Indians. Already maddened by the unfortunate gift of blankets they considered the source of smallpox, they became depredators. Late in 1854, a band of Utes under Chief Tierra Blanco swooped down on the handful of unwary souls who had gathered again at El Cuervo.[23] They killed those they found, then set fire to the buildings. The warriors went on to El Pueblo where the few remaining residents were already celebrating Christmas with spirituous rather than spiritual fervor. The Indians insinuated themselves into the festivities and repaid their hosts by killing most, taking three hostages, and driving off the cattle and horses from the ranch that Marcelino Baca had established east of Fountain Creek.

The Utes returned to the Wet Mountain Valley for a victory feast. Later, Arapahoes, encouraged by their white friends, surprised them as they camped near Grape Creek, southwest of present Canon City. Although Tierra Blanco escaped, the Utes were soundly defeated. The Arapahoes drove off the stolen horses and cattle that survived the battle, leaving the ground littered with carcasses of men and beasts. After all this mayhem, most of the remaining settlers left for safer territory. Doyle and others retreated to Fort Barclay. Few stayed to buck the braves.

Alec Barclay died at Fort Barclay in 1855. Sometime after his death, Joe Doyle sold it to yet another in-law, William Kroenig, who had married Teresita's daughter, Rafaela Kinkead. Young Rafaela died in 1858 after the birth of their second child.

Some say that Elena LeDuc also died in 1858. According to one story, Maurice had continued to adore her although she tried to keep her hard-earned money from him. When she died, he was so heartbroken that he lost his skill as a hunter. According to another account, he claimed that he left her because she got to be a "damn bitch" and he lost his power to kill game because of poor vision and the injury to his elbow that required him to shoot lefthanded. Whichever was the truth, LeDuc took his two children to the Hardscrabble to live in the ruins of El Cuervo. By that time Indian hostility and the Panic of 1857 had halted all traffic along the Arkansas.

LeDuc came upon the bones left from the Ute's premature victory feast celebrating the Pueblo massacre as he attempted to hunt in the Wet Mountain Valley in 1859. After his hunting proved unsuccessful, he moved down to a log cabin on Adobe Creek where he tanned hides for a meager living. He was virtually alone on the Hardscrabble when some Fifty-Niners, including Jack Templeton and Henry Burnett, moved in. A Texan lived in a couple of the best preserved rooms at the Plaza that winter while he ranged his cattle nearby.

By the time the gold rush renewed men's interest in the area, there was little evidence of much travel, except by Indians, along the Arkansas above the Cimarron Crossing where the broad highway of wagon ruts marked the Santa Fe Trail. George Simpson, hoping that his Plaza property was on the Nolan grant, returned in 1860 to see about the possibility of recolonizing it. He saw only "Old Francisi" there living in a tepee with his two motherless ragamuffins. Simpson had the misfortune to break his leg before he was convinced that his land was beyond the grant and returned to Taos.

Others arrived soon after, however, for Henry M. Burroughs, apparently no relation to the earlier John Burroughs, was the first to record a water right from the Hardscrabble on May 1, 1860. Fall found a new growth in population as miners came down from the mountains to winter. The new supply town of Cañon City, platted by William Kroenig and others at the mouth of the Grand Canyon of the Arkansas, was busy and bustling. The banks of the river were crowded with tents. Such newcomers as James Alfred and Mary Toof, Alf's bachelor brother, George, and their friend Lew Wilmot, who had been mining in Georgia Gulch, learned that the banks of the Hardscrabble offered a pleasant haven. They soon built a cabin on Adobe Creek. Young Wilmot found work with G. H. Vickroy[24] who paid him fifty cents a cubic yard to dig the mill pit for a grist mill he was building to process corn raised by Mexicans there.

That winter there were a good number around to hear old LeDuc spin tales of his experiences. Some, like Wilmot, returned to the mountains in the spring to continue mining. Others, like the Toofs, remained to farm. They stayed another year before moving down the Arkansas to ranch near the mouth of Beaver Creek.

Antoine Lebrie, Leon Constantin, Leandro Beral, and Louis Clothier, who had freighted Bent's buffalo hides to Kansas City, settled accounts with Bent in the spring of 1860 and headed West with a load of groceries and whiskey to Cañon City.[25] They built a one and a half story store on six lots given them by the town company. By fall they were ready to catch the trade of the miners and prospectors coming down from California Gulch. However, when they were unable to sell their goods at high enough profit they went to the Hardscrabble where there was good ranch land and adobe houses awaiting rehabilitation.

The four failed to find the overgrown irrigation ditches used by the earlier farmers and had a meager crop without water. They sold out to Vickroy in the fall of 1861. Vickroy moved into the house built by Baca on the rise. He seems best remembered for his skill in preparing bogus gold dust from the yellow rocks of Hardscrabble Cañon to pawn off on the celebrating miners at the Cañon City saloons. He and his partner, Hammit, used adobes from the Plaza to repair their house and fetched what logs remained from El Cuervo and LeDuc's place.

Vickroy and Hammit didn't stay long either. Vickroy could well be the

20

George H. Vickroy who, with Thomas J. Barnum of Cañon City, was awarded a contract on April 24, 1862, to carry U. S. Mail over the Santa Fe Trail.[26]

William Bruce later ranched on the Baca property and had a sawmill in Hardscrabble Cañon near where he was murdered in 1863. Henry Burroughs, who married Bruce's granddaughter, later acquired Bruce's ranch property.[27]

John Reeves Witcher arrived on the Hardscrabble after having been captured by Union forces in the Texas panhandle.[28] He and his brother, William, had come from Georgia to mine near Montgomery. Soon after the start of the Civil War they had joined a Confederate company organized near Fairplay. William died of smallpox on the way to Texas. John's group was captured and released on the condition that the men return to Colorado. In 1864, John Witcher and Thomas Virden bought the Castle Rock Ranch on the north side of the Arkansas northwest of later Florence.

Dick Harrington ranged his cattle along the creek in 1863-64 to supply the ready market at the mines.[29] Few but ranchers found the area attractive until the 1870's when homesteaders began to arrive. Then, after minerals were found in the Wet Mountain Valley, the Hardscrabble Cañon Road was fixed up and made passable in the winter of 1872-73 by subscriptions from Rosita and the newly formed Hardscrabble Mining District.[30] In April, Rosita began to bloom near the source of Hardscrabble Creek in the low hills of the Sierra Majada.

A number of rich and educated Englishmen were attracted to the valley, perhaps as a result of the enthusiastic efforts of the Territory's Board of Immigration represented in London by Edward Reed. So many younger sons, accustomed to high tea at four, populated the place that it was nicknamed "The Valley of the Second Sons."[31]

Shortly after the road was opened, Judge Hoyt of Rosita came to the rescue of one Englishman who had set out without his groom. He was having difficulty with his mule team because the playful near mule wouldn't let him tighten his trace. Another Englishman, Reginald E. Neave, with Dr. William A. Bell who had a ranch in the area, established The Colorado Cheese Factory, the first of its kind in the Territory. After Neave was murdered by whiskey inflamed twenty-eight-year-old Theodore D. B. Pryce in February, 1874,[32] the curing room, with its forty thousand pound capacity, was idle. The cows had grazed too greedily on wild onions, flavoring the milk from which the cheese was made.

While other men adapted their plans to the possibilities, LeDuc chose to remain a hunter and trapper even when such an occupation barely earned him a living. He still trapped beaver when the fur was good, but he no longer tilled his fields. The gold excitement didn't interest him so he soon left for other parts. One-eyed by 1880, he packed his burro and set out to visit a son in Cimarron. According to one account, the once intrepid trapper became confused, lost his way, and became snowbound in the mountains.[33] He was never seen again. By the time he died, the Hardscrabble had become a place of quiet farms and ranches.

Nearly all traces of the Plaza have long since vanished. Only a pattern of packed earth suggests its possible location. As for El Cuervo, the only clue to its location is a bowl-like depression in the earth where once the cistern supplied water. The dust storms of the 1930's pretty well filled the deep excavation and the drought killed the cottonwoods that shaded the place.[34] The whole Hardscrabble valley is now poorly watered with streams that run freely only in the spring and in the upper reaches. The modern highway cuts a straight line across the upland so that little is seen of the once lush river bottom that attracted the early traders.

FOOTNOTES

1. The settlement wasn't officially merely Taos until the 1880's. See Morris F. Taylor *First Mail West*, p. 186 footnote.
2. Spelled Kincaid in some sources. Accounts of his life in the Fremont County area were largely limited to mention in the Francis Whittemore Cragin papers, *Notebooks I-X*, until the publication of Janet LeCompte's chapter, "Mathew Kinkead," in vol. 2 of *The Mountain Men and the Fur Trade in the Far West* (called hereafter *The Mountain Men, etc.*), edited by LeRoy R. Hafen. Kinkead's name in various spellings appears in scattered references in accounts of other mountain men.
3. Although much has been written about William Bent and his brothers, speculation continues concerning this first post. The stockade winter camp between the present locations of Pueblo and Canon City is mentioned in Samuel P. Arnold's chapter, "William Bent," in vol. 6. of *The Mountain Men, etc.* Ralph C. Taylor in *Colorado, South of the Border*, p. 249, places the location opposite the mouth of Hardscrabble Creek. Early accounts of the area indicate that there was a good spring at that spot. The usual seasonal floodings of the Arkansas could have early obliterated any trace of a picket post, as they also destroyed, apparently, any evidence of Pike's construction. William Bent's brothers would not have been with him in this venture since records show them elsewhere.
4. Both Harvey L. Carter and LeCompte have done extensive research on this son of the five-term Chaplain of the United States Senate. See LeCompte's "Gantt's Fort and Bent's Picket Post," *The Colorado Magazine*, 41:111-125, Spring, 1964. Also Carter's chapter, "John Gantt," in vol. 5 of *The Mountain Men, etc.*
5. Cragin's *Notebooks* contain many mentions of Maurice. LeCompte has extended her research from this base in her chapter, "Maurice LeDuc,"

in vol. 6 of *The Mountain Men, etc.* This corrects and amplifies her earlier article, "The Hardscrabble Settlement, 1844-1848," *The Colorado Magazine,* 31:81-98, April, 1954.

6. LeCompte covers the activities of Autobees and Turley in her chapters, "Charles Autobees" and "Simeon Turley" in vol. 6 of *The Mountain Men, etc.*

7. Cragin's *Notebook IV,* p.16.

8. Howard Louis Conard's *"Uncle Dick" Wootton, the Pioneer Frontiersman of the Rocky Mountain Region: an Account of the Adventures and Thrilling Experiences of the Most Noted American Hunter, Trapper, Guide, Scout, and Indian Fighter Now Living* is no more modest nor accurate than its title. The author evidently accepted Wootton's own account of events, not realizing (or caring) that "Uncle Dick" had a tendency to enlarge his part in them. For instance, Wootton claims he started a buffalo farm with the forty-four calves on the site where Pueblo was built twenty years later. Despite such inaccuracies in detail and dates, the book paints a vivid picture of the area under consideration.

9. Cragin's *Notebooks* contain several items on Simpson. The most complete account of his earlier years is Carter and LeCompte's chapter "George Semmes Simpson" in vol. 3 of *The Mountain Men, etc.* Morris F. Taylor's *Trinidad, Colorado Territory* deals with his later life as a citizen of that city.

10. Doyle, a real hustler, appears in many accounts. Carter's "Joseph Doyle" in vol. 2 of *The Mountain Men, etc.* covers the activities of both Doyle and Barclay. Morris Taylor's "Capt. William Craig and the Vigil and St. Vrain Grant, 1855-1870," *The Colorado Magazine,* 45:301-321, Fall, 1968, throws additional light on Doyle's later years.

11. See LeCompte's chapter, "John Hawkins," in vol. 4 of *The Mountain Men, etc.*

12. David Lavender's *Bent's Fort,* p. 214.

13. Cragin's *Far West Notebook #1,* p. 21; *Notebook VIII,* p. 8-9.

14. See Lawrence R. Murphy's chapter, "Charles H. Beaubien," in vol. 6 of *The Mountain Men, etc.*

15. Morris Taylor's "Capt. William Craig and the Vigil and St. Vrain Grant, 1855-1870" and Harold H. Dunham's chapter, "Ceran St. Vrain," in vol. 5 of *The Mountain Men, etc.* indicate the extent of St. Vrain's complicated land speculations.

16. The disorganized and sometimes ambiguous 1881 *History of the Arkansas Valley* may be responsible for connecting these names with the colony.

17. See LeCompte's "Mathew Kinkead."

18. Cragin's *Notebook III,* p. 75; *Notebook VII,* p. 13, 18; *Notebook VIII,* p 8-9. Cragin refers to Whittlesey as El Viejo Wilson in this last entry.

19. Quoted in the Florence *Citizen* of September 11, 1969, Section 3, p. 8.

20. Cragin's *Notebook III* and LeCompte's chapter, "Marcelino Baca," in vol. 3 of *The Mountain Men, etc.*

21. Cragin's *Notebook VII*, p. 16-18.

22. Cragin's *Notebook II*, p. 24; LeCompte in "Mathew Kinkead" quotes Barclay's diary of October 23, 1847, on the same point.

23. Variations of this story appear in Jackson Taylor, Jr.'s "Early Days at Wetmore and on the Hardscrabble," *The Colorado Magazine*, 8:115-117, May, 1931; Ralph Taylor's *Colorado, South of the Border;* and in the Florence *Citizen*, September 15, 1922.

24. Called Vickery in Luther Perry Wilmot's "A Pleasant Winter for Lew Wilmot," he seems to be the G. H. Vickroy whose deed for Canon City property is recorded in the Fremont County courthouse.

25. Cragin's *Notebook IV*, p. 35-37; 43-45.

26. This contract was soon transferred to a group that included three more men, one of them Bradley Barlow. After several changes, this company evolved into the famous Barlow, Sanderson and Company that continued to carry passengers, if not mail, until the end of the stagecoach era. See Morris Taylor's *First Mail West.*

27. Cragin's *Notebook III*, p. 50.

28. Interview with Mrs. J. Tol Witcher, July 30, 1968; Donna Taylor's *Memories from the Foot of the Gorge,* p. 85.

29. Cragin's *Notebook X*, p. 10.

30. George G. Everett's *Cattle Cavalcade in Central Colorado* roams in this area also.

31. See Morris Cafky's "The Railroad That Couldn't Make Up Its Mind," *Trains, the Magazine of Railroading,* 26:38-46, August, 1966.

32. Colorado Springs *Gazette* for February 14, 1874, p. 2.

33. LeCompte's "Maurice LeDuc." There are several alternate versions of LeDuc's last days. This one is based on Cragin's notes and seems as reliable as any.

34. Interview with J. Louis Draper, November 25, 1967. Draper has ranched near the site of El Cuervo since 1929.

Dedication of the Hardscrabble Marker, March 30, 1969
Mrs. John B. Farley of Pueblo, who spearheaded the move for recognition of Hardscrabble's history, addressing the crowd gathered to witness the dedication of the marker erected by the State Historical Society, the Arkansas Valley Chapter of the Daughters of the American Revolution, and the State Highway Department. *Photo by the author.*

CHAPTER III

CAÑON CITY, FRONTIER TOWN

When Texas rebelled from Mexico in 1836, Bell's Springs was close to the border of territory claimed by both Texas and Mexico and largely ignored by both. A handful of Americans may have used the hot springs for tanning skins now and then for a dozen years. The Indians, however, visited the area frequently to drink from the mineral springs on American soil, bathe in the hot springs across the river, and massage themselves with oil from a seep to the north. The Utes in particular believed that such therapy relieved their aches and ailments.

The site of Bell's Springs took on a new significance after the discovery of gold near present Denver in the spring of 1858. It was on a natural route to the diggings that were discovered in South Park the following year. The very name Pound Diggings was itself enough to cause a rush. Greedy gold seekers assumed it meant that a miner could dig a pound of gold a day, unaware that it was named for its finder, Daniel Pound.

The thirty-one year old widower, William Kroenig, seems to have been the first to appreciate the location of Bell's Springs. Kroenig,[1] born in Westphalia in February, 1827, studied for the priesthood at a German Jesuit college but evidently decided to emigrate to America in 1847 instead of taking orders. He was headed for California with the Forty-Niners when a bout with cholera and loss of funds to thieving Indians diverted him to Santa Fe. After several disillusioning experiences as a volunteer with the territorial troops, he settled near Arroyo Hondo. James H. Quinn, a beef contractor who also operated a mill and distillery, set him up as a storekeeper in Rio Colorado, a new settlement that seems to have been distinguished by much robbery and murder.

To provide produce for his store, Kroenig began farming on land loaned by a friend. About 1851, after he had sold all his stock, he joined Beaubien and LeBlanc and a group of Mexicans on a trading trip to the Arapaho and Cheyenne country. In January, 1853, he left Rio Colorado with Charley Autobees who planned to settle on land that St. Vrain and Vigil had earlier promised him. Autobees may not have known that by this time St. Vrain and Vigil had long since deeded their interest in it to others, including the late Charles Bent.

They carried food to trade with the Indians. At Greenhorn they learned that the Utes had destroyed Marcelino Baca's grain and had stolen his horses. As Baca by that time had decided to relocate near old El Pueblo, he invited Kroenig to raise a crop at Greenhorn if he wished since the ditches could easily be repaired and the house was in good condition.

After trading beans and flour to the starving Arapahoes and Cheyennes at Big Timbers, Autobees established the community on the Huerfano where Doyle and Dick Wootton later settled. Kroenig went back to Baca's at Greenhorn. He and LeBlanc harvested a crop there which Kroenig hauled to Fort Laramie to trade. He left the fort with ninety-four cattle and two hundred footsore sheep to join Autobees at Huerfano in an extensive farm operation for which Autobees furnished the peons and Kroenig the seed.

After the 1854 massacre, Kroenig went to La Costilla where he established a store and distillery. A couple of years later he began ranching near Mora. By that time, St. Vrain, no longer associated with William Bent, had a flour mill there. Kroenig and Moritz Beilchowsky were on the spot to buy Fort Barclay from Joe Doyle for a mere $7,340.68. It was near there that Kroenig met and married Rafaela Kinkead.

When word of Pike's Peak gold reached Kroenig, he hurried back to the Huerfano where on one acre of ground he raised twenty wagon-loads of vegetables, finding a ready market for them in the booming gold camps on Cherry Creek. He soon had twenty-five men working one hundred sixty acres while he busied himself with other real estate.

With five others, he laid out Fontaine City on the east bank of Fountain Creek near its confluence with the Arkansas about where Baca had ranched before moving to Rio Colorado following the murder of his brother, Benito, by Indians, a month after the massacre. Midwesterners, hard hit by the depression that followed the Panic of 1857, were flocking to find gold in the Rockies via the mountain route of the old Santa Fe Trail. They were urged on by avaricious outfitters, inflamed by sensation-mongering newspapers, and directed by imaginative authors of fairy tale guide books. Fontaine City failed to prosper at first although some thirty log and adobe cabins were built using the old adobes from the deserted El Pueblo. The prospectors wanted to press on to the mountains.

Kroenig and his companions decided that the entrance to the Grand Canyon of the Arkansas would be a more strategic location for a supply center. The mountains would compel heavily laden freight wagons to stop there. Kroenig, with William H. Young, Robert Bercaw, Charles D. Peck, Josiah Smith and his brother, Stephen, laid out the town of Cañon City in October, 1859, to accommodate some of the estimated 100,000 who crossed the plains that year. They believed it would soon become the "Gate City to the Mountains." They built one cabin, then took off to survey a seventy-nine mile road over Currant Creek Pass to the Tarryall Diggings, about four miles above present Como on Tarryall Creek. They marked each mile with a post.

However, by the time Robert S. Middleton, who had arrived with the vanguard of gold seekers from Lawrence, Kansas, had moved his family into the only cabin, languishing Fontaine City suddenly began to boom.

Despite the marked trail to Tarryall, many of the Pikes Peakers preferred to head north along Fountain Creek to the older town of Colorado City laid out by some of the Lawrence party. From there, gold seekers entered South Park via Ute Pass where volunteers worked feverishly to improve the Ute Trail to accommodate ox teams. Middleton moved back down the river to Fontaine City.

The gate city was about abandoned when winter drove the miners down from the mountains. Many of the disappointed prospectors neither wanted nor could afford town lots. They were simply too poor to return to the States, six hundred fifty miles away. When they realized that the Pikes Peak promotion was a great humbug, they squatted along the Arkansas to farm whatever likely spots they could find.

B. H. Bolin entered the first official farm claim for J. N. Hagius on January 1, 1860.[2] A few months later, Jesse Frazer, Hosea Hoopengarner, Clark Harrington, and John W. Leland filed the first coal claim on land near later Coal Creek, the region's first coal camp.

Gabriel Bowen was out searching for bullet lead when he came upon the oil seep.[3] It can still be seen on Fourmile Creek, now alternately known as Oil Creek. Arrowheads, bone hooks, and hand pieces (some now in the Cañon City Municipal Museum) found in caves and shelters along the creek gave evidence that the Indians had often camped in the area. Bowen acquired title to the oil spring about six miles north of Cañon City shortly after the first successful oil well in the United States was developed in Pennsylvania. He and Matthew G. Pratt attempted to exploit the oil with little success.

Other men found evidence that the region was rich in coal, iron, gypsum, marble, limestone, and granite. What looked good to one, looked good to others. Claim jumping reached problem proportions. Even Kroenig has been accused of jumping the townsite, although his companions seem to have left it to him by default. He interested different men in forming a new company to promote the development of Cañon City.

This company included six members of the Cañon City Claim Club that had been organized on March 13, 1860, to provide a local legal entity. County government in that remote part of Kansas Territory was nominal rather than real. County officers were never known to venture west of the present borders of the State of Kansas. Therefore, thirty-five souls in and around Cañon City undertook to draw up a constitution, claiming jurisdiction over a strip ten miles on each side of the Arkansas from Beaver Creek on the east to the edge of South Park on the west.

Buell and Boyd, who platted Denver and Pueblo, relocated and enlarged the townsite for the new Cañon City Company to include twelve hundred acres on the level ground east and west of the point of rocks above the now vanished soda spring on the north side of the Arkansas.

Wealthy Ceran St. Vrain, well-to-do Joseph Doyle (who by that time had established stores in Tarryall and Denver as well as Cañon City), Alvord and Company, Dold and Company, E. Williams, A. Mayhood, W. H. Young, A. Thomas, William H. Green, James Douglass Ramage, W. W. Ramage, H. E. Easterday, James Graham, M. T. Green, and Harry Youngblood seem to be those who were associated with Kroenig in this new venture. They were an assorted group of solid citizens, promoters, and adventurers. Youngblood's real name was known to few. He was thought to have been connected with the murder of Joseph Smith, the founder of Mormonism.

This new company, with J. D. Ramage as president and W. W. Ramage as secretary, did little more than the previous one to induce immigration. But they didn't need to. With riches discovered in California Gulch, the Pikes Peak gold scramble was again in full swing. Prospectors swarmed through town bent on cramming their pockets with gold nuggets and returning home rich men as soon as possible. Hard on their heels came the merchants so necessary to support prospectors and miners.

Frederick Z. Salomon,[4] an employee of Doyle and Company, left Denver in the spring of 1860 by Central, Overland and Pike's Peak Coach. Six days later he was in St. Joseph purchasing three hundred head of cattle and goods to fill thirty-five wagons to supply Doyle's branches in Cañon City, Mountain City, and Golden Gate. Wolfe Londoner, another early member of the area's early Jewish community, had already been to California three times before he set out from St. Louis with a wagon train of goods from Hanauer's company there. Londoner was sent by the firm to represent them in Cañon City. He soon had a solid business in the first stone building to be built in the town. Evidently he took only his business seriously, for he soon had a reputation as a practical joker. His boisterous pranks kept his friends howling with pain or delight. Some had serious repercussions. Years later, for instance, he became Mayor of Denver, the result, he claimed, of a retaliatory trick played by his poet friend, Eugene Field.

Stopped by the steep trail to the diggings, freighters stored their large stocks in sheds in the city. Forwarders packed the goods to the mountain camps. Farmers planted seed as soon as they could. They hoped to sell their produce in the gold camps at highly inflated prices. Easterday, for one, advertised in the *Rocky Mountain News* in April that he had on hand in Cañon City a large supply of flour made at his mill in New Mexico. Such flour sold for twenty dollars a sack in the South Park mining camps. In the midst of all this bustle, Indians by the hundreds arrived to occupy their traditional campgrounds round about, much to the consternation of the newcomers. Fortunately, they proved to be a nuisance rather than a menace.

When Anson Rudd[5] arrived with his wife at Cañon City in August, 1860, the place was booming. The Rudds were actually headed for California when they heard of the new gold strike in the mountains of present Colorado. They spent some weeks around Buckskin Joe (near present Alma) but heard of Cañon City and decided to winter there. When Harriet Rudd saw how mild the climate was, how bountiful the supply of fish and game, and how rich the soil, she declared she wanted to stay. California could be no better. Her husband, who had spent some time on the west coast before returning to claim her and end their eighteen year long engagement, agreed. He was sure that Cañon City would become the most important city in the proposed Jefferson Territory. He and his friend, Benjamin Griffin, whom he had known in Kansas, hauled logs from the Shadow Mountains (now the Greenhorns) and built cabins on adjoining lots. Rudd's cabin, moved from its original site on the northwest corner of Fourth and Main, still stands behind the present Municipal Building near his later stone house. It now may be visited as part of the Cañon City Municipal Museum.

One time Rudd was physically as well as intellectually impressed by the place as indicated by this story that he often told on himself. Once when he was hunting, he mistook the back of a jackass in the sagebrush for a bear. He crawled on hands and knees until he was near enough, carefully fired, and shot the jack. Unfortunately, he reared back at the blast and sat on a cactus. When he rose, he found his breeches pinned to his skin. It took two friends twelve hours to extract the spines with tweezers. And it was two weeks before he cared much for sitting down.[6]

With a building boom on, the town company offered an original share in the town as an inducement for the establishment of a sawmill in the vicinity. Henry Harkens, Asa C. Chandler, J. B. Cooper, and J. C. Moore brought a mill from Minnesota and installed it above the Soda Spring near the mouth of Sand Creek. R. R. Kirkpatrick set up a shingle mill on the adjoining claim.

To establish an air of law and order in the city, the citizens in September drew up a code of laws, established a people's court, and selected Warren R. Fowler as chief magistrate. Fowler had recently arrived in Cañon City from Chicago after having lost a fifty thousand dollar Forty-Niner-made fortune in the financial crises of 1857-58. A deacon of the Presbyterian church, he held what religious services there were.

One of Fowler's first cases concerned Dr. James L. Dunn, the area's first oil well promoter, "of pleasing address and smooth exterior" who was accused of selling counterfeit U.S. scrip in the amount of three hundred dollars.[7] Dunn spoiled the show for some by making reparation before he could be tried.

H. S. Millett, with Chandler and Chambers, published the first issue of the *Cañon Times* on September 18, 1860. This was considered a "racy little sheet" where miners could publish their claims as required by law. Of the three newspapers published at that time in Colorado outside Denver, it was the only one to survive 1860. Its early issues depict a rapidly growing community.

There was a daily stage from Denver and one three times a week from Colorado City. With no Highway 115 then, it was a long trip down the Fountain and up the Arkansas. L. Calkins and Company had a steam saw mill known as the Pioneer Mill and a timber claim six miles southeast of town. Kroenig's new business house boasted an excellent cellar, not for wines but for vegetables. Mr. Corley's Cañon City Saloon supplied the "superb drinkables."

McFarland and Corvan's bakery and W. N. Bercaw built new adobes. George A. Hinsdale, later to be Governor of Colorado, completed a new frame building, Rudd and Allen a one-story commission house. Thirty residences were completed during the last half of September alone.

Although no scalps were lifted when a large band of Utes in war paint camped near the hot springs that fall, many scalps did tingle with fear at the disquieting beat of the tom-toms. The Utes moved east, returning in a few days with a fine collection of Cheyenne scalps. The following month, the Cheyennes returned the visit. They offered horses and equipment to any white who would join them in fighting a small band of Utes camped on Oil Creek. Some of the mine-toughened hot-bloods were spoiling for a battle, but those acquainted with Indian character cooled them off. The Utes lost three dead before they drove off their attackers.

When the mines at California Gulch, Fairplay, Tarryall, and Blue River closed for the winter, the population of Cañon City swelled to seven hundred fifty, making it a close rival to Denver. Business flourished. The post office, with Matt Riddlebarger as postmaster, opened in one of the hundred fifty completed buildings. G. D. Jenks opened the hotel. Wolfe Londoner, later a prominent Denver grocer for fifty years, then presided as manager of Dold and Company's store. Custer and Swisher ran the meat market. Jim Briner and John Larley, jolly bachelor blacksmiths, kept busy shaping old shovel blades into hoes as men turned from mining to farming. Jesse Frazer hauled coal by ox team to the blacksmith shop.

William C. Catlin, a Bostonian with an English wife, arrived about this time. He did what he could to earn a living. Among other things he freighted butter and eggs to trade in Denver for other staples. One round trip took him seven weeks and led his worried family to believe he'd been captured or killed by the Indians.[8]

Winter weather didn't completely cool the gold fever. Three sharp characters carefully leaked a story of their fabulous find up Grape Creek. During the night, every man in town stealthily moved in to plant his stakes. By sunup, a two mile stretch of the canyon was completely filled with claims. The initial site was soon seen for the hoax it was and the rush became the joke of the town.

One of the perpetrators didn't laugh long. One morning as he cooked his breakfast, his revolver slipped from its holster, struck the bake-kettle, discharged, and killed him instantly. He may have been the first white man buried in Cañon City. He soon had company. One of the wintering miners was notably hot of temper. On different occasions within a year, Charles Dodge shot and killed three men who irked him.[9]

Calkins and Company opened a quarry to get stone for a three-story hotel expected to cost at least fifty thousand dollars finished and furnished. L. W. Calkins didn't have the respect of his fellow citizens for long. When he was entrusted with four hundred dollars worth of gold dust to carry to its owner, he claimed that Londoner had swiped it from him. A jury acquitted Londoner. His lawyer, Major Miller, remarked that Calkins was "an ass, a knave, or a fool" to have left the gold where he said he did.

That night Miller was almost assassinated as he slept in the room behind the printing office with the editor and others.[10] The balls missed the men, lodging in the wall a few inches above the bed. W. W. Ramage was arrested without due process of law the following day but was released for lack of evidence. Editor Millett, who continued as editor through several changes of ownership, denounced Cañon City's depravity. After his scathing remarks appeared in the paper, Matt Riddlebarger, thought to be the local agent for the so-called Taos Lightning, and known to be a Southern sympathizer, acquired a controlling interest in the *Cañon Times*. There was soon so much news that Millett added another press, previously used at Golden City, to his equipment.

That winter Cañon City was a wide-open, wild town. Every department of pleasure ran at capacity. Beaver and deer skins, as well as venison, were legal tender. Now and then some unfortunate soul discovered he had accepted as payment some of Vickroy's bogus gold dust. Others found brass filings padding the pokes or discovered that the nuggets they had accepted were mere spelter, an alloy of copper and other metals.[11]

The census for 1860 shows only one hundred twenty females in a total of seven hundred twenty-seven souls in the entire Cañon City Claim Club area. How popular they must have been at the gala Christmas Ball!

After an abortive attempt to form Jefferson Territory, the Pikes Peakers had a government of their own when Congress passed the Colorado Bill in February, 1861. Claim jumping was such a problem that George Hinsdale, Wilbur F. Stone, later a Colorado Supreme Court Judge, and John Howard agreed to set up a people's court until the Territorial Organization could furnish a District Court. This new people's court functioned for about two years in the area from Cañon City to Beaver Creek and from the Oil Wells to Hardscrabble.

R. O. Olds soon haled Calkins into this court. Olds, who had opened his business with a hop and oyster supper, accused Calkins of generously using Olds' whiskey as a persuader in an effort to defeat the city code on election day and not paying for same. Calkins didn't stay around town long. He started thirty or forty two-story stone buildings under contract, finished only two. His men had completed the first stories of the rest when he couldn't, or wouldn't, pay them. He collected what money he could and skipped town.

George F. Hall opened his El Progresso saloon in one of the completed buildings with a gala dance. The Kitchen Brothers also held a "coarse haired" dance when they opened their saloon in the other one. Alex Majors bought out James H. Reid's dray business. The first express coach drawn by four white mules arrived May 13, 1861.[12] Although only two passengers were aboard, the inauguration of the Kansas City, Santa Fe and Cañon City Fast Line service[13] called for a celebration at the Jenks House with a buffet and dancing until dawn. Cañon City at last had a direct connection with the East.

The county records show a brisk trade in real estate. Lots sold for cash, credit, or anything of value. Albert F. Bercaw received twelve hundred dollars, plus three pairs of oxen at two hundred twenty-five, two stoves at ninety dollars, one hundred pounds of white lead at twenty-four dollars, two boxes of glass at twenty-eight dollars, one Sharps rifle at thirty-five dollars, a watch at fifty dollars, one hundred pounds of sugar at thirty-five dollars, and ten gallons of brandy at eight-fifty a gallon for sundry lots he sold to William R. Demitt and Matthew G. Pratt.[14]

Speculation drove the price of city lots sky high. A group of men tried to lower them by formally platting the Town of Delray near the Oil Spring to provide cheap suburban lots. They were too late. The tide of immigration turned.

With spring, the residents headed for the hills or sought open space for farms and ranches. Anson Rudd, a man of wit and learning, stayed. Since he wrote poetry on any and all occasions, he was called the Blacksmith Poet after he opened a smithy in Middleton's old cabin. Rudd did his bit to stabilize the population. His son, Anson Spencer Rudd, was born on June 23, 1861, the first white child born in Cañon City to survive infancy.

M. D. Swisher's child had received a town lot in celebration of his being the first born, but he didn't live. He was probably buried near the hog back, likely the location of the burial ground claim entered by the Cañon City Claim Club. Baby Charles Bowen was buried there in 1861 and his father, Gabriel, aged forty-five, two years later. Charles' brother, aged twelve, joined them the following year. Their graves were discovered some forty years ago when a road grader widened the exit to the Skyline Drive.[15]

The day after he became a father, Rudd, who enjoyed good jokes and pranks, acted as clerk of the court to witness John Howard's divorce papers. When Mary Howard sued John for divorce in Denver, he responded by issuing a quit claim deed for "that ancient estate known as Mary Howard." This document, with its salty description of his discovery and possession of this property, was couched in legal phrases and properly executed at Cañon City.[16] However, no actual divorce seems to have been granted.

When the first Territorial Legislature met in September, among other things it divided the Territory into seventeen counties, choosing Cañon City to be the seat of Fremont County. Cañon City is one of the few originally designated to continue as a county seat. Some of those then named soon ceased to exist. It looked for awhile as though Cañon City too would meet that fate.

Activity slackened in the summer. No buyer made an offer when the newspaper was offered for sale in late August. There was no more pay dirt for the poor man to pan. Colorado's remaining gold lay locked in ores that required smelting processes beyond the knowledge or means of the casual miner. The threat of war between the States quickened the return of many to "America."

While the court continued to cope with crime, horse stealing called for direct action. One horse thief escaped from custody, stole another horse, and lit out for the new town of Pueblo.[17] Gentleman Charley Harrison, a visiting gambler who always dressed like a city clergyman despite his reputation as a desperado, offered to ride the only good horse available for pursuit. He overtook the horse thief near the Beaver Creek Ford where the road to Pueblo crossed from the south to the north side of the river. He covered the villain with his Winchester, tied him with one lariat, and strung him up with another.

Charley led the stolen horse back to the sheriff and reported that he'd tied his man to a cottonwood. He suggested that the sheriff take a wagon to fetch him, hinting that the fellow's feet would be too cold for anything else. The sheriff's posse buried the victim at the foot of the tree. He may have been James Dover of Missouri since the *Cañon Times* of September 5, 1861, reported that he had been hanged on Beaver Creek for horse stealing.

With diminishing news and little business, the owners of the *Times* took their press to a more profitable place, after publishing ads for Army volunteers in the last issue on October 7, 1861. C. P. Hendron's Company was one of the first to be formed. While it awaited orders in Cañon City, the men spent their time as pleasantly as possible. When the company left for Fort Garland, ninety-one strong, most of the men were well hung-over, suffering the sour stomach and headache that follow too much Taos Lightning.

By the end of November, two more companies had been recruited at Cañon City. Captain James H. Ford's and Captain Theodore H. Dodd's Independent Companies were nondescript and ill-equipped, like many that fought in the Civil War. Captain W. H. Green of the second town company was with the men who repulsed the Southern troops at Glorieta Pass in New Mexico to save the riches of the mountain mines from falling into Confederate hands. Not all the residents were Union men. Those of Southern sympathies who wanted to evade the recruiting officers crossed the river near the Soda Spring quietly at night and headed for Confederate country. Some went secretly down the Arkansas to cross at Chandler Creek to rendezvous at A. C. Chandler's ranch.

Despite an exodus that depleted the entire Territory, Cañon City remained one of the leading communities. The First Territorial District Court convened in Murray's Hall above his saloon where at other times balls and other social events were held. Judge Moses Hallett sometimes had to send the bailiff down to ask the boys to quit whooping it up so loudly that they drowned out the testimony.

George Phillips' feed and slaughter pens furnished meat for whatever mining operations continued in South Park and California Gulch, but in December, James Graham, then president of the Cañon City Company, was glad to sell his undivided half-interest in the Cañon City, San Juan, and Grand River Waggon Road to Green for seven hundred fifty dollars. Early in 1862, when a newly built three-story flour mill burned to the ground before it was ever used, it wasn't rebuilt.

These troubled times didn't prevent Governor William Gilpin from appointing Rudd, Cooper, and Lewis Conley (who had a grist mill on Beaver Creek) to determine the bounds of Fremont County. Their original survey included present Custer County, and more. The Cañon City Claim Club turned over its records to the new government when the county actually organized on January 25, 1862.

George Vickroy and Thomas Barnam with their partners[18] received the U.S. Mail contract for the route along the Arkansas from Pueblo. Beginning July 1, 1862, their coaches carried mail and passengers from Pueblo, serving Beaver Creek and Cañon City as well as a number of gold camps en route to Breckenridge. The slump in trade because of the Civil War soon caused a revision of the schedule.

By fall the county seat was practically a ghost town. Few came to replace the many who left. When the Rev. Mr. R. M. Slaughter came from Colorado City with the idea of organizing a Methodist Episcopal church, he talked to all who were in town, the Rudds and their baby son, Felix J.

Burdette, and a deranged soul who sometimes called herself Queen Adelaide.

When Jenks, the last member of the town company, departed, he entrusted the town records to Anson Rudd. Rudd seemed likely to stay, mainly because at the time he couldn't afford to leave. Optimistic, he homesteaded one hundred sixty acres and formed a ditch company. He stoutly held that Cañon City would prosper once again. For awhile it looked as though he was mistaken. The first ditch company's plans fell through after it had made a survey and dug a quarter of a mile of ditch.

Contrary to oft told tales, Anson Rudd did not have sole possession of or live alone in Cañon City. Rudd himself recalled twenty years after the exodus that there were twelve others who stayed but since they were crippled or deranged, and he was the only sound one, he claimed to be the only *man* left. This bit of his wit seems to have long been misinterpreted.

The scattered few who remained in Fremont County were to endure a time of terror. In the spring of 1863, Judge William Bruce of Cañon City was killed near his sawmill at the fork of North and South Hardscrabble. Friends searching for him found his body on the frozen creekbank, a crude cross carved in the flesh of his chest. He was buried near the Bowen baby. In the middle of March, Henry Harkens, who was moving his mill nearer Colorado City, met a similar fate. Weatherworn, his gravestone, reinforced with concrete, is alone on a rise east of Highway 115 in El Paso County in what has since been called Deadman's Canyon. The stone once read, "Henry Harkens, murdered Wednesday eve March 19th, 1863."[19]

Joseph M. Lamb, an early resident of Cañon City, was with the posse that tracked the trail of those responsible for a number of like killings. He shot Vivian Espinosa, the younger of two brothers who had vowed to kill six hundred Americanos in vengeance for some undetermined affront.[20] Felipe eluded the posse, paired up with his young nephew, Julian, and some time later fell to the deadly aim of the scout, Tom Tobin, Charley Autobees' half brother, who wintered in Cañon City between 1860 and 1868.[21]

Although Tobin took the heads in a gunnysack to the Commandant at Fort Garland as proof of his prowess, he was unable to collect the twenty-five hundred dollar reward. The Territory was too poor to pay. He waited thirty years for most of it and never did get it all.[22]

With the troops off fighting a war, the Indians grew increasingly hostile and managed to virtually isolate Cañon City from the outside world. This pinching off of the southern route to the mines seriously affected the development of Fremont County. It diverted travel to the Platte River route and put rival Denver in a position of advantage. Mail went via ship to San Francisco then overland to the Rocky Mountains. Only now and then did a covered wagon or a small freighting party pass through. Such travelers usually rested in one of Cañon City's abandoned houses a few days before moving on. Evidently Rudd couldn't persuade anyone to stay.

Alexander M. Cassiday was around part of the time. He had bought out Bowen in 1862, sold a large interest in the operation to a Boston company, and kicked down a fifty foot oil well. Part of the original wooden casing of this well is now in the Cañon City Municipal Museum. Neither Bowen nor Pratt had the means or the knowledge to develop the oil claim, but Cassiday, who had worked with the oil crew in Pennsylvania, built a primitive refinery of equipment made in Denver. He sold partially refined coal oil throughout Colorado Territory for a dollar and a quarter to three dollars a gallon.

Others began to drill, hoping to find a larger pool. Some of them struck salt water instead. That wasn't a total loss, for salt, which was used for treating gold ores, was worth fifteen to twenty cents a pound. Cassiday's crude pump brought in about a barrel of oil a day. He could realize a profit of about a hundred dollars on this, although his product had to be freighted seven to twelve hundred miles, at a freight cost of a dollar to a dollar and a half per gallon. It was refined by the Colorado Coal Oil Company, six miles north of Cañon City.[2 3]

Cassiday sold out when the price rose to five dollars a gallon during the Indian wars of 1864. Although he sold that oil claim, he was to be active in Fremont County's oil history for many years. He formed a company in Boston and, with eastern capital, returned to drill again only to have litigation stop him until he obtained proper title to the land. His undaunted perserverance led to the later development of the notable Florence oil field.

FOOTNOTES

1. Charles Irving Jones derived Kroenig's very interesting story from notes Kroenig made with the evident intention of one day writing his reminiscences. This is found in "William Krönig, New Mexico Pioneer, from his Memories of 1849-1860." *New Mexico Historical Review,* 19:185-224, July, 1944; 19:271-311, October, 1944. According to Cragin's notes, Kroenig some time later married the daughter of Sam B. Watrous, *Notebook XI,* p. 1.
2. The records of the Canon City Claim Club as well as the *History of the Arkansas Valley* throw light on the early days of Cañon City. See George L. Anderson's "The Canon City or Arkansas Valley Claim Club, 1860-1862," *The Colorado Magazine,* 16:201-210, November, 1939.
3. Bowen's oil claim of 160 acres was first recorded in the Mining Companies book at Delray where Bowen lived near the seep. Fremont County records reveal that the oil property changed hands many times. Microfilm of *Grantees Book I, January 1862 – June 1880.*

4. Ida Libert Uchill's *Pioneers, Peddlers, and Tsadikem* indicates the important part Jewish merchants played in supplying goods to the Fifty-Niners. Salomon was probably "the company" in Doyle & Co.

5. Rudd's son's account, "Early Days in Canon City," doesn't agree in detail with the version on the Rudd cabin flyer prepared by Rudd's granddaughter, Jean Rudd Bogeart.

6. See Alice Polk Hill's *Tales of the Colorado Pioneers*, p. 265. The *History of the Arkansas Valley* gives a variant version of this tale, p. 550, as does *Southern Colorado*, p. 9.

7. *Southern Colorado*, p. 11. This 1879 book is the source for many of these tales. Anderson's "The Canon City or Arkansas Valley Claim Club, 1860-1862," reveals additional peccadillos of Dunn and his fellow townsmen.

8. See Donna Taylor's *Memories from the Foot of the Gorge*, p. 88.

9. *Southern Colorado*, p. 12.

10. *Cañon City Times*, March 21, 1872, and the *History of the Arkansas Valley*, p. 559.

11. Cragin's *Notebook XVIII*, p. 8.

12. *Cañon City Daily Record*, September 16, 1962, Sec. D., p. 1. This 72 page special edition, "One Hundred Years of Progress," contains many items of historical interest.

13. See Morris Taylor's *First Mail West* for earlier service from Denver and Colorado City as well as details of the eight day schedule from Canon City to Kansas City.

14. Microfilm of Fremont County Records, *Grantees Book I, January 1862 - 1880*. Deed dated March 11, 1861.

15. Unidentified clipping in the Canon City Municipal Museum. There is now no record nor indication of this first burial ground.

16. *Southern Colorado*, p. 19. This forerunner of the *History of the Arkansas Valley* is similar in information, prejudice, and inaccuracy.

17. Wilbur Fiske Stone's *History of Colorado*, v. 1, p. 740. Stone reviews much of the early history of the area and includes anecdotes not found elsewhere.

18. The group included Bradley Barlow. Jared L. Sanderson also evidently had an interest in the line. As Cottrill, Vickroy and Co., the company provided express coach but not mail service from Pueblo to Denver. Vickroy gave up his membership in the firm July, 1863. See Morris Taylor's *First Mail West*, pp. 88-90, 95.

19. Henry Priest gives details in his "The Story of Dead Man's Cañon and of the Espinosas," *The Colorado Magazine*, 8:34-38, January, 1931.

20. There are several reasons advanced for the Espinosas' actions but little indication that the motive was ever really revealed. The most fanciful account is Wootton's as recounted in Conard's book.

21. J. Andrew Smith's "Joseph Milton Lamb, Pioneer Fremont County Citizen, Miner, Indian Fighter, and Civil War Veteran," is based on information provided by Lamb's son, Frank.

22. Interview with Frank Lamb, April 10, 1968. In late 1899, there was renewed interest in these heads. A clipping from the *Times* contained correspondence revealing that one head had been given to Dr. McLean, then contract post surgeon, who had kept it in alcohol in his office. The doctor died not long afterward of blood poisoning. No one knew what became of the gruesome souvenir.

23. [C. P. Sykes], *Petroleum in Colorado Territory*, p. 1.

CHAPTER IV

RESURRECTION

The sere summer of 1863 was perhaps the low point in Fremont
County's history. Crops shriveled. People and animals suffered. Bears in
particular were a nuisance and a real danger, especially to a poor shot. The
next year was but little better.

It was too wet, and in addition to warped Mexicans and savage Indians,
dangerous desperadoes sometimes threatened those who remained on the
widely spaced farms and ranches. In July, 1864, Jim Reynolds, who had
earlier worked as a laborer in the rich placer mines, led twenty-one rough,
tough, and nasty men, ostensibly Confederate guerillas, back to Colorado.
They plundered wagon trains, stages, and mail coaches. Five of the gang,
including Reynolds, were tracked to Cañon City. A posse captured one of
the men there, Al and George Toof took three more near their place at
Beaver Creek with the help of Lewis Conley and Pete Baltof. The
remaining two were captured in Butte Valley, the earlier haven of rascals,
now a refuge for rebels.

The Utes grew overbearing. Their signal fires by night and smoke by day
kept the nervous settlers aware of their presence. Always bothersome
beggars, they became worse. The Baptist preacher, Matthew Rule, was
calling on a woman on Eightmile when a large band pushed into her house
to demand food. They were so sure her husband was out that they were
unhappily surprised when Rule whomped the first Indian with an ax-helve
and flailed the others near the door. The Utes not only left, but treated
Rule with deference from then on.[1]

Settlers in eastern Colorado were scalped and mutilated. Women were
kidnapped and violated. Homes and hayfields were burned. The ruthless
retaliation of the troops, such as the still controversial Sand Creek
slaughter, bred but fresh furies. Lack of communication led to confusion
and contradiction in governmental policies.

Despite the dangers and the distance, immigration to Colorado resumed
even before the close of the Civil War. James Alexander McCandless[2] was
one of the first of the newcomers. Son of a North Carolina schoolteacher,
he was known as J. Leroy McCanles when, not yet eighteen, he married
Sarah Franklin, some years his senior. They had two children, James
Wellington and Mary Jane, before Leroy followed his brother, David
Colbert, West in 1859. After a quick look at the Pikes Peak region, Leroy
returned to settle near Colb in Nebraska Territory at the Rock Creek
Station of the Central Overland and Pikes Peak Company's Pony Express.
After he fetched Sallie and the children with Colb's family from eastern

41

Tennessee, the two brothers set about building a toll bridge on the Oregon Trail at Rock Creek. Leroy moved to Crab Orchard, Nebraska Territory, late in 1860 after a quarrel with his brother. Colb remained, only to be killed in cold blood by James B. Hickok, a Red Leg guerrilla, not yet known as "Wild Bill."

Leroy ventured West again in 1864. After outfitting at Kansas City, he and his household, which included pretty little nineteen-year-old, Catherine J. Garrett, left in April with several families to join a large wagon train at Great Bend. The McCandless family left the group at Fort Larned where the rest of the wagons took the trail toward Fort Sumner, New Mexico. When they were delayed by Indian outrages against earlier travelers they didn't reach the Arkansas until it was in flood. This was the same high water that washed out Colorado's first orchard planted by William Lee below Cañon City. With the river three miles wide, they had to head up Sand Creek where they camped for a couple of weeks among Arapahoes and Cheyennes. When they finally reached the dozen or so houses that marked Pueblo, McCandless paid some Mexicans ten dollars to help him herd his oxen across high Fountain Creek.

Rudd, Jothan Draper, and Burdette were the only men in Cañon City when McCandless, (from then on known as James) moved into Londoner's empty house. Several women remained in town while their husbands sought work in the mines. Rudd, who had been sheriff, continued to seek whatever office was open. In April, 1864, the Federal Government had appointed him inspector of distilled spirits and oil for the upper Arkansas Valley. He would be County Commissioner for two years and hold other public positions in turn.

The McCandless family also headed for the mines after Kate Garrett gave birth to a daughter, Julia, on July ninth. They were back to winter in Cañon City. In the spring James butchered meat for the miners at Buffalo Flats. In the fall of 1865, they returned to Fremont County to ranch in Eightmile Park[3] where James ran sixty head of cattle on the lush grass. They weren't lonely. Chiefs Ouray and Colorow and several hundred Utes camped nearby. Fortunately, twenty-nine-year-old McCandless, with his long straight black hair, appeared to them to be part Indian. They dubbed him "Ute's Mac" and were unusually friendly. McCandless soon took another ranch to the west at Twelve Mile Ford near present Parkdale. Here Wellington and Mary Jane climbed the rugged rocks at the upper end of the gorge with their Indian companions.

Men who remained in the Territory were divided on whether it should seek statehood or maintain its territorial status. The slavery issue made it of importance to the entire nation. The southern counties were opposed to the idea of statehood when Henry M. Teller of Central City was nominated for the senate by the Union Party. Teller and his brother Willard both lobbied against statehood when the question rose again in 1866.

By August, 1864, when Rudd became postmaster of Cañon City, a train of some twenty families arrived in Fremont County. When Thomas Macon had decided to head for Colorado with his young wife Mary Virginia and their two small children, his recently widowed mother-in-law, Mrs. Anna Harrison, accompanied them with her three sons, John Henry, twenty, James, and Robert. Tom's brother, Augustus, who had practiced law in Omaha, Nebraska, also joined the party.

They had their share of Indian scares during the two and a half months it took them to reach Denver from Missouri. They were delayed a day when one of the young Macon children turned up missing. Signs showed that the boy had been taken by some Indians. The Macons tracked them down. The baby was with a squaw who said she took him because he was such a fine baby. When dainty Virginia Macon faced up to the squaw and said she thought so too and wanted him back, the squaw handed him over.

When they reached Fremont County, some of the families found Beaver Creek to their liking. Thomas Macon led the rest up the Arkansas through Fourmile to Cañon City. While the community of Fourmile never had a post office, almost as many people lived there in the 1860's as in Cañon City. Its bottom land appealed to farmers and ranchers. In fact, the first milch cow in the county is said to have been brought in by Jesse Rader who built himself a log cabin close to Fourmile Creek after mining for five years near Breckenridge. When his cabin was ready, he returned to Missouri for his wife Elizabeth and their several children.

Mary Merrell, a widow, had patented the land next to Rader with scrip from the War of 1812. George H. Green and George B. Green held adjoining places nearby.

Rudd warmly welcomed the Macons, the Harrisons, the McClures, John Wilson, and others. He saw in them the resurrection of the town. With a number of fundamentalist faith among them, they proved to be resurrectionists in a different sense as well.

These stable families saw in the once bustling gate city precisely what they were looking for, a ready-made community with plenty of range and crop land nearby. They took possession of the vacant stone buildings. There were few wooden ones left. Since those could be moved or disassembled, most had been appropriated for use on outlying farms and ranches. Unlike the roistering miners, these families sought not instant riches but the steady gains to be had in business, farming, and cattle raising. They had brought with them the horses, cattle, implements, and goods necessary to make a good start in a new place.

For instance, twenty-four year old William McClure had three yoke of oxen and a small supply of goods. He traded much of this in Breckenridge, bought salt at the works in South Park, freighted it to Denver where he invested in more goods, and returned to open a notably successful mercantile establishment in Cañon City. He sold this in the early 1870's to his brother, John, and turned to the brokerage business.

But despite a solid start, not all were contented. According to a later account by Thomas Macon,[4] many of the families subscribed to an old fashioned orthodox Baptist creed. They thought the earth belonged to the saints and that they were the saints. When Satan in the guise of a Universalist preacher arrived, they quickly sent for a preacher of their own faith.

When the Rev. Mr. M. B. Adams arrived in the spring of 1865, young William McClure helped him establish a Baptist congregation. A religious war of conflicting creeds followed. According to Macon, the Baptists bested the heretics of other faiths and politicians found it politic to adopt that religion. However, with no one to quarrel with, the Baptists began to bicker among themselves. By the spring of 1868 all but four families of that faith that had arrived together had sold out and gone to Missouri.

Cañon City proved hardly more godly than most frontier towns. It wasn't because the churches hadn't been trying. The Reverend Mr. George Murray's struggling little Methodist Episcopal congregation had bought a stone store building at 228 Main Street. They fitted it out as a permanent place of worship that may have been the first to be dedicated in the Territory south of Denver.[5]

The Reverend Mr. B. F. Moore had gathered eight Presbyterians together on January 23, 1867, to organize the Mt. Horeb Cumberland Presbyterian Church, the first Presbyterian congregation in the county.[6] Rudd donated land at the northwest corner of Macon and Fifth Streets where the church building and parsonage were built with lumber hauled many miles.

Tiny Virginia Macon continued to outwit the Indians even after she was at home in Cañon City. She was a splendid musician and the Indians loved to hear her play the great square piano, the first in town, that had been hauled by oxcart. She seldom refused to play when she saw them coming but one day she was simply too tired. Since she didn't want to flatly refuse, she popped her mother cat and kittens under the piano lid. By the time the Indians were at the door the animals were howling over the strings. She pretended to be frightened as she pointed to the piano, telling the visitors that bad spirits had entered it. Her unbidden guests departed and never came to hear her music again.[7]

About the time young Henry Harrison became the partner of Tom Macon's brother, Joseph, who had brought in goods to open a store, the United States government included the site of Cañon City in a survey. Rudd, along with William Catlin, Benjamin Griffin, and Jothan A. Draper, promptly pre-empted it under the Homestead Law. Catlin may have by then established his brickyard near his home. The ruins of it may still be seen on South Second Street. Griffin had already moved his log cabin across to the south side of the river. An 1869 plat shows that Rudd claimed the entire NE quarter of Section 32, R 71 W, T 18 S; Catlin the NW quarter of the SE quarter; Griffin the NE quarter of the SE quarter; and Draper the NE quarter of the SW quarter. This gave them a controlling interest in the main part of town. They deeded the improved lots to their individual owners, holding the rest for sale. Among the many recorded property transfers of that decade is that of Ceran St. Vrain to H. E. Easterday.

Rumors of a possible transcontinental railroad renewed the hopes of this new town company. The Cañon City and Four Mile Ditch,[8] optimistically put into operation at this time by a company spearheaded by Augustus Macon, still serves the city. Rumors of an Indian invasion quickly squelched any hopes. Cañon City's scared residents used the vacant stone houses as fortresses whenever the Indians threatened to repossess their homeland but no actual assaults took place.

The gate city again looked like a town with a future as more families arrived after the war ended. The Colorado Coal Oil Company continued to refine petroleum from the wells north of town. The town soon boasted forty families, many with children. There were enough to warrant reopening the postoffice, inactive during the lull, in the basement of the Fremont Hotel at First and Main.

Catlin, Griffin, and Rudd established the first school district in the county in 1866, although as early as 1864 Thomas M. Richardson had held school in a log cabin.[9] Hiram Morey was apparently the first county superintendent, serving before the local districts were formed. The first district school was held on River Street at a now unknown location, then moved to adobe Bates Hall when that building was built in 1870. School was held there for five years. Warren Fowler, former magistrate, served as school superintendent from 1867-1873.

There was great jollification, including heavy consumption of William A. Helm's seductive native wine, when the Cañon City and South Cañon bridge opened. Helm had come to Colorado in 1860, then returned East for his family and settled on a farm near Cañon City to raise fruit.

More arrived after being mustered out of the army. Captain B. F. Rockafellow tried mining with his father, George, before settling down. He went East to sell the mine and to marry Kittie King. He returned to build a rather pretentious house at 121 Main Street and to become one of Cañon City's leading citizens. By the time he and Warren Fowler became interested in property across the river, the South Cañon Ditch was furnishing water to irrigate the fertile fields. Colorado farmers were numerous enough to encourage the Colorado Agricultural Society, organized in the spring of 1863, to hold the First Territorial Fair at Denver.

By 1869, Cañon City was once again a trading center as new mining activity flourished in South Park and the San Juans. Henry Harrison dissolved his partnership with Joseph Macon to join Rockafellow in the mercantile business for a while. Farms spread in the natural parks that surrounded the town. The cattle industry became well established in the county on both sides of the Arkansas. The Garden Park Ditch was built to serve the open valley to the north. New school districts formed in these outlying communities.

Rockafellow sold half of his ranch, where once part of Delray had been platted, to John Gravestock and his son. The Gravestocks were the first large scale gardeners, florists, and horticulturalists to take advantage of the favorable location for fruit and truck growing.

Cañon City residents were quick to catch the fever of interest in the proposed transcontinental railroad. They were sure that the only feasible route through the Rockies lay in the Grand Canyon of the Arkansas. Thomas Macon, Rockafellow, and the Rev. Mr. Adams comprised a committee to approach the Kansas-Pacific Railroad in an attempt to convince the company of this. Dapper young General William Jackson Palmer, managing director, and W. H. Greenwood, chief engineer in charge of construction, were interested enough to send engineers to survey the scene in 1868 but nothing came of it. The Eastern officers decided to head for Denver instead.

While Cañon City tried to gain a railroad, Denver and Golden vied for capital status. Thomas Macon, then a member of the legislature, offered to support Denver interests in exchange for their help in securing the Territorial Prison for Cañon City. The strategy was successful. Governor Frank Hall appointed Rudd, with Samuel N. Hay, and James M. Welson of Arapahoe, to select the location. Rudd persuaded Draper to provide the necessary twenty-five acres from his land east of the hogback.[10]

The prison wasn't established quite soon enough. As promptly as Indian marauders had been moved out, white cattle rustlers moved in to deplete the growing herds along the Arkansas. Notorious bands of desperadoes stole cattle as far west as Fremont County when they weren't busy robbing travelers along the Santa Fe Trail. William Coe, the leader of one of these gangs, was captured and jailed in Pueblo. Some visitors who called on him took him for a ride in a wagon and left him dangling from a cottonwood tree, thus removing this threat to Fremont County's cattle interests.[11]

Ever since discouraged prospectors had released their gaunt beasts to fend for themselves over the winter on seemingly sere grass and had found them not dead but fat and sassy in the spring, the grassland of Colorado had been recognized as good grazing ground. In 1869, Charles Goodnight, Elton and Edwin Beckwith, Ira Mulock with his brother, the Eddy brothers, and other cattlemen drove herds as large as three thousand head

46

to Colorado to feed the hungry miners. The lush Arkansas Valley and South Park beyond served as open range for an increasing number of cattle.

With the promise of railroads, colonization came to Colorado. The colony plan made sense in a land where farmers depended on irrigation projects often constructed by cooperative effort. Colonies appealed to the less rugged pioneers, providing as they did instant community life complete with schools and churches.

Carl Wulsten organized one of the first of the agricultural colonies of Colorado among the poor German workingmen of Chicago in 1869. When an advance group came to Fremont County to select an appropriate site, Rudd, who had had a hand in locating county roads, led them to the Wet Mountain Valley, then still a part of Fremont County. They found forty thousand acres to their liking. Although Congress refused them a grant of the land, two hundred fifty bound themselves to work together for five years and headed West anyway.

The following spring, Vice-President Schuyler Colfax used his influence to have government wagons escort the first eighty-six families to the chosen spot on the upper reaches of Grape Creek. In his honor, they called their company The German Colonization Colony of Colfax, Fremont County, Colorado Territory, but it was commonly known as the German Colony. Although the members called their town Colfax, it lasted hardly long enough for them to write the full name of the company. One hundred more members had scarcely arrived before dissension over mismanagement of the semi-cooperative colony caused it to break up.

Although the German Colony disbanded as such, many of the individuals, not discouraged by the difficulty of raising crops at an altitude of eight thousand feet, stayed in the area. The post office moved to Palmer Ranch in 1872 where it became Blumeneau.

Mrs. Gottlieb O'Graske was concerned that there was no church. She wrote to request a Lutheran missionary to serve the several Lutheran families. The Rev. Mr. J. Hilgendorf came to Colorado to investigate and organized a congregation of fourteen families in November, 1872. It joined the Missouri Synod in 1879. After several moves, in 1917 the congregation built the stone-faced church that still stands in Westcliffe.

Blumeneau was a community of fifty by 1884. Later the post office returned to the original site and name of Colfax. Today there's no trace of either place.

After Harrison and Rockafellow dissolved their partnership in Cañon City, Harrison planted much of his land to orchards. Rockafellow prepared for an expanding population by platting seventeen hundred acres of bottom land southeast of Cañon City, naming it Lincoln Park after the late lamented President. He baptised it with water from Mill Creek but, despite its favorable and attractive location, he could do little with it until an adequate water supply was provided three years later.

Settlers continued to come to Fremont County by wagon. Many stayed in the Cañon City area which then boasted two stores, three churches, a post office and drug store, one hotel, one saloon, and some still unfinished large stone buildings. They were convinced that there would soon be a railroad through the Grand Canyon of the Arkansas, seemingly the most promising route for a line to serve the increasing number of mining camps in western Colorado. Others, undaunted by the difficulty of travel, pushed farther westward into the convoluted country along the river.

FOOTNOTES

1. *History of the Arkansas Valley*, p. 623.
2. Commodore Byron McCandless, grandson of Colb, expended much effort after his retirement in 1946, particularly after seeing the television program perpetuating the erroneous story of Wild Bill, in compiling the true facts of his family's migration. Many of his letters concerning this were made available to the author by his brother, Charles G. McCandless. The Fairbury, Nebraska, *Daily News,* July 13, 1961, presented a complete review of the actual event in connection with a pageant at Rock Creek celebrating the one hundredth anniversary of Colb's murder. In 1927, the *Nebraska History Magazine* devoted an entire issue to the Rock Creek Ranch fight. The first debunking of Wild Bill's claim to fame may have been Nobel Burns, "The Greatest Single-handed Fight in American History," published in *The Dearborn Independent* in 1924.
3. Not to be confused with the valley of Eightmile Creek east of the gorge.
4. Alice Polk Hill's *Tales of the Colorado Pioneers,* p. 269. Mrs. Hill interviewed a number of prominent persons in Canon City during a visit in 1883.
5. *Canon City Daily Record,* February 25, 1971.
6. Much information about this denomination is found in a history of the Presbyterian Church in Cañon City prepared by C. Arthur Frederickson in 1962.
7. Janet Sterling recounts several such tales in her *Legends of the Royal Gorge Region.*
8. Incorporation papers on file in Colorado State Archives and Record Center.
9. Unidentified clipping dated March 17, 1938. Further information about all the county districts was compiled by the last County Superintendent, A. V. Wilson in his unpublished *One Hundred Years of Fremont County History of Education.*
10. *Canon City Daily Record,* September 11, 1962, Sec. C, p. 7, and other accounts present these facts that refute the popular yarn that

Cañon City had a choice between the penitentiary and the university and chose the pen because Colorado had more candidates for that institution. The university was not established until several years after the prison was built.

11. Other sources claim that two of Coe's gang were strung up on new telegraph poles near the Drovers Hotel in Pueblo. See Ralph C. Taylor's column "Colorful Colorado," *The Star-Journal and Sunday Chieftain* (Pueblo), March 1, 1970, Section D, p. 12.

CHAPTER V

WAITING FOR THE TRAIN

While the residents of Cañon City waited in resignation for the rails to reach their town, they sipped sodas made with water from the natural Soda Spring at the ice cream parlor hard by that popular spot.[1] They contented themselves with looking forward to the nearer day when Barlow and Sanderson would make arrangements for a first class four horse coach line connection with Pueblo.

No Chamber of Commerce existed to tell prospective settlers of the salubrious climate and the plentiful natural resources. In addition to abundant range for cattle, rich crop land with an adequate water supply, there were copious deposits of coal, iron ore, and petroleum, unlimited stone for building and decoration, with ample amounts of gypsum, silver, and other minerals. Dr. F. V. Hayden noted in his U.S. Geologic Survey of 1870 that nearly every formation in the geological scale outcropped nearby.

Those who lived there didn't need a weather bureau to convince them that here was a large amount of sunshine, low humidity, and much less wind than elsewhere in the West. They left the extolling of Colorado Territory's resources to the land development companies connected with the railroads.

As the rails crept across the prairie, these companies grew lavish with fact and fiction. They had large acreages to sell and needed not only cash, but settlers to provide business for their lines. In the meantime, railroad construction itself created an enormous demand for wood, first for ties and later for fuel. In order to bring the wood down from the well-forested mountains, companies that contracted to supply ties usually had to build roads first. These roads opened up yet more land for settlement. Between the mines, mills, and railroads, the demand for wood began to exceed the supply. Railroad officials turned their eyes toward the coal fields along the Arkansas. Cassiday and others drilled a nine hundred foot well with Isaac Canfield near the Arkansas but found no oil.

In the meantime, the first prison building, built of granite from the nearby hills, opened on June 1, 1871, with the U.S. Marshal in charge. The forty-two cells proved completely inadequate for frontier conditions although they included some dungeons with leg irons. There was no wall around the property until the prisoners' work detail built one.

In January, 1872, Cañon City's population reached six hundred. A new *Cañon City Times* noted that until the previous summer the locality had been one of the most desolate looking places in the country "always excepting Colorado City."[2] The editor did what he could to inspire immigration. He reported, "There are one hundred and twelve bachelors whose ages range from 25 to 50, residing in Cañon; while but two maiden ladies, a few widows and young ladies are alone left to comfort them. Hear, oh ye school marms of New England, seize your carpet satchels and blue umbrellas, and rush to the relief of suffering humanity." Not many rushed.

Residents accused Denver of circulating cock and bull stories of Indian raids designed to keep settlers and visitors away from Cañon City. In truth, outsiders paid little attention to the gateway city, if they ever heard of it, until a correspondent of the *Chicago Tribune* visited there and wrote an article that was widely reprinted. He allowed that the town languished because it had depended too much on its natural resources and not enough on puffery. Among the many attractions he described was a conical mountain of magnetic ore located near Grape Creek. Its pull was so powerful that a paper of needles thrown on the rocks would stand on end "like the quills of a fretful porcupine."[3]

Perhaps this report was the kiting that Cañon needed. The *Times* was soon reporting that the famous Soda Spring at the west end of town was a favorite place for lovers' twilight strolls. There the soda water, considered similar to the highly regarded waters at Saratoga, gushed into a large rock bowl in a rock nook paved with flagstone. The Soda Spring and the adjacent Iron Spring remained a popular spot through a progression of later embellishments until the springs were destroyed in the name of progress.

George Rockafellow was elected Cañon City's first mayor when the town incorporated on April 1, 1872. Having thus come of age, the small city felt venerable enough to promote an Old Settler's Reunion to celebrate the Fourth of July. The original celebration grew into the Wild West Show, the Royal Gorge Roundup, and still later, the Pioneer Celebration and Rodeo.

When the transcontinental railroad had finally reached Denver in August, 1870, thirty-six year old William Palmer, formerly of the Kansas-Pacific, conceived the daring idea of linking the several transcontinental lines either completed or contemplated. He organized the Denver and Rio Grande Railway Company to build from Denver to El Paso, Texas, and eventually to Mexico City. This bold venture, backed by private enterprise, chose the less costly narrow gauge to compete with railroads largely subsidized by generous government gifts of public domain. The D & RG puffed into Pueblo late in June, 1872, after crossing a magnificent amount of practically uninhabited land.

Forsaking for the moment his plans to continue south, Palmer turned to the west to exploit the coal fields along the Arkansas. As early as May 1871, Palmer men had inspected the area around Cañon City. He had his engineers stake a survey all the way through the Grand Canyon of the river as far as Twelve Mile Park to see if a line to the mines on the Upper Arkansas was practicable. It seemed unlikely. At one point along the way, there wasn't even room for a narrow gauge track. However, the General saw that his Central Colorado Improvement Company, formed in November, 1871, snatched up any real estate that might later gain in value from the presence of a railroad. This included coal lands, potential townsites, and the rich magnetic iron deposit near Grape Creek.

The Atchison, Topeka and Santa Fe, building along the Arkansas through Kansas, had crews cutting ties near Oro City and California Gulch. The virgin forests fell to supply mines, mills, and railroads. On August 6, 1872, the first twenty-five thousand ties were started on their way to Fort Dodge.[4] Some twenty men were wet to their chins every day for thirty-six days as they guided the ties down the river. Jams in the narrow throat of the gorge added danger to their discomfort. By the time the first ties passed Cañon City in September, one hundred thousand were in the water.

Some residents felt that Cañon City's Main Street was almost as hazardous as the river. They complained that it was horribly muddy because of careless irrigation. Between the cross ditches and the chuck holes, wagons and buggies were broken and the passengers thrown out unless extreme caution was used. They cynically asked whether Main Street should be a public thoroughfare or a water course.

Despite such criticism, Cañon City continued to grow. Many new houses were built. Real estate additions took form in all directions except west. The early plat notwithstanding, little developed beyond the hogbacks. New residents and businesses, to say nothing of churches, arrived in increasing numbers.

Mrs. Anna Harrison, who was a charter member of the Mount Horeb Presbyterian Church, was one of ten charter members to organize the First Presbyterian Church of Cañon City on Sunday, August 18, 1872. The new organization increased as slowly as the old and for some time met alternate Sundays, by agreement with the Baptists, in the adobe building in the six hundred block of Main Street. However, by the following year, the Baptists wanted full use of the building they had been occupying since about 1870. The Cumberland Presbyterians were gracious enough to invite their rivals to use their building on the fourth Sunday of each month.

Rudd began to see the activity that he had long predicted. He felt his faith in the town was justified when it incorporated in the not wholly unwarranted expectation of becoming the capital when Colorado became a state.

With all indications that the railroad would soon reach Cañon City, Rudd, Rockafellow, Thomas Macon, J. Marshall Paul, and William H. Greenwood organized the Cañon City, Oil Creek and Fairplay Railroad

Company. They saw a ready market for the million dollars worth of stock since Palmer's Central Colorado Improvement Company was opening immense tracts along the way. Although the president of the CC, OC & F made a trip to England to raise capital, the Panic of 1873 put an end to all railroad schemes for the time being.

Cañon City remained the only community of consequence in Fremont County. After the rails arrived and later continued west, new communities grew rapidly as men moved in to supply the demand, first for coal, then for other resources. Some of the place names of this era have been long forgotten, others have stayed in man's memory, some continue to make history.

FOOTNOTES

1. *Cañon City Daily Record,* September 16, 1962, Sec. D., p. 6.
2. The new editor, in several numbers, reprinted items from the earlier *Times* to give a history of Cañon City's early days.
3. Quoted in Don and Jean Griswold's *Colorado's Century of "Cities,"* p. 39.
4. *Cañon City Times,* September 19, 1872.

PART II

ROUTING THE RAILS

CHAPTER VI

ALONG BEAVER CREEK

As the Denver and Rio Grande railroad inched along the Arkansas, it revealed what had been while it shaped what was to be in Fremont County. Beaver, just west of the county line, was Fremont's first railroad station. The fertile valley of the Beaver had appealed to a number of early settlers. Lewis Conley had set up a grist mill in 1860 before the county was formed and served as postmaster for the post office at Beaver Creek. William May, flooded out upstream in 1861 with William H. Phelps, had bought Clark Harrington's Boulder Ranch south of the Arkansas below Beaver Creek. His partnership was again dissolved by flood waters during the wet summer of 1864, the year that the Toof brothers foresook the Hardscrabble and bought William Burdick's ranch near where young Richard Toof had settled. Old State Highway 120 now provides a view of this by-passed deep valley at the mouth of the Beaver where the Toofs' well-run ranch was a favorite stopping place on the road between Cañon City and Pueblo. However, by the time the rails arrived over a right of way through lands owned by Devella and Richard J. Toof among others, Beaver Creek no longer had a post office for its population of twenty-five. The Toof and Juniper post offices that later served lower Beaver are also long since gone. Little but the sandy, shadeless cemetery remains to mark the measure of the community, and even there many of the soft sandstone monuments have weathered to blend with the sand of the soil. One sturdier stone marks the grave of Mary Toof, the first to be buried there when she died in May, 1865.

The second grave was dug the following October for James Henderson who fell victim to a marauding bear. The wounded beast he tried to shoot turned on him, broke his hip, shoulder, and jaw, and tore off his scalp and ear in a single piece. Although Hiram Morey and other neighbors cared for him carefully, he succumbed to blood poisoning after nine days of terrible suffering.

When John V. Callen saw the abundant deer and antelope grazing in the kneehigh grass produced along the creek by the unusual amount of moisture, they felt there would be plentiful pasture for their stock. The Callens and their three children left the Macons and other companions of the trail in Cañon City returning to settle on the flats along Beaver Creek. They raised vegetables to haul by wagon to Buckskin Joe. They opened their home to the first Sunday School held in the area. Other neighbors included Jack and Henry Tremayne who made a circuitous trip by wagon

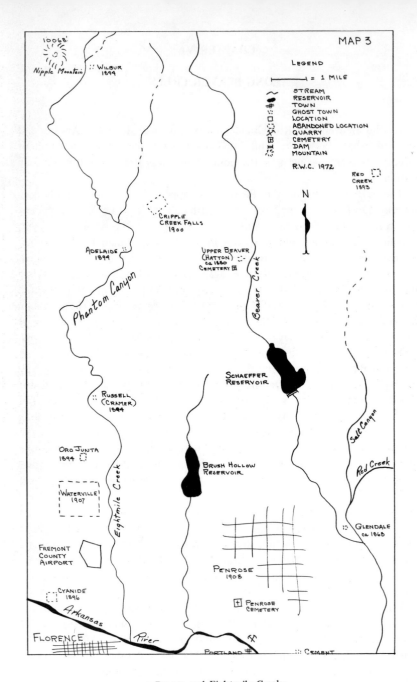

Beaver and Eightmile Creeks

Before the flood of 1921 when Schaeffer Dam broke, the Beaver Creek drainage, settled in the 1860's, provided fruitful fields. Treacherous Eightmile was a more frequent flooder. Despite this, the Florence and Cripple Creek Railroad climbed its canyon profitably for a few years.

58

up Ute Pass, down Currant Creek, and through the then deserted Cañon City. The Callens are among the early settlers buried in the Middle Beaver Creek Cemetery now within the bounds of the Fort Carson Reservation.

Jesse Kelley, who had freighted from Kansas City to Denver in 1860, and had carried the mail on a mule from Pueblo to Buckskin Joe, soon met young Martha Jane Callen and married her in 1866. Little Mary Ellen Callen also grew up to marry a one-time freighter.

LaFayette Uriah Coffman had come to Fremont County in the fall of 1860. He freighted to California Gulch, gardened in South Cañon on the Catlin place, hauled stone for Cañon City buildings, and otherwise hustled a living until he enlisted in Wilson's Sharpshooters. After serving in the Second Colorado Volunteers, he returned to Fremont County, freighted to Fairplay, and worked in the mines. He had a cattle ranch on Grape Creek by the time he married Mary Ellen on January 19, 1873.

Mary Ellen found life on the ranch lonesome and longed for her family. The Coffmans sold out then moved to Glendale where they raised seven children and spent the rest of their long lives.

Bucolic Beaver Creek country had no real center until John C. McClure, who had bought his brother's mercantile business in Cañon City, built the McClure House at Glendale to accommodate travelers on the Granite-Colorado City stage road which had been constructed by Bob Spotswood and William McClelland in 1873 over roughly the route of the more recent Lytle Road.[1] The two-story, sharp-gabled structure of pale stone from nearby quarries stood surrounded by lawns and flower gardens on the east bank of Beaver Creek above its junction with Red Creek. Below it, where the road forded the creek, large barns and corrals held a thousand head of mules and horses for exchange teams. Mining activity along the Upper Arkansas brought an enormous amount of traffic through this stage stop. During its heyday, D. S. Coffman, then its proprietor, served more than a hundred passengers a day. In addition, the spacious, well-furnished rooms made it a popular spot for local weddings, dances, and occasional gospel meetings. It was frequented by Indians and cowhands as well as more cultured ladies and gentlemen.

Not all the travelers who stopped there were to be trusted. Two men who presented a one-hundred dollar bill in payment for a twenty-five dollar gun were on their way with the gun and their change when the century was found to be spurious. They were caught as counterfeiters and sent to the pen.

Glendale remained a lively place until the railroad reached Leadville and there was no longer need for horsedrawn vehicles to carry men and goods to the mining towns.

Lower Beaver Creek was the scene of a crime in the fall of 1888 when an alleged miner made a contract with young Charles R. McCain of Pueblo for the use of his two wagons and teams for hauling ore. On October 26, McCain kissed his wife goodbye and left Pueblo, never to be seen alive again. His body was found near Beaver Creek. His wagons and teams were traced to George R. Witherill who had been released from prison in the spring of the previous year after serving a sixteen-year term for an earlier murder in Douglas County.[2]

In 1871, on a fair September Sunday, young Witherill and his friend, Jack Wight, had shot a literary neighbor in the back to acquire his herd of sheep and his supposed fortune. Later evidence indicated that after Witherill's release he had killed a woman and her grandson in Denver, then had gone to Silverton and induced Marius Jensen to haul ore with him to Pueblo. Jensen was never seen again either and Witherill had sold those teams.

Despite his bloody record, Witherill never served a life sentence. He was lynched at the southeast corner of First and Main in Cañon City on December 4, 1888, by a mob of angry men who easily broke into the county calaboose. A sadistic souvenir hunter removed Witherill's upper lip with its walrus moustache which along with his wide suspenders and other items in tasteful array, was displayed behind glass in one of Cañon City's hotels for many years. This artistic item now graces the lobby of the Frontier Hotel in Denver.

David Fleming Hall[3] was but twenty-three when he and his younger brother came to the Beaver in 1883 to rent a farm and raise truck for the Leadville market. They soon saved enough to buy a place of their own. After his brother married, Dave returned to North Carolina to do likewise on January 1, 1889. When he brought his petite wife back to Beaver, they spent the night at the Toofs' two-story stone house, then set up housekeeping in a log cabin near by.

In 1892, Dave built a house near his brother's on the east side of Beaver Creek on the farm they owned together. He bought a place on Red Creek, homesteaded land near by and proved up. He soon sold that and bought a larger place on Upper Beaver where he raised stock as well as fruits.

Upper Beaver families around the little post office of Hatten kept busy in the 1880's and 1890's growing fruit, truck, and meat for Leadville and Cripple Creek. The log school house of School District #6, now owned by a Pueblo man, still stands less than a half mile north of the Upper Beaver Cemetery where a number of early residents lie buried. Once on a through stage route to Colorado Springs, this deserted community is near the end of a long dead end gravel road replete with sandy washes.

Not far from Hatten, William W. Williamson platted the typical grid town of Red Creek[4] near the head of that stream in 1893 to provide housing for those working on Turkey Creek placers. Although fifteen lots were sold when they were first offered to the public on June 22, and a week later a contract was let for a two-story hotel, the local architecture was not elaborate. In August, a young man was killed there when heavy rains caused his dugout to cave in on him.[5] In recent years, gypsum has been mined near that little developed and long forgotten town located across Highway 115 from present Camp Red Devil close to the El Paso County line.

Beaver Creek farms began to languish when railroads increasingly carried competitive products. About the turn of the century, Dave Hall began to buy up homesteads between Upper Beaver and Eightmile Creeks. Among the first he bought were those of Mittie Merrit and Nannie Gambill. Perhaps he foresaw the future value of Beaver Creek's water rights and was preparing another profitable move. However, there was little activity along the creek again until 1907, when J. Q. MacDonald of Florence[6] saw a future in fruit raising on the slopes where relatively low altitude permitted early crops that would bring premium prices in Denver and Colorado Springs. He interested Spencer Penrose, later famous as the builder of the Broadmoor Hotel, and other Colorado Springs men of wealth, in the idea of forming the Beaver Creek Land and Irrigation Company. They bought out Dave Hall and others who had water rights along Beaver to supply the underground irrigation system to water fruit crops.

Clayton Hollifield put two horses to his wagon and hauled the surveyors over the prairie that was to become Beaver Park after the water was turned into the ditches in 1908. Hollifield was one of five ditch riders during the busy years, and evidently liked his job. He completed fifty-six years with the company before retiring.

The Beaver Park Land and Water Company platted Beaver Park on November 2, 1907, in the heart of the natural park's eighteen thousand acres of rich agricultural land. The following June, The Fremont Townsite Company superimposed the Town of Penrose on the larger plots of Beaver Park.

In 1909, Spencer Penrose with his friends built the Beaver, Penrose and Northern Railroad to connect the town to the D & RG at Beaver Station. Until it was ready for business, those who lived in the area had to make an all day trip by team to trade in Florence. The tyro railroad tycoons also planned a connecting line west to Oro Junta which never developed. The BP & N owned but two pieces of rolling stock, a locomotive and a combination chair and baggage car. It leased freight equipment from the D & RG as needed. The short line ran only until 1919, always losing money, even after it switched from steam to a Cadillac flange-wheeled auto car as its major piece of equipment.

When the railroad failed to create the expected demand for small town lots, subsequent amendments vacated many blocks and reduced the size of the town. D. E. Gibson, the Canon City lumber dealer who had opened a new yard near the Penrose depot, closed it a few years later after a couple of expensive fires, and the anticipated building boom failed to materialize.

While the town didn't grow, fruits and vegetables did. The D & RG's Beaver Station for many years served as a busy shipping point for Beaver Park's apples, cherries, and small fruits. After World War I, increased use of refrigerated railroad cars to bring produce from distant points cut the premium prices for early fruits. Without that higher market, agriculture subject to the vagaries of mountain weather ceased to be very profitable. Drought, frost, and flood made crops a gamble.

One of the most spectacular and damaging floods occurred in 1921. Days of rain, heaviest along Upper Beaver, continued to saturate the earth. Cloudbursts caused Eightmile Creek to overflow its banks and great rocks to roar down the gulches to be carried on by the Beaver, swollen into a raging river. Dams filled to overflowing. Although the spillways at Schaeffer Dam, completed in 1913, were opened to relieve the pressure, they proved inadequate. At 9:30 a.m. on Sunday, June fifth, when the dam broke the twenty to forty foot wall of water swept all before it, leaving sand, gravel, and boulders where grassy meadows and alfalfa fields had been. Orchards and cultivated fields were damaged beyond salvage.

The combined water from Red and Beaver Creeks swept away everything at Glendale except the one-time McClure House that for many years remained a lonely reminder of the past and an inspiration for ghost stories. The flood demolished other buildings, including the stone Toof house at the mouth of Beaver Creek. Then it joined the high water of the Arkansas to race on to Pueblo to add to the previous destruction.

There was a decline in fruit farming for two or three years with a shift to other crops. The Beaver Park Company built a diversion dam and the Brush Hollow Reservoir to supply irrigation water. It later rebuilt Schaeffer Dam. As late as 1927 Beaver Park outclassed the rest of the State with the community exhibit at the State Fair and by 1930 was noted for raising Hubbard squash for seed. But is was a question of either too much water or not enough. The 1930's brought a drought as damaging as the flood. The Penrose Canning Factory lasted only two years, as did the alcohol distillery optimistically established by Western Distilleries, Inc., in 1934.[7] The productivity of Penrose declined until Ma and Pa's Cherry Cider Stand on the highway was almost the only visible sign of industry, although there remained small farms and orchards.

Penrose retained much of its rural charm through the post World War II years. Today the gaunt remains of Glendale, now on private ranch property, present a nostalgic contrast to smart new homes and the trim factory of the country's largest manufacturer of model rocket kits and one-shot propellant engines.

FOOTNOTES

1. See Sterling's *Legends of the Royal Gorge Region,* p. 55, and the *Canon City Daily Record,* January 27, 1969, for stories of Glendale. Mrs. Ada B. Shadford kindly loaned the author her unpublished accounts of pioneers in the Penrose area.
2. D. J. Cook in *Hands Up; or, Twenty Years of Detective Life in the Mountains and on the Plains* tells of Witherill's earlier crimes. Sterling and several newspaper articles tell of his capture and lynching.
3. Mabel Hall's *Story of Phantom Canyon* supplies much information about Beaver Creek and Fourmile families.
4. Stump Witcher, Canon City lawyer, kindly loaned the author his plat book.
5. Colorado Springs *Weekly Gazette,* August 3, 1893.
6. MacDonald was the general manager of the Union Metallic and the National Mills of the U. S. Reduction and Refining Company, vice-president of the First National Bank of Canon City, and general manager of the Greenhorn Artesian Water Company, according to *Canon City Illustrated, 1905,* and a director of The Florence Portland Cement Company, according to incorporation articles.
7. *Canon City Daily Record,* July 7, 1971.

Concrete

A modern ghost town that was active from 1905 when the U.S. Portland Cement Company built the mill until operations ceased about twenty years later. *Photo by the author.*

Portland

Production of cement here began in 1898. The Ideal Cement Company bought out the previous companies in 1924 and has continued to upgrade and update the facility since. *Courtesy of the Florence Pioneer Museum.*

CHAPTER VII

CONCRETE AND PORTLAND

The gaunt cement remains of a modern ghost town stand a short distance west of the site of the old Beaver station. They mark the location of Concrete, once a busy community of workers employed by the U. S. Portland Cement Company. Roland Blunt, later quarry foreman, was one of the construction crew when the mill was built in 1905.

The still very much alive town of Portland is a mile farther west on the south side of the Arkansas. In the mid 1880's, while planning the Florence water system, Geddis and Seerie, Denver builders and contractors, noticed that all the elements needed for the manufacture of cement were available in the vicinity. The raw materials outcropped on the bluffs along the river. In 1898, they began to make cement with lime, silica, aluminum, iron, gypsum, and two other unrevealed elements. It equalled the famous Belgium cement then being imported.

The followng year, William F. Geddis with Joseph A. Thatcher and others incorporated the Colorado Portland Cement Company,[1] capitalized for $100,000. This was increased in 1901 to $125,000, perhaps to compete better with The Portland Cement Company incorporated for $500,000 by James A. McCandless of Florence, Lyman Robison of Canon City, and others. This company in turn increased its capital to $1,000,000 two years later. They also platted eighteen lots along Main Street facing the railroad tracks west of the station of Cement. They called their town Portland for the cement process that produced a material resembling the natural stone found on the Isle of Portland off the coast of England. The next year, McCandless, as president of The Portland Land and Investment Company, platted additional lots across the street.

The cement company modernized its huge quarry in 1904, switching from wheelbarrows to horse drawn cars for hauling ore to the mill; and in 1910, advanced to the use of a steam shovel.

Charles Boettcher was president of both companies in 1908 when the Colorado Portland Cement Company dissolved. The Portland Cement Company voted to change its name to the Colorado Portland Cement Company. This firm platted a third subdivision in 1911 at the junction of the D & RG with the Santa Fe railroad. It accommodated a total Portland population of 250 families.

The Ideal Cement Company, active in the area by 1910, was incorporated in 1924 and bought out both the Colorado Portland and the U. S. Portland Cement companies. To consolidate operations, it abandoned the Concrete site. In 1948, Ideal spent ten million dollars on a new plant. The Portland plant continued to grow, making a large contribution to both payroll and pollution in Fremont County.

There's no mistaking the product in this company town. The houses, now home to only fifty families, are made of cement block and stucco. Even the benches and barbecues in the shady park, where more company houses once stood, are made of concrete. Visitors are always welcome to enjoy the spacious park facilities and groups are invited to use them with company permission. Tours of the works can be arranged.

Harry E. Born, the chief chemist at the Ideal plant, who had started at Concrete in 1918, may be one of the best remembered from earlier days. In 1931, when the Alexander Aircraft Company of Colorado Springs was hurting from the depression, Born bought a four thousand dollar Alexander Eaglerock plane for fifteen hundred dollars. He flew from a strip about a mile and a half east of Penrose and took in a few extra bucks with his five dollar flights from the Royal Gorge airport. He gave sightseers many a thrill over the Gorge until he was transferred to another Ideal plant in 1936.

Although Hardscrabble Creek joins the Arkansas just west of Portland, it is now reached more readily from Florence. In 1868, however, there were enough people living at Lower Hardscrabble near the confluence to warrant the formation of a new school district which later became the Portland School District.[2]

Despite the interest of Fred Walters, longtime postmaster at Wetmore, in the site of the old trappers' fort, El Cuervo's significance was little known to the local residents until young James McFall drew a scale plan of Walters' archeological measurements of the fort as an engineering school project. Years later when his brother Jack found the drawing, he had it reproduced and distributed to interested persons. Harry Chalfont undertook to make a model from the plan.

Hardscrabble's history as the earliest settlement in Colorado would still be unknown to the casual passerby except for the ample information sign beside Highway 67 just north of the Custer County line. The shallow depression that marks the site of El Cuervo is on private land, some distance west of the marker. No other evidence of the early inhabitants remains.

A small church with its sizeable cemetery speaks of the influx of more pious souls to found the community of New Hope in the 1870's and 1880's. When the Southern Colorado Baptist Association met in Cañon City in 1872, the New Hope church, east of the creek, established the previous year, had twenty-two members, outnumbering Cañon City's nineteen. By 1900, New Hope was no longer considered a community.

In the next decade, the development of Beaver Park again stirred men to activity on the Hardscrabble. Emmet E. Jennings, Alva Koontz, and Louis R. King became directors of The Hardscrabble Irrigation District, organized on petition of residents of the District.[3] They appointed Arnold Benton McFall, a civil engineer of experience in Fremont County, father of James and John McFall, to survey an area approximately eight miles long by three wide along, largely in Fremont County east of Hardscrabble Creek, and to ascertain the feasibility of constructing a reservoir to control the stream's flow.

Jennings, who had farmed there since 1883, King, who had lived in the District since 1895, and Koontz, who owned one hundred acres farmed since 1876, all recognized that Hardscrabble's flow was erratic. A large volume of water over the years had carved a course some seventy-five feet below the gently sloping land where Kinkead was among the first to value the flourishing native gramma grass. However, the flow was never steady. There was too much water in the late winter and early spring. Late summer storms in the well-named Wet Mountains sent floods roaring down the creek. Only those who farmed the bottom land from five hundred feet to half a mile in width could count on water during the critical growing time and their fields were always in danger of being flooded out.

McFall's survey showed that a reservoir constructed east of the town of Wetmore in Custer County, fed by a one and a half mile long diversion canal, would indeed make irrigation of the upland in the District possible. On the strength of his survey, some of the large holdings were subdivided into tracts of five to forty acres designed for intensive farming and the raising of orchards and small fruits. In 1912, when a special election approved the issuance of $950,000 worth of six percent bonds, an elaborate prospectus was prepared.

A quarter section within the District was designated the townsite of Mountain View, approximately a mile northeast of the still standing New Hope church. The town of Mountain View remained on paper with Mountain View Reservoir #1 an unfulfilled dream of the promoters, as the bonding company considered the available water inadequate for the proposed project and refused to sell the bonds. The residents then had the District legally dissolved.

Here trappers and hunters like Maurice LeDuc once ranged to take what they could when they would. Now even the federal trappers of the Bureau of Sports, Fisheries and Wildlife Management and Enforcement must have a state permit to trap, because in 1925, an act of the State Legislature created the Newlin Creek State Game Refuge. This extensive area includes private and public lands high in the mountains centering at the headwaters of Newlin Creek, a tributary of the Hardscrabble.

Market hunting of deer had nearly depleted Colorado's game by the turn of the century. In 1905, the legislature closed the state to hunting for a five year period. Game animals were in even shorter supply at the end of that time because any hunter could claim to be after predators if he wasn't

67

found with illegal game in possession. To eliminate this excuse, the legislature created game refuges where all birds and animals are protected. Only certain predators can be taken and those only by permit. Because this action proved effective in reestablishing the deer herds in particular, the refuge lands have been open for controlled seasons since 1937.

Where once the traders made illicit whiskey available to the Indians, there later thrived another illicit whiskey business. During Prohibition a number of hidden stills and vats produced a generous supply of White Mule and Dago Red.[4]

Vegetation has been sparse in the valley since the 1930's and the land is eroded. Amateur archeologists like Walters have long since sifted the ant hills for beads and other evidence that gave credence to the rambling tales told by LeDuc to the gold rush pioneers.

There are now some scattered ranches, a grange hall, with a few houses of relatively recent vintage, in addition to the church, to give even a semblance of community to this area that has been the longest inhabited by whites of any in Colorado. The New Hope area seems but a rural suburb of newer Florence.

FOOTNOTES

1. Incorporation papers on file in the Colorado State Archives and Records Center.
2. Wilson's *One Hundred Years of Fremont County History of Education,* p. 3.
3. Interview with John R. McFall, November 14, 1969, and his *A. B. McFall, Pioneer Civil Engineer, Florence, Colorado;* also, the prospectus of *The Hardscrabble Irrigation District in Fremont and Custer Counties, Colorado.*
4. Conversations with John R. McFall and Charles G. McCandless.

CHAPTER VIII

FLORENCE AND VICINITY

Although there was no town of Florence until the approach of the railroad, the site had early been settled by farmers. The first to recognize its agricultural potential was Jesse Frazer, who in 1859 married Mrs. Ash in Denver. The following April he brought her and her son, Will, to squat on a broad bottom on the south side of the Arkansas about eight miles below Cañon City. Frazer fashioned a cottonwood fork into a plow and turned the first farm furrow in what would become Florence.

He sold his vegetables and Mexican corn to the gold seekers at an enormous profit. After he and his friends filed on their coal land, he kept busy in the off seasons hauling coal to Cañon City. Once he was nearly drowned fording the river in the process. The success of his first crop prompted Uncle Jess to make long range plans for raising fruit as well as vegetables. Twenty years later he had two thousand bearing apple trees as well as other fruits. He developed the delicious Colorado Orange apple, known only locally but highly regarded by those privileged to taste it.

William Ash took over his stepfather's claim and sold part of it to Isaac W. Chatfield and Clark Harrington in 1863. Uncle Jess moved to the next place below. Harrington sold his share to Chatfield in 1866, then made yet another move, this time to lower Hardscrabble. Perhaps he found as much profit in land as in cattle for three years later he moved on to upper Hardscrabble. Ash patented his 120 acres in 1867.[1]

When Stephen Frazier with his wife and sons, Reuben, Henry, and Gideon, came from Iowa in 1860 to settle above Frazer on the ranch first claimed by William Costan, the area became known as Frazierville. This name was reinforced after Jesse Frazer sold his second claim to Henry Frazier in 1862.

Accounts of these two notable families are confused since both spellings were used indiscriminately. Stephen Frazier was to become a ruling elder of the Cañon City Cumberland Presbyterian Church, and Gideon a member of the Rocky Mountain Presbytery of that church when it was incorporated in 1876. Jesse Frazer was considered "the salt of the earth" by all who knew him.

William May and two companions took up a claim along the river well above Frazierville. After May was flooded out in the spring of 1861, John Howard and Wilbur F. Stone agreed to improve a claim on land below that location for P. A. McCumber. However, when McCumber decided grub was too scarce to feed help, he took over the claim himself.

John Witcher raised wheat on his Castle Rock ranch north of the

Arkansas. He had his wheat ground in Johnson's mill. He and young William Stump freighted the flour to Fairplay in time for Christmas, 1865. Two oxteams pulled Witcher's wagon and one pulled Stump's across the solidly frozen river. Although the men almost froze themselves, it was a profitable trip. They sold the flour for twenty-five dollars a hundredweight as fast as they could unload it. Stump, originally from Virginia, had come from Ohio to avoid fighting relatives in the Civil War. He bought some cattle from Charles Goodnight, who in 1868 headquartered on the earlier Nolan Grant about five miles west of Pueblo,[2] and established a ranch.

Witcher married Purlina Foster in 1866. The following year he moved eight miles north to take squatter's rights on land near the present Phantom Canyon to engage in the cattle business. His brother Taliaferro (pronounced Tolliver) who had been a messenger for Confederate General J. E. B. Stuart, soon arrived by oxtrain to establish a squatter's right near him. T. Witcher became the partner of Adam Stultz, a sturdy homesteader straight from Germany.

In the spring of 1866, James McCandless[3] paid Henry Johnson two thousand dollars for ditch rights and the one hundred sixty acres first claimed by Antoine near the mouth of Chandler Creek. He hired Mexicans, bought enough seed to plant one hundred acres to wheat, and harvested a fair crop despite rain damage. In the fall of the next year, he went back East to gather some forty-five relatives: Greens, Woods, and Hartleys as well as McCandlesses. His father and mother, James M. and Selina McCanles, returned to Colorado Territory with him.

Some of the relatives wintered with him on his Big Spring Ranch at Twelve Mile Ford on the only road then leading to the Wet Mountain Valley. In the spring, he and others, while looking at land in that valley, managed to get lost in the trailless upland park. James A. bought Harrington's ranch on the upper Hardscrabble but soon disposed of it to William Vorhis returning to the Frazierville area. Others of the family settled in Pueblo County and elsewhere.

James M. McCanles, an amateur poet of some talent, died at Booneville, Colorado, in 1869. He was buried in the Chico Cemetery near present North Avondale. James A. refused to attend the funeral, having taken umbrage at the chiding poem his father had written on the subject of his infidelity. His parents seem to have been as ill-pleased as was his wife at the *ménage à trois.* As far as can be determined, Kate Garrett was still around and her daughter Julia was accepted as one of his children. His wife, Sarah, like others in her position, lacking skills, education, or resources, was unable to initiate divorce proceedings or to support herself apart from her husband. She did let it be known, however, that she intended to leave James as soon as her daughter Mary Jane was married and could offer her a haven.

In 1870, McCandless bought three hundred twenty acres, which included Jesse Frazer's original claim, and three shares of Union Ditch[4] stock from Chatfield. He paid for this with one hundred steers at thirty-five dollars a head and his Big Spring Ranch valued at fifteen hundred dollars. The following year, he sold his wheat land, bisected by the proposed railroad right of way, to W. R. Brewster, more than doubling his money. These would prove to be smart moves.

Orphaned early, Edwin Lobach learned the trade of saddler and harness maker. In 1854, too poor to ride, he walked most of the way to California. He returned to Pennsylvania after four years and in 1859 headed West again to mine near Central City. Fortune continued to elude him. He found greater returns in hauling government freight and working on the Union Pacific grade.

When the railroad reached Denver, Lobach gave up freighting to start a stock ranch. At thirty-eight, he married nineteen-year-old Nancy Crouch. In 1872 he bought Stephen Frazier's place. There he ran a dairy, and raised Berkshire hogs and fine horses. His tireless energy and determination soon built it into one of the finest ranches in the county. Others came to farm at Frazierville, drawn by the 168 day growing season, unusual in mountain territory.

When William Palmer built the Denver and Rio Grande Railroad, he cannily kept his rails outside any existing community. He and his various companies invested in thousands of acres of inexpensive land, including a healthy portion of the Nolan Land Grant south of the Arkansas. He used his Central Colorado Improvement Company to create such townsites as Colorado Springs, designed for resorts and residences, and South Pueblo, designed for industry. This practice of bypassing previously established settlements caused much disgruntlement in the affected localities.

After Palmer temporarily abandoned the idea of continuing south in favor of exploiting the coal resources along the Arkansas, his CCI, in customary fashion, planned a new townsite, Labran. It was about a mile and a half east of Frazierville on land purchased from John Locke. This time the ploy didn't work. McCandless had the foresight to plat a rival townsite on thirty of his acres near Labran. He wielded enough influence to prevent an exodus to Palmer's property. He considered Frazierville as the name for his town until the engineer who did the survey suggested that he name it for Kate's cute little daughter, Minnie Florence, born in Pueblo on October 3, 1871. The post office thus became Florence, a development the D & RG seems to have ignored. Once his town was established, McCandless opened a store where he served as the first postmaster in the adobe building on the south side of Main Street.

The D & RG referred to the end of the tracks simply as Coal Banks (for the deposits to the south originally worked by Frazer) and proceeded to

71

David Colbert McCanles
In 1861, Colb McCanles was killed in cold blood by James B. Hickok, later known as Wild Bill. *Courtesy of Carol McCandless.*

James Alexander McCandless
Once known as J. Leroy McCanles, Colb's brother later became the founder of Florence, Colorado. He was a State Senator when this picture was taken between 1878-1882. *Courtesy of Charles G. McCandless.*

set up Labran station in 1872 in a boxcar. However, the town of Labran failed to develop. This was a blow to Palmer whose railroad was, as usual, hard pressed to find funds. The Union Contract Company, actually set up to build the thirty-six mile spur from Pueblo, retained possession of it until 1874 when the final payment was made.

By this time, because Sarah McCandless had long since had enough of her husband's adultery she promised to make good her threat to leave him. She kept her word when Mary Jane married William Delos White, the son of William B. White of California Gulch, in March, 1873.

James, in simulated wrath at Sarah's departure, sued for divorce the following fall, claiming that she had deserted him and refused to live with him although he was willing to have her as wife. She didn't contest the action. Her nephew, James Green, testified that she had gone to Greenhorn to live with her daughter. The Hon. Moses Hallett, Chief Justice of Colorado and Judge of the Third Judicial District, granted the divorce on November 14, 1874.[5] Meantime, James had been well consoled by Kate. Their third child, Evelyn, was born in Florence in April of that year.

Sarah subsequently married a Mr. Arthur about whom little is recalled. She lived for many years across the street from her former husband before she died at the Hardscrabble ranch of her daughter in 1914 at the age of eighty-one.

The Florence Citizen claims that several accounts give LeDuc credit for refining oil for improvised wick lamps at El Cuervo around 1841. If he did, he must have had better luck finding oil than did A. M. Cassiday who had early exploited the Oil Creek seep. Cassiday induced four associates to buy large tracts near Florence between 1871 and 1874 but their probing produced no oil. Cassiday, undaunted, incorporated The Colorado Oil Company in 1877 to continue boring.

When the Panic of 1873 interrupted the search for oil and prevented the further extension of the D & RG, it stimulated prospecting for the more readily retrieved minerals such as gold and silver. With the discovery of precious metals in the Wet Mountain Valley, interest shifted there. New towns sprang up. The panic didn't prevent production of McCandlesses, however. James kept busy in bed as well as at business. Kate became the mother of Julius Victor in 1875 and Ida in 1877.

Julius McCandless, who had been nine when Hickok murdered his father, Colb, came to Florence in 1876 to work for his Uncle Mac. He did the actual work at the post office and whatever else James McCandless required of him. He was eager to make his fortune so he could marry his Nebraska love, Mary Andrews, in Endicott on Thanksgiving Day, 1880.

The D & RG's affiliate, the Canon Coal Railway Company, built about two and a half miles of track to connect the main line with the coal mines in 1876. The station at Florence then became Coal Junction. With greater

Julius McCandless

Son of Colb, Julius here assumes a preacherlike pose in his later years. *Courtesy of Charles G. McCandless.*

Byron, Beatrice, and Charles McCandless

Julius' three children grew up in Florence, Byron to become a famous Navy man, Beatrice to die in the flu epidemic, and Charles to serve in the State Legislature and to be honored as a distinguished pioneer. *Courtesy of Charles G. McCandless.*

activity at the coal banks, James McCandless could no longer prevent an exodus, that left the town's business buildings deserted and forced the residents to travel to Coal Creek to trade. Florence, in truth, was little more than a coal junction for awhile. Julius, aggravated by the railroad's attitude toward Florence, flagged down the train one day to inform the crew that he was tired of going to Labran for mail meant for Florence.

When the tiny town was incorporated in 1877, James Alexander McCandless, then in the livery business, was its most prominent citizen. As such he aspired to political eminence as well. He was elected County Commissioner. Before his term was up, he ran for a seat in the Colorado House where he served two terms.

The D & RG was soon able to entertain further plans for expansion. It tried to head off its rival, the Atchison, Topeka, and Santa Fe, by occupying all points of advantage, especially mountain passes. However, in 1880, the Santa Fe built an expensive branch from Pueblo to the newly opened mine a mile west of Coal Creek. Shortly after that, the Grand Canon Coal Company struck a basin of lubricating oil at 1450 feet. The Colorado Coal and Iron Company hit gas veins in borings below the coal.

In 1881, Isaac Canfield hired Cassiday to drill for water at the Canfield Coal Mine about four miles south of Florence. Cassiday, discouraged in his search for oil, was glad to use his rig for water. He had about given up on that, too, when, ironically, he hit a substantial flow of oil. He recovered several barrels of oil before he lost his tools in the hole. Although litigation prevented development of this well, it marked the first real find in the Florence field.

David G. Peabody of Cañon City noticed traces of oil near Brush, Eightmile, and other creeks near Florence where he thought he'd hit the fringe of a vast petroleum deposit. He was sure that sinking a well would tap it. He went to Pennsylvania to consult with experts, returning to organize the Land Investment and Coal and Oil Mining Company.

Ed Lobach was among the principal investors when that company, using modern equipment, began a hole in his cornfield in November, 1882. They found oil at 1205 feet in April, at a drilling cost of $20,000. They torpedoed this well and later lowered it to increase production. It still produces, upholding Florence's reputation as the oldest continuously producing field in the world.

The company raised its capital from $100,000 to $1,000,000 and developed other wells near town, starting a boom that was to last fifty years. Eventually the company went broke developing a new well. Meantime, Cassiday organized the Arkansas Valley Oil and Land Company which owned seven wells within two miles of Florence. The first refinery there was built by the Arkansas Valley Oil and Land Company.

Oil companies proliferated as oil fever struck U. S. investors. Many mining men switched from gold and silver to the black magic rush. Not all the oil companies were successful. Although it was widely believed that there was a vast lake of oil under Florence, it is, in truth, a freak field. Oil is found only in fissures where it has been forced by natural pressures.

However, there was enough activity in the area to warrant a new real estate addition, platted by the Colorado Coal and Iron Company in 1884, mostly along Railroad Street. There was then no town water supply. Individuals dug wells or stored water in barrels or cisterns, taking the precaution of adding a stalk of cactus to clear the water. By 1886, there were enough children in town to require the establishment of a school district and the building of the school house now owned by the American Legion.

The Colorado Oil Trust Company, capitalized in 1887 at $3,000,000, became a few months later The United Oil Company headed by Nathaniel P. Hill, the renowned mining expert who had solved many of the problems of Colorado's difficult ores. McCandless platted an addition to his original townsite, then built the two-story McCandless Building to house his Florence Mercantile business. He also became a banker and began the first of two terms in the Colorado Senate.

The Democrat editor of *The Florence Oil Refiner* put out Florence's first newspaper on December 5, 1887. He spared no language in expressing his opinion of Republican McCandless. He modified his diatribe only after Wellington, McCandless' thirty-three-year-old son, undertook to beat him up.

By 1889, James McCandless had prospered enough to replace his attractive log cabin, which is still standing, with an elaborate brick mansion to house his family, by this time augmented by Colbert, born 1879, and Dora, born 1886. However, he soon felt the competition of another imaginative opportunist.

Augustus Rose Gumaer,[6] had attached the property of the Colorado Oil Company in order to recover several hundred dollars he'd loaned at ten per cent interest. He then incorporated the Florence Oil and Refining Company for $500,000 with F. M. Brown, E. C. Gray, William E. Johnson, and T. M. Harding of Cañon City. The following year, the directors called a special meeting and voted to reduce the number of directors to three and changed the official office from Cañon City to Florence, newly arrived at municipal status. At the same time, A. H. Danforth, who had been vice-president and general manager of the Colorado Coal and Iron Company for the previous nine years, was elected president with Johnson as secretary.

Gumaer's company drilled well #16, one of the most productive, back of the present Florence Hotel. He wanted to buy up adjoining land but not the improvements thereon. Somehow the empty buildings including that of the mercantile establishment which had moved to Coal Creek, conveniently

James A. McCandless' Log Cabin
J. Victor McCandless, born in this cabin, later added another old log cabin to enlarge it, and in time died there. *Photo by the author.*

James A. McCandless' Mansion
The McCandless family were proud of this house, the most imposing in Florence when it was completed in 1889. Courtesy *Florence Citizen.*

77

burned. Later, James McCandless's son, Victor, who owned land across the tracks from Gumaer's #16, tried to tap the same fissure. However, his driller got nothing but mud and water. After repeated attempts, Vic knew they were stumped. They finally lost their tools and the well, but they figured it had been worth the chance to discomfort the thoroughly disliked Gumaer.

Gumaer had arrived in Cañon City in 1881 to be cashier of Ira Mulock's new bank and soon acquired a reputation for sharp trading. As Mulock and his three sons prospered in the cattle business at the head of Badger Creek they had money to lend. An educated young man from Port Jervis, New York, where his French Huguenot ancestors settled about 1690, Gumaer had married Mulock's daughter, Ella, in 1874.

According to some accounts, certain papers came into Gumaer's possession when the bank failed breaking the affluent Mulocks. About a year later, Gumaer was on hand to bid in the ranch at a sheriff's sale for a small sum which he soon recouped from the sale of beef. W. H. Huff, James K. Robinson, with Gumaer's associate, William E. Johnson, incorporated The Boston Land and Cattle Company in 1892. Gumaer, as was his wont, liked to remain in the background to manipulate his many interests. Although he persuaded Eastern money to invest in the cattle company, he seems to have been the principal owner and to have operated the IM ranches under that company from then on.

The City of Florence grew steadily with the continued development of the oil field despite the determined opposition of the Pennsylvania producers. Gumaer took credit for having thwarted John D. Rockefeller's attempt to buy the product of the Florence Oil Refinery at his own price. An argument followed Gumaer's refusal to cooperate.

Rockefeller, of Standard Oil fame, with the connivance of the railroad companies, drove the price down to five cents a gallon locally. Gumaer countered by furnishing coal oil free to Florence customers. In those days, housewives brought out their gallon cans, spouts corked with raw potatoes, to be filled when the horsedrawn wagon reached their doors. By this time, the Florence Oil and Refining Company had a substantial still east of Gumaer Avenue near the present location of the bulk plant of Sasser and Nelson. Here, too, Gumaer, a sporty sort, kept race as well as draft horses in the sturdy brick stables that are still there. And there he developed a track where the race horses could work out.

Not all the petroleum was processed locally. The Rocky Mountain Oil Company, with producing property near Highland Cemetery, laid a four inch pipe line to its refinery at Overton, north of Pueblo, in 1892 despite the kerosene war.[7] The Cleveland capitalists involved, like others, believed their well tapped a large lake of oil. But contrary to their expectations, the early pipe line operation was not profitable. The cutthroat competition became even sharper. Then the depression that followed demonetization finished it off. The refinery operated through most of 1893 before the plant closed and the business was abandoned.

Although oil had encouraged her growth, Florence didn't really boom until gold was discovered in Cripple Creek. The new mining district had neither the coal nor the water needed for smelting the precious ores. Florence which had both, determined to become the smelter center for the mines in addition to being the "derrick town of Colorado."

Senator McCandless incorporated his banking business as the Bank of Florence. Lobach, with Julius McCandless, by then proprietor of the Florence Hardware store, promptly incorporated the Florence Land and Improvement Company to deal in real estate.

Early in 1892, James McCandless, Canfield, and other businessmen, combining civic pride with self interest, incorporated the Florence and Cripple Creek Free Road Company as a non-profit company to compete with Cañon City's toll road to the District. They hired Ben McFall, then but a newly graduated civil engineer who had bribed a brakeman with a dollar for the privilege of reaching Florence in a boxcar, to survey the least costly route along Eightmile Creek.

Adam Stultz had remained in his two-story log house on his homestead at the canyon mouth. John Witcher had long ago moved his family to West Four Mile in Teller County and T. Witcher had traded rights with Jack Bernard for a place west of Cañon City. Nannie Gambill, T. Witcher's niece, kept house for Stultz and mothered T. Witcher's sons, Otis and T. Lee, ten and eight when they came to live at Stultz's in 1891 after their parents' divorce.

Those who had laughed at the idea of building a road up the high-walled, narrow, rocky, winding canyon of Eightmile Creek had nothing but praise for the enterprise when it was completed in six weeks for less than ten thousand dollars using voluntary labor. Every morning crowds gathered at the stage office at the Florence Hotel to watch the Concord coach take off behind three span of horses. Much freight arrived at the D & RG depot to be carried to Cripple Creek although the steep road had hairpin turns so sharp that the lead team had to be unhitched to get the rig around the bend.

Within a year ore production taxed the capacity of the freight wagons and coaches plying the Free Road. David H. Moffat, although no longer connected with the D & RG, tried to interest the line in building a railroad from the Arkansas to Cripple Creek but the Gould interests had other ideas. Both McCandless and Johnson joined some of Moffat's business associates in incorporating the Florence and Cripple Creek Railroad Company.[8] The directors of the Free Road Company turned over their road to the railroad so that it might be used as a roadbed. Construction began on

New Year's Day, 1894. Young Ben McFall served the company as civil engineer until late the following year. To hold down cost, the narrow gauge line partly followed the creekbed despite flood danger. The roundhouse and other facilities were built at Main and Second Streets in Florence.

McCandless was so busy that he sent to Nebraska for Julius's brother, Charles, Colb's youngest son, to help with the mercantile business. All this activity may have been what brought Billie White and Mary Jane back to Florence from Maysville about 1893 to open a coal, feed, freight hauling, and road contracting business. Their ample building stabled thirty-six horses and housed such equipment as wagons, dump carts, scrapers, etc.

Gumaer, the Johnson brothers, and others formed The Florence Improvement Company to deal in real estate and to build and operate street railroads, water works, electric light and power plants, and to deal in franchises. Gumaer signed the articles with the bold Spencerian flourish that gave clue to his character.

The very next day, McCandless, always closely competing with Gumaer, signed articles of association with Canfield and others for The Florence Rapid Transit and Power Company. They proposed an electric railroad from Florence to Union Highland Cemetery and the nearby coal towns. Such a railroad would have been a boon since, aside from the steam trains, horses provided the only transportation available— except for two bicycles, one owned by a blacksmith and the other by a teacher. The bicycles were difficult to maneuver in wet weather when the mud was knee deep in Main Street.

People in town could board their saddle horses at the livery stable for twenty-five cents a day or rent a horse and buggy for a dollar and a half a day. Four to six jerk line teams hauled hay and grain from Westcliffe and returned loaded with coal, coal oil, and other supplies.

Of course, electric railroads required an adequate supply of electricity. This would be available at the plant of the Arkansas Valley Electric Light and Power Company, completed in 1892 on South Union Avenue. Although no electric railroad materialized, the power plant did brighten the town when the twin carbon arc street lights were installed. William Russell McCandless, son of Charles, was long employed at the power plant.

The Johnson brothers became directors of The Florence Land Company whose purpose was to deal in real estate and securities. Another of the directors was James B. Orman, later Governor of Colorado. Lobach heightened the competition by platting Castle Rock Park which includes West Third and Fourth Streets and Lobach Avenue. Stephen Frazier subdivided some of his land. Everyone wanted in on the Cripple Creek boom.

The Panic of 1893 had little immediate effect on Florence or the construction of the railroad. Gold ore flowed unabated from Cripple Creek to Florence's nine mills. When the railroad was ready, the first freight climbed from Florence's 5199 foot elevation to Victor's 9700 feet on May 11, 1894. No passenger train made the run until the first of July. The first one called for a big celebration. The joy of this was marred when the next day the coaches left the tracks near Anaconda, killing one and injuring many.

Florence flouished after the railroad was in operation. And so did the ranchers along Eightmile, Sixmile, and Upper Beaver. They did a thriving business in draft stock and driving horses and found a ready market in the mining towns for their large herds of beef cattle. When Stultz sold out to Russell the depot and switches near there took the name of Russell until Cramer bought the place.

The hastily built railroad all too soon felt the press of competition. Only three days after the forty mile line was completed, the Midland Terminal Railway from Colorado Springs reached Gillett with a standard gauge road. Despite this, plenty of high grade ore reached Florence in sealed box cars that were carefully cleaned for gold dust after they were unloaded.

The Florence Oil and Refining Company, with Gumaer as president and his wife as secretary, platted land along the F & CC right of way. The company also platted an addition near its refinery south of the Santa Fe tracks. This included a club house for the horsey set near the race track, not far from Gumaer's walnut grove and fenced game preserve.

The Triumph Oil Company, of which Isaac Canfield was president, platted Florence Heights. McCandless built a new brick building at 110 Main Street. He moved his mercantile business to the first floor and provided hotel and office space on the upper floors. In 1895, his odd marital arrangements long forgotten or forgiven, he was honored by having the new school named after him. He had earlier served as president of the board of School District #2.[9]

Moffat and his associates built a 170 ton capacity mill on the F & CC two miles above Florence. Here their Metallic Extraction Company used the new cyanide process of ore treatment. The Florence Oil and Refining Company platted the town of Cyanide near the mill in 1896.

Freight trains and narrow gauge Pullman buffet cars from Denver rode the rails between Florence and Cripple Creek at all hours of the day and night. Then, in late July, 1895, a cloudburst above Adelaide sent a flood down Eightmile Creek. It left three hundred feet of track suspended above the torrent at Russell and completely tore out a half mile of track above that. It swept away the boarding house at Adelaide, drowning three people. In all, twelve miles of track were washed out or damaged. The helper engine had a wild ride down the grade ahead of the water but managed to outrun it.

Although the tracks were patched in fifteen days so that trains could run, raising the road to a safer level didn't commence until the following spring. Much of the ballast used to bolster the tracks was actually low grade ore that could today be profitable processed. After the disastrous April fire in Cripple Creek, in addition to the usual traffic, the F & CC used about thirty-four locomotives, some leased, to haul building materials to crippled Cripple Creek.

By the following year, a number of reduction mills were running at their top capacity of about fifty tons a day. However, the El Paso Reduction Company's could handle twice that. With ore processing and oil production, Florence continued to boom. With the boom came the inevitable saloons. All fifteen of them remained open around the clock. All offered poker games. Some had gambling equipment in basements or upper floors. The more benevolent had high board bullpens in back where drunks could sleep it off to avoid being robbed by sluggers waiting in the dark vacant lots separating the scattered adobe or frame business buildings. If slick gamblers in the saloons didn't gain the part of the paycheck the saloon keeper left, a man could easily lose it betting on the horse races held every few days. Ladies of the night housed near the railroad on Union and other streets, also helped diminish the take home pay.

Jesse Frazer's estate, Gumaer, Lobach, and McCandless continued to add grid-like additions to the city for the next few years. Only the United Oil Company's Mesa subdivision southeast of Bridge Street seems to have used the contour of the land to advantage by platting curved streets. A less formal addition was a tiny tent town, occupied by those chasing the tuberculosis cure, crowded onto the tract where the Methodist Church now stands.

By 1900, Hill's United Oil controlled most of the production in the Florence field, although small independent companies continued to proliferate. Among them were the Blaney Oil Company, Centennial, Central, Columbia, Creed, Crescent, Doctor, Empire, Fremont, Frazier, Hiawatha, Keystone, Lobach, Majestic, National Oil Creek, Stadicona, Union Oil and Coal, Victor, and West Lebanon.

For awhile it seemed as if the F & CC would serve a new town, Cripple Creek Falls, elaborately platted at a location about halfway to Victor but never developed. In 1899, a seven mile branch from Oro Junta did connect the F & CC with Cañon City. In August, however, it was Florence, not Cañon City that sent fire engines on a special train to fight the Victor fire. Unfortunately, a rock slide on the tracks prevented the train from reaching Victor in time to do any good.

The Florence Electric Street Railway Company was organized to carry on business in Fremont, Teller, El Paso, Pueblo, and Custer counties. Stock at one hundred dollars a share financed a survey by Ben McFall and his partner, Robert S. Kelley. They mapped the proposed route from Florence to Cañon

82

City via West Third Street to Cyanide Avenue, north of Castle Rock, then along present Highway 50 to Cañon City, circling back through Lincoln Park, North Brookside, and Brewster.

When Cripple Creek reached its peak of production at the turn of the century Florence reflected that activity. McCandless's bank became the First National Bank of Florence. The city's reduction works were in full operation. The many men who were employed to dig a couple of reservoirs to store Newlin Creek water lived in a tent city of their own. Their horse drawn scoops had already completed Reservoir #1 when McFall was appointed assistant construction engineer. Florence, with seven thousand souls, was then the greatest industrial center in Colorado and trading center for a melange of miners from Italy, Ireland, Scotland, England, Austria, and a variety of other countries.

Gumaer, who had been a grocer before he came to Colorado, opened the Boston Market at 124 East Main Street as an outlet for his cattle company beef. This proved to be one of his more enduring projects. When Charles J. Butz, Sr., arrived from Pennsylvania in 1910, he worked there for Gumaer and a few years later bought the market. It remained in the Butz family until it closed in late April, 1967.

The Fulton Market at 122 East Main Street was a long time competitor, remaining at that location for fifty years before its owner, Dan Morganstein closed it in 1950. It had served as an outlet for Price and Morganstein's feed lot and slaughterhouse on South Union.

According to the pamphlet *Colorado, Its Resources, Its Men. . . A Lesson in Prosperity,* published by the authority of James B. Orman, Governor of the State of Colorado, in 1901, for free distribution at the Pan-American Exposition in Buffalo, New York, Gumaer was considered a Colorado financier in a class with Carleton, Guggenheim, and Reed. He was credited with controlling the townsite of Florence (which was expected to rival Pueblo within a decade) and the Cotopaxi Mining and Milling Company as well as his oil and cattle kingdoms. He was reported to be "shrewd, firm yet kind, always aggressive." Those who dealt with him were inclined to be less than kind in their estimate of the man.

Gumaer built a fine home in Florence. It still stands on Main Street next to Coal Creek. He or his cattle company owned vast tracts in Fremont, Chaffee, Custer, Park, Teller, El Paso, and Pueblo counties, including the Castle Rock Ranch originally owned in 1863 by John Witcher, the Stirrup Ranch in Park County, and much of the Arkansas River bottom near Florence. He acquired it largely by tax title or when it was sold following foreclosure. He would often grubstake a man for a homestead knowing full well he would starve on land that required at least three thousand acres for a living instead of the Homestead Act's one hundred sixty. Gumaer was always content to let others assume the risk.

Ready for the Big Parade
Judging by the bunting, this Star Works wagon was decorated for the Fourth of July
parade. Courtesy *Florence Citizen.*

The Florence Oil Refinery Stables
These sturdy brick buildings still stand, although little else remains to indicate the
extent of Florence's oil industry. *Photo by the author.*

Gumaer also built a ranch house, strong as a fort, on the Hardscrabble. It was just south of the Custer County line, where W. E. Draper first filed a claim in the early 1860's not far above the site of El Cuervo. Although the lumber visible in the attic is all plainly marked Boston Land and Cattle Company, he seems to have developed this ranch for his own pleasure. He directed Danforth, his business manager, to tear down barns already started and replace them with a crenellated concrete construction similar to some he saw in Old Mexico. He ordered a building that looks like a Spanish chapel to accommodate the grooms.

He raised fine horseflesh and trained his trotting horses on the quarter mile track behind the concrete barns. He raced his horses throughout the West and shipped them to his brother, Peter, to race in the East. There were slaughter pens to supply the Boston Market.

Most of these buildings which are now occupied by ranchers J. Louis Draper and his son, can easily be seen west of Highway 67. The "chapel" has been remodeled as a house. Louis Draper, who worked in the area with the Hatchet Cattle Company for fifty-two years, is no relation to the Draper who first filed on the place.

A dressy man who always wore kid gloves, Gumaer was often seen driving a spirited pair between this ranch and Florence. He invariably wore a veil when he drove, a habit he continued after he had a car and chauffeur. He claimed that it kept the dust off his face but the popular opinion was that he preferred not to be recognized because he was always afraid for his life.

It soon appeared that he had built the ranch house for his niece. She had come from the East for a visit. Gumaer had been so completely smitten that his wife Ella returned to New York to contemplate divorce. Some who still remember the man recall him as a flamboyant character who bought everything and paid for nothing.

After McFall became the proud owner of a 1912 Ford, he filled the tank at the Florence Oil Company whenever he could charging the amount against the sum Gumaer owed him for engineering services. When Homer Pierce worked for him, Gumaer paid him a dollar now and then but not in full until Homer asked for a layoff so he could get a job to earn money for clothes. Another unpaid cowboy had occasion to feel Gumaer's wrath. He made the mistake of stealing some Boston Land and Cattle Company cows. When Gumaer found out, he took everything the man had and literally cleaned him out.

One legend recalls that Gumaer, who had an apartment at the Brown Palace, went into a jeweler's in Denver and ordered all the shop had of a certain silver pattern. When the jeweler demurred, Gumaer allegedly bought him out, then and there. No one seems to remember if the deal went through or if the check bounced. By that time his fantastic financial empire was constantly being dissipated in litigation and unfortunate investments. Few men in Fremont County gave so much work to the courts. He spent thousands of dollars either as a complainant or defendant in a variety of civil cases which he felt concerned his property rights.

At the turn of the century, Florence's seven reduction plants handled over 1300 tons of ore daily. In addition to the Metallic Extraction Company, there were the Union Mill, Dorcas Mill, National Mill, the Beam Milling Company, Florence Mill, and one true smelter, the Rocky Mountain Smelter Company.

Unfortunately, when Cripple Creek began to wane, Florence did too. In 1901, the F & CC headquarters moved to Cañon City. That was a blow to Florence's pride as well as a financial loss. The following year a ten thousand dollar fire destroyed the still house at the Florence Oil Refinery when oil overflowed into the fire below. This same still had been the scene of a lesser blaze only two months earlier.

In a joint venture with the city, the street car company replaced the bridge over Coal Creek. It laid track from the bridge east on Second Street to the Santa Fe tracks before it ran out of resources. The tracks were later taken up. Only the bridge remained to remind Florence of the long heralded street railway.

When the F & CC's holding company was foreclosed in 1903 the line was sold to the Cripple Creek Central Railway Company. Local interests again became associated with it. However, it lost an important customer when the mill at Cyanide burned. The mill was never rebuilt although its tailing pile was later reworked. Only the Union and Dorcas mills still operated.

As the incandescent bulb began to replace the kerosene lamp, the gas buggy began to gain on the horse. Men looked again to oil. McCandless incorporated the McCandless Oil, Gas and Refining Company in 1904. He continued his interest in breeding fine stock. His Holstein cattle and Cleveland Bay and coach horses took blue ribbons at exhibits.

A series of disastrous fires retarded the development of the area. At midnight on St. Patrick's day in 1906, two wooden passenger trains collided head-on east of Florence.[10] This splintering wreck quickly caught fire, killing thirty-five and injuring many more. It did little to endear the D & RG to the public. People were outraged when the railroad sent the eighteen-year-old telegraph operator to Kentucky on a free pass. A coroner's jury found him guilty of negligence because he slept so soundly on the job that he was not awakened when the train thundered past only twelve feet from him. He had been on duty eighteen hours, six more than had been permitted by rules. The railroad's signal system was too antiquated to give adequate warning. Other fires took a toll in buildings.

Florence flourished as a derrick town. As many as four hundred wells had been sunk in the Florence field since 1862. Seventy-five of them produced, about three thousand barrls or some 120,000 gallons a day for the United Oil and Florence refineries.

Bull Wheels

This primitive machinery was used to drill Florence's early oil wells. An example is preserved behind the Florence Pioneer Museum. *Courtesy Florence Pioneer Museum.*

C. J. Frederickson of Cañon City continued to have faith in the region although he had been drilling unsuccessfully for oil for some time. One of his more spectacular holes produced exceedingly hot mineral water. Frederickson had all too often met water where he expected oil but, undaunted, he decided to develop this artesian bonanza.[11] He platted Watersville Subdivision along the F & CC right of way south of Oro Junta, a couple of miles north of present Highway 50. Orchards he planted on the flat expanse were irrigated with the hot water. There no smudge pots polluted the air. The vapor from the hot water amply protected the trees from frost.

However, Frederickson had counted on obtaining additional potable water from a ditch development promoted by the Cañon City orchardist, Dall DeWeese. When DeWeese, who had lent his influence to several real estate schemes, ran into water right problems he was unable to deliver the anticipated volume. Long before the water situation was straightened out, the hot mineral water proved so potent that it ate out the well casing, causing the flow to quit. As the orchards shriveled so did Frederickson's resources. He could do nothing but abandon the project and buckle his belt a little tighter.

The F & CC suffered further misfortunes. Competition from other lines pulled traffic away. Lodges and other groups were encouraged to charter trains for picnics or athletic events. Specials ran from Cripple Creek for celebrations and fairs. By 1910, traffic on the main line was limited largely to delivering coal to the District. Ore was going to more modern mills in Colorado Springs and Victor. Florence, although reduced to a population of but 3500, continued to serve as a center of the surrounding coal towns and could boast of being the largest oil producer in the state.

The Baptist and Christian churches of Cañon City chartered a train for a picnic excursion in July, 1912. Both these denominations believed in immersion and that day they almost got it. A sudden storm cut the picnic short. By the time the train had reached the end of the canyon, the cloudburst north of Adelaide sent a wall of water rushing down the creek. Because the force of this made the trestle on the Cañon City branch unsafe the excursionists were diverted to Florence.

The damage to the narrow gauge line was disastrous. The railroad couldn't afford the $110,000 repair bill. With no trains running, lack of ore soon reduced the Union Mill to treating its own dumps.

The F & CC petitioned to abandon the road. Cañon City fought the petition and the PUC ordered service resumed. The F & CC fought back. Finally, in 1914, the Auto Club in Victor proposed turning the right of way into an auto road. This proposal was enthusiastically supported by Vic McCandless. The F & CC would agree only if Cañon City would refrain from trying to have the PUC decision enforced. Early in 1915, railroad interests offered to turn over the road bed and bridges. They agreed to construct the highway as well. However, when Cañon City and other

United Oil Company

Florence was crowded with oil tanks and stills during the height of the exploitation of the second oldest oil field in the United States. *Courtesy Florence Pioneer Museum.*

Fremont County interests continued to force the rebuilding of the railroad, the F & CC legally dissolved, leaving the PUC and Cañon City with neither road nor railroad.

After he sold his holdings on Upper Beaver, Dave Hall bought out Cramer at the original Russell Station. When the railroad finally folded, Clarence Bond, Sr., bought the town of Wilbur which in 1900 had boasted a population of sixty. Hall soon bought out Bond, plus twenty-two hundred acres atop Cooper Mountain and added other properties until he owned over fifteen thousand acres.

Finally, in the autumn of 1918, the State Highway Department completed the present Phantom Canyon Highway.[12] This, too, has suffered from floods from time to time. All too often, chunks of the road, bridge timbers, and cattle (grazed on the open range until the Taylor Grazing Act of 1934) were carried the length of Eightmile Creek. After the great flood of 1921, the counties had no funds left to repair this road. Volunteers who undertook to rebuild the damaged parts completed the work in three months.

After the Taylor Grazing Act convinced homesteaders that they couldn't make a living on fenced land, they sold out to cattlemen who were willing to acquire adequate acreages. When a cloudburst closed the Phantom Canyon Highway in 1942, it wasn't reopened until the end of World War II,. Today it is a scenic fair weather road which provides plenty of thrills for tourists from the flatlands and excites railroad buffs who know the history of the once highly profitable Florence & Cripple Creek Railroad.

Oklahoma A & M College opened a geology camp in 1949 across from the old schoolhouse where Edson H. Burnett had homesteaded at the Eightmile water gap. The camp has been busy every summer since. The Burnett homestead is now owned by Eric T. Kelly, Sr., a distinguished pioneer who was instrumental in founding Pueblo Junior College in 1933 and the College of the Canons in 1965. On a knoll behind the house, two unusual monuments carved by Mabel Burnett to mark the graves of her little brother and father remind visitors of earlier days. After Mabel married, she turned her artistic talent to barbering in Pueblo.

Before the F & CC was washed out, Gumaer had undertaken to develop Rainbow Park as a residential area. This land east of Florence was advertised as inexpensive irrigated orchard and garden tracts on the "Santa Fe Trail of the Rainbow Route of the D & RG." Gumaer entertained plans to develop a resort spa at the east end near Highway 115 where mineral springs had been discovered in 1889, but he couldn't raise the necessary capital.

McCandless, with Kate and son Victor, incorporated The James A. McCandless Investment Company to deal in real and personal property.

They were ready to cope with the situation when World War I increased the demand for oil. The Continental Oil Company then played a large part in the Florence picture. Robinson Avenue was closed off to accommodate a supply pipe from the Standard stills to the Continental works.

This war brought glory to the McCandless name when Julius's son, Byron, earned the Navy Cross for conspicuous heroism. Perhaps it was this that triggered the idea that they should move Mary's body to rest beside Colb, her first husband. Mary, a pipe-smoking, uneducated Irish woman, had remarried a few years after Colb's murder in 1861 but had come to Florence to live for some time before her death in 1907. Byron, his brother, Charles G., and their sister Beatrice, who later died in the flu epidemic in 1918, wanted to dispel their reputation as descendants of the desperate McCandless gang. Although their efforts brought to light the true story of the killing, the public preferred to accept Wild Bill's highly distorted self-glorification. The monument they erected over Colb and Mary's grave soon was disfigured by souvenir hunters who didn't hesitate to chip off pieces to exhibit to friends.

Gumaer no longer spent much time in Florence. His wife remained in the East still contemplating divorce. A butler took care of his mansion. By 1916, Gumaer was loaded with debts and deeply involved in expensive litigation. Although he had pneumonia that summer he didn't think his condition was serious and went about his business. However, the disease progressed to a point that drove him to Salida for treatment on July 25. He seemed to improve enough to attend to some legal matters in Cañon City and suffered a bilious attack at the Strathmore Hotel. He returned to his suite at the Brown Palace where his Denver doctor summoned his old friend, Dr. F. N. Cochems of Salida. He took Gumaer to the Red Cross Hospital for treatment that included tapping his ulcerated lung three times.

By October Gumaer's condition was critical but he was confident that he would recover. He died suddenly on October 13, 1916, at the age of sixty-four. At that time the Boston Land and Cattle Company had been consumed by the Gumaer Estates Company of which he was, of course, the principal stockholder. The company owned some fifteen thousand acres of oil and farming land in Fremont County, the refining plant of the Florence Oil Company, and a large amount of city property. He had long had the reputation of letting his taxes go, then making a deal with the county commissioners to pay a lesser amount.

His personal holdings included the copper mine at Cotopaxi, the famous Ella W. mine in Cripple Creek, and two hundred fifty head of standardbred stock at the big ranch near Wetmore. His town house was empty of the elaborate furnishings. The beautiful lawn and expensive shrubbery had been allowed to go to ruin. His wife and his brother Peter, Mayor of Port Jervis, New York, arrived for the funeral at Cañon City but were undecided whether to ship his body East. Although the newspapers reported that he would be buried in Port Jervis, he actually lies alone in a small plot in Lakeside Cemetery in Cañon City.

He left no direct heirs. Gossip says that he had given so much to his niece that his wife inherited only his debts. The Decree of Final Settlement, filed in 1928, indicated that Ella Gumaer had received $2123.57 although she had expended $2134.52. Although Gumaer had skyrocketed to financial fame by the turn of the century, his spectacular manipulations had turned to char in the legal crunch. Scarcely a soul in Fremont County recollects his name today. Mrs. Gumaer is remembered more kindly as the donor of the lot at Second and Pikes Peak on which the small Carnegie Library stands.[13]

About 1917, Louis Miller made plans for an amusement park at the soda springs at the east end of Rainbow Park. Although this never materialized the springs were developed as the Mineral Health Springs. At one time the Hygienic Plunge was one of the largest swimming pools in Colorado. It was filled with eighty-five degree mineral water aerated with carbon dioxide and touted as being equalled only by Bad Nauheim in Germany. Until recent years, the adjacent American Nauheim Baths provided capable attendants for those who preferred to soak in privacy. Danforth, president of the Gumaer Estates Company, promoted the nearby Sunnyside Addition, but Florence had passed her prime.

When James A. McCandless, long called "the father of Florence," died at his large brick mansion of old age on February 22, 1922, the population of his town had shrunk to three thousand. He was buried on his eighty-sixth birthday in Union Highland Cemetery following an impressive funeral. His Kate joined him there two years later. Their fine home now serves as a funeral parlor.

Then the cost of dying was much less than later, especially for members of a burial organization such as the Spanish speaking inhabitants formed about 1923 to provide care and improvement of the little, barren, sunbaked cemetery west of the old Hardscrabble Road, a short distance south of Florence. The by-laws, in Spanish, provide for a $5.50 charge for digging a grave. A grave space was free to members, five dollars to others. In 1940, Continental Oil Company granted the society a quit claim deed to the land. At that time the fences and gates were replaced and the burial ground was named San Juan Bautista.

As coal mining declined, the Continental and Standard Oil refineries became the mainstay of the area's economy. After an explosion and fire at the Standard stills on June 25, 1925, which left three men dead and completely devastated the site on east Main Street (now occupied by the Florence Lumber Company), Continental controlled the Florence oil business. The granddaddy of all Conoco wells was #86 on the Cherokee and Pittsburgh lease drilled in 1895.

Oil production gradually dropped off as holes drilled relieved the natural pressures which had forced the oil into the fissures. The oil companies shipped in oil from Wyoming to the refineries. Finally Continental pulled out. It was more economical to build a new plant in Denver. Florence's oil heyday had passed. Pictures of the town's derrick days in the Florence Pioneer Museum with the weathering bull wheels behind it are practically the sole reminders of Florence's oil field fame.

Julius McCandless's younger son, Charles G., won a seat in the state legislature in the late twenties. Not to his surprise, he, a Republican, was reelected during the Roosevelt landslide. After all, he was related to a vast number of the voters in his district.

Despite the stockmarket crash, Dr. Y. Nabona of Colorado Springs, referred to as the "internationally known Indian doctor," planned to build a $40,000, twenty-room, Spanish style sanatorium across from the Hygienic Plunge. Dr. Nabona's own crash stalled this development when an auto accident hospitalized him in Tucson.

New Deal days saw the few ranchers who had replaced the many homesteaders driving their drought-gaunt cows with scrawny calves to the railroad at Florence. There, government officials bought cattle that might have cost the owners as much as seventy-five for ten dollars a head. Piteous calves too weak to ship were shot and cast aside for later disposal, a sight heartbreaking to ranchers who had struggled through the drought-plagued summer to save them.

Florence went into a deep slump after that. Area coal production declined further. When at last there was water again, the poorly drained irrigated fields became increasingly saline and were thus lost to agriculture. Then World War II brought new activity to the oil field and new glory to the McCandless name.

Ninety-year-old Julius listened to his radio on December 12, 1942, to hear Admiral Ernest J. King present his grandson, Commander Bruce McCandless, with the Congressional Medal of Honor for bringing the *San Francisco* safely out of the Battle of Lilacs after his superior officers had been killed or injured. Julius died the following February.

When his son, Commodore Byron McCandless, retired from the Navy in 1946 after serving as commander of the San Diego Destroyer Base, he was renowned as an authority on flags. He had designed the President's Flag in 1915 at the request of Franklin Delano Roosevelt, Secretary of the Navy, and he had later written the famous flag article for the October, 1917, issue of the *National Geographic Magazine.* Retired, Byron turned his attention to further disproving Wild Bill Hickok's version of the Rock Creek incident. Before he died in 1969, he had the joy of having *his* grandson, Bruce II, selected for the astronaut program.

Ben McFall's son, Jack, also brought honor to the community by earning the U. S. Treasury Department's highest citation before he retired, the Albert Gallatin award.

Despite fire and flood, and busts as well as coal, gold, and oil booms, Florence has had the stamina to survive. The attractive little town appeals to retirees who are proud to point out that, in terms of sunshine, it's second only to Yuma, Arizona, where the sun shines eighty percent of the daylight hours.[14]

FOOTNOTES

1. The succession of ownership in this area is told in *History of the Arkansas Valley, p. 643 ff.*
2. Ralph C. Taylor's "Colorful Colorado" column in *The Star-Journal and Sunday Chieftan* (Pueblo), March 1, 1970, Sec. D. p. 12.
3. In addition to public records in the State Archives and Record Center and at the Fremont County Courthouse, much family information was gathered from interviews with Charles G. McCandless, nephew of James, and from an unpublished account by Mrs. Genevieve A. Carlin, granddaughter of James and Kate.
4. This ditch dates back to November, 1861. It still provides some water for the City of Florence which acquired rights dating back to 1862. See Bob Cruzen's "Florence Prepares for Future with New Filtration Plant" for the complete story of the town's water supply difficulties.
5. James A. McCandless vs Sarah McCandless *Divorce Proceedings* at the Fremont County Courthouse.
6. Information about Gumaer is surprisingly difficult to find, considering his financial activities, business enterprises, and flamboyant life style. His name is frequently misspelled and thus stories are hard to identify until they have been cross-checked. Recollections of the man vary considerably. His admirers paint him as a financial giant without whose promotional ability Fremont County would have prospered less. His detractors feel that he invariably took advantage of the less sophisticated and was adept at manipulating situations for his own gain.
   Mrs. Grace Bennett of the staff of the Ramapo Catskill Library System in Middletown, N.Y., furnished the original information that led to local sources. Bits and pieces of information from interviews helped round out the picture. Especially helpful were the interviews with J. Louis Draper and Charles G. McCandless. Everett's *Under the Angel of Shavano* and Epperson's *Colorado As I Saw It* as well as scattered references in the Florence and Canon City newspapers were also useful.
7. Interview with Edgeworth Westwater, November 14, 1969. There is an account of the Overton operation in the *Pueblo Chieftain,* September 21, 1964.

8. Morris Cafky presents an exhaustive account of this line in his *Rails Around Gold Hill.*

9. Wilson's *One Hundred Years of Fremont County History of Education,* p. 12.

10. Robert G. Athearn covers this in *Rebel of the Rockies, a History of the Denver & Rio Grande Western Railroad* more objectively than did the contemporary news reporters.

11. Interview with C. Arthur Frederickson, son of C. J., September 8, 1969.

12. The depot, station platform, and water tanks were removed from Adelaide at this time, *Canon City Daily Record,* April 27, 1971.

13. *The Occasional Leaflet of the Colorado Library Association,* 2:126, November, 1919.

14. Brochure of the Florence Chamber of Commerce [1959].

William May's Cabin
May built this cabin when he settled on Oak Creek in 1866 after being flooded out of earlier Fremont County locations. *Photo by the author.*

CHAPTER IX

COAL TOWNS

The widespread distribution of coal south of the Arkansas in what is now Fremont County was obvious to the settlers who grazed their stock in the foothills. Antelope hunters, too, saw the many outcroppings exposed by erosion. Except for Jesse Frazer's claim, the coal was there for the taking. All a man had to do was load his wagon and haul it home across the rolling grassland.

Frazer and his companions sold out to Joseph R. Musser. He freighted coal to Denver in an ox-drawn cart for forty dollars a ton which helped to build the fine reputation of Cañon coal when he received several premiums of silver medals at the Colorado Territorial Fairs.

Musser (who later was murdered by a man with whom he had a slight misunderstanding) sold out to Palmer's Central Colorado Improvement Company which first worked the mine in 1872. The following year, George Hadden, a Scot, came to serve as superintendent for the subsidiary Colorado Coal and Mining Company which continued to open mines in the Cañon coal field in a systematic manner.

That field developed rapidly to fill the demand of the railroads for fuel, a demand that was no longer met adequately by wood from forests depleted for mines and smelters. The coal companies not only supplied coal for locomotives and communities along the railroad, but tried to corner the smelter market in South Park and the upper Arkansas. Their steam coal was well known by 1874. Locomotives got eighty-five miles to the ton in contrast to forty miles to the ton produced by the more expensive and inferior coal available formerly.[1] The solid lump of coal 8'9" by 4'4" by 6' that CCI sent to the Centennial Exposition in Philadelphia in 1876 attracted still more favorable interest.

When the Canon Coal Railway Company's track reached the mines that year, the area was populated by miners working the Cañon City Coal Company, the Grand Canon Coal Company, and the Colorado Coal and Iron Company mines. The latter company was the result of a consolidation of several of Palmer's interests: the Central Colorado Improvement, Southern Coal and Town, and the Colorado Coal and Steel Works companies.

While the advent of the railroad permitted large mines to employ hundreds of men and to ship hundreds of tons of coal economically, small mines continued to operate. These wagon mines were usually worked by the owner or lessee who employed fewer than two dozen men. Wagons hauled the coal to private homes for cooking and heating, sometimes as far as Colorado Springs or Pueblo, and to the mills in Florence.

With oil in the offing and the coal mines prospering, Henry M. Teller, the Colorado politician, platted the Town of Coal Creek on November 15, 1878, with his brother Willard, to accommodate the influx of workers to the area where the Coal Creek school already served the second largest district in the county. There were daily stages to Cañon City, Florence, and neighboring towns.

Joseph Blunt was one of the many English immigrants attracted to the area, arriving in 1879. His son Roland, almost twelve and big enough to tote a lunch pail, went to work in the Canfield mine. Charlie Cowan, a Scot, brought in his family about the same time.

By 1883, the weekly *Coal Creek Enterprise* furnished the news to the several hundred inhabitants. Caldwell's Addition provided for the expanding population. Coal Creek was a sizeable town when it incorporated in 1889. It enjoyed a degree of culture for a decade or so. The Coal Creek Hotel often housed opera stars and traveling stock companies who performed in town.

It's hard to understand how culture could compete with the saloons, considering the lot of the miner in those days. Men and boys, some as young as ten, walked as much as three or more miles to the mines before daybreak and didn't return home until after sunset. The face of the coal might be another mile or so from the mine entrance. There, in unpleasant heat, sometimes in water, often on his hand and knees, the miner dug coal. He was paid sixty-five cents a ton for digging and loading the coal by hand with no pay for loading dirt, rock, pea coal or slack. Usually he was in debt at the company store, a slave to its policy of extending credit.

The miner struggled for odd jobs when the mines closed down in the summer because there was no demand for coal for heating. With luck, he might pick vegetables on a farm for a half cent a pound. At least, doing that, he could enjoy the sunshine.

Despite such pay scales, by 1890 Roll Blunt had saved up enough to marry sixteen-year-old Elizabeth Cowan, and to go bouncing in a buggy to Canon City for a wedding picture.

Considering conditions, it's no wonder that the miners listened to the union organizers. A decade after the formation of the Western Federation of Miners, all Colorado's mining camps were again tied up in strikes. There was violence in various degrees when management attempted to operate mines with strike breakers. When the mines finally reopened, the miners had gained enough to keep them quiet for another ten years.

There was more than coal in the hills around Coal Creek. Wild burros abounded. These sure-footed, strong, stubborn, braying beasts were descendants of the "Rocky Mountain canaries" which had carried supplies for many a prospector in the high country during the gold rush days.

Burros were often turned loose when a prospector had no further use for them. Snows drove them to lower elevations where they found protection from predators near the settlements. They propagated until there were enough— and more— for all who cared to catch and gentle them. Some were used in the mines during the working months then hitched to a spring wagon to take folks fishing in the summer when the mines closed, or were used for hauling.

Local boys rode their burros to visit other coal camps. Boys from Florence often raided the burro herds near Coal Creek. The Coal Creek boys responded by hiking to Florence to look for the missing burros. This got to be quite a sport that fortunately led to nothing more serious than fist fights.

This free transportation disappeared when burro baseball became popular. Some burros were bought from their owners but most of them were simply hauled off by the truckload. These winsome little animals were so popular that raising them was suggested as a livelihood for invalids seeking out-of-door life.

In 1907, Coal Creek suffered Fremont County's most destructive holocaust. Flames from an unknown cause broke out one June Saturday afternoon in the roof of Alf Salmon's bottling works. Before the volunteers could check the flames, the $200,000 fire had consumed 102 buildings, causing a tremendous loss to the 5,000 residents. The town never rose again to its former prominence, although the Rocky Mountain Fuel Company platted its own Town of Coal Creek. In 1917, the Colorado Fuel and Iron Company platted an addition on top of an earlier one. Neither of these plans on paper showed much consideration for existing buildings. The D & RG abandoned the Coal Creek branch in 1913 and removed it in 1924.

Perhaps the last notable event in Coal Creek was the 1923 funeral of Dr. A. A. Eddy. All coal mines and places of business closed for it. All the principal officers of the CF & I were in attendance.

Coal Creek shrank with the closing of the various mines as the demand for coal lessened. With a diminishing tax base, the town fathers found it increasingly difficult to supply public services. The antiquated water supply could no longer adequately supply even the greatly reduced population. Only recently have government funds made possible the drilling of a new well that could permit doubling of Coal Creek's 1969 population of about one hundred thirty.

Evidently inspired by their success at Coal Creek, Henry and Willard Teller soon platted the extensive City of Williamsburg. It was the terminus of the coal branch of the D & RG's Oak Creek branch built in 1881. It was essentially a shipping point and a residential development where houses rented for four to six dollars a month. Williamsburg's population claimed assorted nationalities: Welsh, Irish, English, Scots, and German. One part of

Rockvale, 1880

By this time, May was surrounded by Rockvale platted by the Cañon City Coal Company of which he was a stockholder and director. *Courtesy Florence Pioneer Museum.*

Oak Creek Slope

The very productive coal mines around Rockvale were acquired by the Colorado Fuel and Iron Company in 1896. *Courtesy Florence Citizen.*

town was known as Little Italy. Most of the residents worked in the dozen or so coal mines circling the town.

Of the few privately built dwellings, perhaps the most distinctive was the stone house built in 1890 by Louis Francisco whose family had been Venetian mosiac artists. Proceeds from his saloon permitted mosiac floors in his mansion.

Williamsburg had water problems from the beginning. The town marshal, in addition to trying to keep the lid on a lively coal camp crossroads, was expected to serve as water hauler. He drove a team with a tank wagon to fill the barrels buried in the ground at each home with drinking water from the town well at twenty-five cents a barrel. The women and children were expected to haul water by bucket or donkey cart from other sources for washing clothes and such.

Like many a mining town, Williamsburg developed its Stringtown of less desirable habitations. There, several saloons competed with the ice cream parlor in Williamsburg proper. In 1888, the town invested ninety-seven dollars in a small rock building to serve as a two-cell jail. Deputy marshals were hired as needed to guard homes quarantined for small pox and to help police the Stringtown saloons.

Incorporated in 1889, Williamsburg continued to grow with the Rocky Mountain Fuel Company's additions. Despite the conglomerate of nationalities, fifty some families of blacks who were brought in by the Rocky Mountain Fuel Company to work the struck Ocean Wave mine during the labor troubles of 1902-1904 were resented by all. The resentment was due not so much to their color as to the fact that they were strike breakers willing to work for what the miners felt was unacceptable pay. Undeterred by the ill feeling, a community of blacks settled near the Ocean Wave. Although the formal name of that mine, sold by the CF & I in 1903, was the North Magnet, it was called the Ocean Wave because of the large quantity of water that had to be pumped from it.

Not all was work in Williamsburg. The town sported a top notch baseball team sponsored by the Gold Label Beer Company which furnished the brilliant red uniforms complete with gold sox.

Five years after the Santa Fe began construction of its Oak Creek branch, the D & RG abandoned its two and a half mile spur serving Williamsburg. This did not leave the residents completely without service. The Chandler branch and the spur to the Fremont Mine in Bear Gulch passed nearby.

The CF & I provided about thirty company houses for the miners in Bear Gulch who preferred not to commute, although about three hundred men worked there during the height of production. On the whole, miners considered working conditions in the CF & I mines as good as any in the area. Most had good air, an important consideration, and most of them were connected by an air course. Miners could walk underground from the Coal Creek mine to Rockvale to Bear Gulch.

However, fires caused considerable damage. The tipple at Bear Gulch burned in 1908. The underground mule barns, home to twenty-four mules, burned in 1910 with the loss of two men and five mules.

There was much labor unrest throughout Colorado during 1913-1914. Miners in the southern Colorado coal fields demanded recognition of the United Mine Workers of America, ten percent increase in wages, an eight hour day, a check weigh man to insure honest weight, and the privilege of trading or boarding where they chose.

When the miners struck, more negroes came in as strike breakers. According to the Florence *Paradox,* one hundred fifty armed men halted a train carrying some negroes headed for Radiant near the Ocean Wave on January 31, 1914. The train crew reversed the engine and returned to Florence. Shots were fired, but after the event, seemingly in celebration of the enemy's retreat. Later, a train with thirty-five blacks and twenty members of the National Guard got through while a troop of cavalry patroled the track. That same day, strikers shot up a train of empty coal cars en route to Chandler. It, too, rapidly backtracked to Florence with holes in the engine. Increasing incidents of violence culminated in the infamous Chandler March in April.

The Williamsburg town fathers had long planned a water works. The original plan involved purchasing water from the South Canon Water Company and tapping two artesian wells on Chandler Creek, nine miles away. Since this line would also serve some fifty families in Bear Gulch near the Fremont mine, it was logical for the CF & I to agree to pay for for the cost of materials if the town would furnish labor to lay the line.

On January 16, 1914, the town . board approved the survey and specifications submitted by A. B. McFall for the twenty thousand dollar project. However, fear that the CF & I would shut off the supply of water in times of labor troubles deterred them from accepting aid from this source. The town couldn't afford to undertake it alone. The water problem was yet to be resolved when the CF & I platted an addition in 1917.

Finally, in 1921, a thirty-five hundred dollar bond issue permitted construction of a reservoir and pipeline. This brought water from Coal Creek for the high part of town and water from Rockvale for the lower section. When those towns ran short of water, Williamsburg had to haul water from Canon City.

The school district built two new schools to serve the pupils in Bear Gulch as well as in Williamsburg. The Bear Gulch pupils walked to school except in bad weather when the CF & I provided a mule team and covered wagon for them.

That same year the Fremont mine suffered double damage, from both fire and flood. Lightning struck the hay barn in June. Men used the steam pump to supply water to fight the fire. Then the clouds burst, delivering a torrent that threatened to extinguish the fire in the boiler. Runoff from this storm joined the swollen Arkansas and contributed to the damage in Pueblo.

A few years later the Fremont mine suffered again from an overabundance of water when the workings filled with water from the Ocean Wave. This marked the end of activity in Bear Gulch. The company pulled the machinery in 1926-1927. Most of the buildings were moved to other company towns.

Williamsburg had passed its peak. Many moved away when other mines shut down. Some stayed and, like the Scutti family, are there to this day. Theo Scutti was elected mayor in 1929, a position he would hold for close to a half century. Louis became a member of the town council a few years later. Anthony (Ty) and Nick Scutti also were active in the local government. Although others served from time to time, today Scuttis largely govern and populate the place. Williamsburg still lives although it's but a remnant of its former size.

For years William May ranched in undisturbed bachelorhood at his small cabin where he had settled in 1866, hoping that Oak Creek wouldn't flood him out. He got along well with the Utes who frequently passed through his pastures. They never failed to close his gates which was more than he could say for some whites.

Then in 1880 Benjamin Rockafellow and others organized the Cañon City Coal Company. Forty-eight-year-old May became a stockholder and director, possibly in exchange for land. M. D. Thatcher was secretary of the company, an enterprise that provided a base for his later fortune.

This company platted the Town of Rockvale, modest in area, only a few months after the founding of Williamsburg just to the north. Allegedly named by Rockafellow for Rockvale, Maryland, the town became the center of the company's operation and the terminus of the Pueblo and Arkansas Valley Railroad, a subsidiary of the Santa Fe. Rockvale's population was only one hundred to Williamsburg's five hundred, but by 1888 the Cañon City Coal Company platted an addition and incorporated the town. That year, Colonel May died, and was buried, still alone, in Cañon City's Greenwood Cemetery.

Coal production continued to increase. The depression that followed 1893 failed to diminish the output. Meyer Guggenheim's smelter in Pueblo added to the demand.

John C. Osgood, began investing in Colorado coal lands in 1882. Ten years later he merged his Colorado Fuel Company and other holdings with Palmer's Colorado Coal and Iron Company to form the Colorado Fuel and

Iron Company. He continued the aggressive policies of the CC & I and in 1896 acquired the Cañon City Coal Company mines at Rockvale. By 1903, he had relinquished control to the eastern Rockefeller and Gould interests but the CF & I remained a force in the mining area for many years. Rockvale, essentially a company town, provided miners from many countries with a club house, scarlet uniforms for the band, and a baseball team that competed with all the neighboring communities. An Opera House pleased large audiences with motion pictures and phonograph entertainment. The *Paradox* published the news.

Except during the strife torn days of 1904[2] and 1914, shared by most of Colorado's coal towns, life was good in Rockvale. Records of those earlier days were lost in 1915 when the projector showing movies upstairs in the Rockvale City Hall caught fire, destroying the equipment, the building, and all the records.

There were other casualties, too. Miners recall many accidents in World War I days. They worked fast and long for the war effort so all too often were tired and careless. The First Aid team had plenty of practice. Rockvale's was experienced enough to earn the First Prize in 1916 at the CF & I field day in competition against a dozen other teams.

Old foundations of some thirty company houses reveal the site of Nushaft, two miles south of Rockvale. In 1912, the CF & I sank a four hundred foot shaft there to shorten underground hauling. This large but short lived operation, served by a spur of the Santa Fe, was shut down about 1931 as the company had promised because the miners carried out their strike threat.

The fifty to sixty mules used underground hadn't seen the light of day for five years. They literally went crazy when they were pulled out of the tunnels and released above ground. Lessees later worked Nushaft until it was finally sealed in 1951.

During Prohibition, adopted in Colorado four years before the Federal Amendment took effect in 1920, Gus, Joe, Charlie, and Sam Salardino opened The Gold Nugget in Rockvale, billing it as The Gay Spot of the West. It was a high class place with music and a good floor show every night. There were special productions for Christmas and New Year's Eve. The brothers also provided back rooms for gambling for those who were allowed past the guards at the door. It was a popular place with movie actors on set in and around Canon City as well as with the sports in the area. Business fell off as more and more mines shut down. The Salardinos closed The Gold Nugget in 1940 and razed the building.

As mines continued to close, the tipples, railroads, and other signs of Rockvale's heyday were dismantled. Colonel May's log house, now owned by the town and used as a storehouse, and Chiri's Place next to the newer

Rockvale's Fire Protection
This hose cart remains as a quaint reminder of the early day volunteer hose companies. *Photo by the author.*

post office stand forlornly near the empty wasteland that was once ahum with activity.

Little remains of another short lived and long forgotten town, Springfield, platted in December, 1887, southwest of Rockvale. Perhaps it died aborning since there was already another town of that name in eastern Colorado.

Traces of the old Santa Fe railroad grade can still be seen three miles south of Coal Creek. A good gravel road crosses the grade near the site of Radiant, later called Pyrolite, where a mine produced five hundred tons of coal a day in 1916 for Osgood's Victor American Fuel Company.

After the Radiant mine closed, only a watchman remained until February, 1931, when the Federal Government leased the town with all its facilities to provide a camp for transient unemployed. During the Great Depression, the trains and highways were crowded with people, many sick and hungry, crossing the country in search of work. The Federal Emergency Relief Administration furnished the old houses. Officers assembled hitch hikers and bussed them to the spot, then known as Kenwood,[3] from Florence and Canon City. The government provided doctors, dentists, a hospital, and a mess to feed the several hundred men and boys. Eight teachers manned school rooms for the boys who were sheltered in sixteen of the houses.

The indigent residents of Kenwood were free to come and go but if they decided to stay, they were required to work or go to school, to fight forest fires, build roads or fences, or do whatever work was needed. They played too. The ball club competed with other teams in the county.

The Park and Forest Service operated the camp from 1935 to 1936. The buildings were eventually moved or demolished for the lumber. More recent strip mining at the site has left the country marred by slag piles and scarred by pits filled with stagnant water. Nothing remains of the company town.

As late as 1945, the railroad was extended past this point. W. D. Corley, jr., of Colorado Springs, had expanded the family's mining interests with the purchase of an 830 acre tract about five miles southeast of Rockvale in 1937. Coal could be found there at less than a hundred foot depth on top of Trinidad sandstone.

Lack of a railroad forced Corley to haul coal a long way. After World War II, he learned that the Interstate Commerce Commission still listed the Santa Fe spur as active and as having an unloading point only a couple of miles from his mines. Corley quietly constructed a road to this location, then cagily requested the Santa Fe to haul a piece of equipment from Colorado Springs to that point.

The Santa Fe responded that the ICC had given permission to abandon the spur. Corley reminded the railroad that such a procedure required it to advertise the spur for sale to any interested party on the route.

He then bought the spur with its four miles of trackage, built an extension with old street car rails from Pueblo, and invested three thousand dollars in a war surplus 1920 American locomotive that had once done duty as a Union Pacific switch engine. Later he acquired an ancient Pierce Arrow "section car" junked from the Midland Terminal in 1949. He leased gondola cars as needed.

This private railroad carried approximately 240 tons of high grade bituminous coal from the completely mechanized mines to the main line in Florence. The two man crew found the boiler's tendency to freeze in winter unless it was continuously fired up a frustrating challenge. A costly wreck that in 1951 toppled eight cars and left the right of way covered with coal to mark the spot today, made Corley consider discontinuing his slow-moving "Corley Flyer."

In 1953, he sold the locomotive for what he had paid for it. The rails were sold to the CF & I as scrap, but both locomotive and rails wound up at the Climax molybdenum plant. The little engine was minus its bell, however. The bell now graces a church in Denver.

A number of other mines are still active on a small scale in that area but there is no settlement near them. The few miners needed now prefer to commute from Florence or other towns.

Although Brewster once boasted the Stratton coal mine, it was primarily a truck farming area. Essentially a suburb of Florence, it was first settled in 1886 by John and Melby Smith. They sold to John K. Brewster, husband of Mary McClure. He platted it as a subdivision in 1894 during the Cripple Creek boom. At one time both the D & RG and the Santa Fe had loading docks there to pick up the produce shipped by the vegetable growers.

Fawn Hollow forms a natural amphitheater a short distance west of Brewster. This was the scene of a pageant in August, 1925. Each town in the area contributed a segment of "The Awakening," a fantasy with an ecological message, written by Edgar Carlisle MacKechen of Denver. While the theme would be appropriate today, the characters of Mr. General Public, Spruce Tree, Demon Fire, and such would seem a bit quaint.

The Florence and Canon City Music Clubs which promoted the pageant hoped to develop an attraction that would draw a crowd to the region. They weren't disappointed. An audience of two thousand applauded the whole show. Although the well organized production proved that Fremont County people could work together, those participating felt that it was too much of an undertaking to attempt on a regular basis.

The Hollow is now more visibly marked by a coal mine and a tavern, both abandoned, than by the rock formation in the form of a recumbent deer from which it gained its name.

Brookside, about halfway between Rockvale and Cañon City, was an

1888 project of the Cañon City Coal Company although there had been homes there since the mine opened on the west side of Spring Creek when the Santa Fe branch was constructed. The whole area actually was controlled by the Santa Fe. A no saloon edict was in effect. However, a survey showed a half acre that had been overlooked by the company. That tract, soon full of saloons and wild women, earned the name, Hell's Half Acre. Although every building housed either a saloon or a dancehall, the madams who provided other attractions brooked no nonsense. When one shopped for a revolver at the Florence Hardware, she spurned the proffered pearlhandled model, declaring that she wanted "something that would make a hole the size of a saltcellar." History has failed to record if she ever had to use it.

The Brookside mine closed in 1911 when water shut many sections. However, parts were later leased for operation as small wagon mines. This activity was discontinued in 1940 when Federal and State mine inspectors ordered every entrance sealed because of a fire in an outcrop vein.

After the F & CC Railroad was built and before the mine closed, the Santa Fe used a third rail on the Brookside spur to accommodate F & CC cars carrying coal to Cripple Creek. The boxcar depot dispensed tickets at $1.50 for popular Sunday summertime excursions to Victor or Cripple Creek.

The five cent beer with the free lunch at the Fremont Saloon in Hell's Half Acre was a particular favorite with movie men who were shooting two reel Westerns in Canon City in 1910. Among them was Pennsylvania-born Tom Mix who had drifted West after the Spanish-American War. He had joined Selig-Polyscope as safety man after that company had used Mix's Oklahoma ranch for a documentary film. Mix caught their eye when he won the rodeo championships at Canon City and Prescott, Arizona, in 1909.

Mix and Woody Higgins, one of the local ranchers who furnished horses for the movie company, liked to place a lemon on a glass at the end of the bar in the Fremont Saloon and take turns shooting at it. The poorer shot had to pay for the drinks. The saloonkeeper objected until he found that the target practice drew a crowd. One customer failed to be frightened when Mix pulled his gun on him. He stared Mix down and coolly said, "I think I'll shoot the buttons off your shirt." Mix put away his gun. The two became friends before the evening was out.

Hell's Half Acre was an oasis during Prohibition, too, but now all signs of this once wicked spot have faded. Today, rural Brookside is known in a more worthy way. Sometime after its school district consolidated with Canon City's, the old schoolhouse became the New Hope School for the retarded.

According to an early history, John Mills located on Chandler Creek in

1865, possibly after A. C. Chandler had left to fight for the southern cause. Mills, a friend of William May, had the misfortune to die of "knotting of the bowels for which there was no help." Little other mention is found of the Chandler Creek area until the Western Fuel Company platted the town of Chandler west of the mine workings in August, 1890. This was considered the prettiest of all Colorado coal camps after it was acquired by the Victor American Fuel Company. The only commercial buildings there were the large general store, boarding house, and a single saloon. The several hundred residents took pride in their neat homes and tree lined streets. The mine was worthy of pride, too, for it was second only to that at Rockvale in Fremont County production.

Charlie Cowan sank a new shaft about a mile south of Chandler in 1903. His son-in-law, Roll Blunt, lived there at Cuckoo with his family. Their baby daughter, Ada, was born in makeshift lodgings and shortly died of pneumonia. Their five-year-old son died there the following spring. In those days lack of medical care with difficult living conditions contributed to an unplanned zero population growth.

Frank D. Heath organized the Great Western Coal Company in 1904 to develop this property. He obtained a charter for a railroad into the camp from Chandler. This short line was impressively called the Canon City and Great Western Railway. However, when the coal soon gave out the shack city disappeared. Heath next planned to mine his 360 acres at Heathton.

By 1905, the Chandler mine had a payroll of 175 men. There were thirty-six miles of tracks in the maze of rooms, slopes, and bores. A hundred mules hauled ore cars underground, never seeing the light of day.

Less than a decade later this ideal community was the site of the murder that precipitated the longest trial in the history of the old Fremont County Courthouse. The infamous Chandler March came on the heels of the Ludlow massacre where fifty were killed. The Victor American Fuel Company continued to insist on an open shop to the annoyance of the United Mine Workers of America which was trying to unionize all the mines in Colorado. UMW agitation threatened to bring about a repetition of the troublous times of 1904.

When the union members struck, the Victor American mine at Chandler continued operation with a hundred strike breakers. So much bad feeling existed between the striking miners and the adamant owners that State Militia was sent to protect the mines and the strike breakers. The miners formed vigilante committees and bought up what firearms they could. The situation was tense but didn't become violent until a few weeks after the Militia had been withdrawn.

On April 15, 1914, a mob of sixty masked men attempted to lynch Charles Ragland, a negro, who had been arrested at Portland on the charge of murdering Joseph A. Petty of Florence. They stormed the Fremont

County jail with sledge hammers, breaking down the doors. Sheriff William Newcomb gave alarm and sounded the steam whistle on Canon City's electric plant, thwarting their plans.

Terror spread throughout Colorado over the battle to unionize the mines. The strike situation was so bad in the state that a bill was introduced in Congress proposing that the government operate Rockefeller's mines. Unreasonable violence reached a peak with the infamous April 20th shootings at Ludlow where nine hundred men, women, and children, evicted from company quarters, lived in tents and shanties.

Victor American shut down its Chandler mine as the officers prepared to protect their property. Later that week, Sheriff Newcomb went to Chandler to warn the women and children to leave. The Chandler school closed. The striking miners voted at Florence to attack Chandler. Strikers guarded the route when, at dawn the next day, one hundred strikers moved first on Rockvale. After Black Hand letters had warned of the attack terrified residents of Rockvale and Williamsburg moved in fear to Florence.

Telephone wires were cut, hundreds of shots were fired. Rumors were rampant that after attacking Chandler, the strikers would invade Canon City to blow up the courthouse, power plant, and other buildings. Amazingly, there was only one fatality in the thirty-six hours of shooting, which could be heard as far away as Canon City. At four in the afternoon of the first day, twenty-six-year-old William King, a non-union underground miner, was shot in the forehead as he carried coffee and sandwiches to the bivouacked mine guards on Tank Hill overlooking the Victor American operation.

At six a.m. on April 27, General Chase, on orders of Governor Elias M. Ammons, arrived at Canon City from Ludlow with two hundred nine men. By that time the mine office was riddled with bullets. All the company houses were ransacked, but no mine machinery nor buildings had been damaged.

The striking miners lined the hills around Rockvale, Coal Creek, and Williamsburg to hold off the militia. After Chase had dispatched the cavalry, the Governor unexpectedly ordered him to hold his troops in Canon City. Although the armed cavalry had no trouble in entering Chandler, the Governor requested Federal aid. The militia pulled out when 175 Federal soldiers arrived on the 29th.

As these men searched the hills for hidden arms, they came upon Half Way House, a saloon run by Kate Bender, less than a mile from Chandler. Since this was a source of supplies for the strikers, they set fire to it although they found little ammunition there.

The strikers, varying in number from three hundred to a thousand according to which account you read, left Chandler for Brookside. Then the verbal brickbats began. They claimed the whole thing started because a delegation had organized in Canon City to exterminate the strikers. The district organizer of the United Mine Workers denied that one of his men had said that union men would take up arms to prevent non-union men from working the mines.

U. S. troops remained at Chandler, Williamsburg, and Radiant throughout the month although the explosive situation had calmed by May 5. On the 27th, after six weeks of study, a grand jury indicted one hundred men for inciting the march and twenty-seven men for first degree murder. Those who couldn't furnish bond were held in the Fremont County jail for several months before they were released for lack of evidence.

Seven against whom charges were actually filed were brought to trial on November 16. It turned into the longest murder trial in Fremont County history. The prosecution hoped to prove conspiracy to prevent non-union labor from working. The defense held that King might have been killed by one of the company's own machine guns and that the battle had been caused by a citizens' alliance formed in Canon City to attack the mines at Williamsburg. The sensational trial finally ended in January, 1915, with the conviction of two for voluntary manslaughter. It also resulted in a change in Colorado law to prohibit an attorney general from confessing error as he did in that trial.

Chandler quickly recovered from the battle after labor and management came to an agreement. The new two-story school was the scene of many a pleasant social. The community was highly sports minded and the rivalry with other coal towns was intense. During Prohibition spectators at the baseball games often refreshed themselves with home brew beer at nearby homes.

Chandler's population of some six hundred vied for the cash awards offered in community beautification contests sponsored by the company. However, by 1942, when the mine was no longer economically productive, Victor American closed the pits. The D & RG pulled out the last loaded coal cars and in 1944 lifted the tracks. The company sold off houses to be moved to reduce the tax load then tore down the buildings that remained. Today all that's left of Chandler is the huge dump, the remnant of the old water tower, and weedgrown streets.

Although a community had existed near the CF & I mine south of Canon City since 1888, it didn't become Prospect Heights until 1905 when Florijan Adamic, an Austrian miner, platted a triangle off Mountain Street. With Canon City adopting local option, saloons in the Heights happily stayed open twenty-four hours a day to satisfy the thirsty from Canon City, the nearby U. S. Smelter, the Nonac, Wolf Park, and Royal Gorge Mines. Literally carloads of beer, wine, and whiskey came in on the Santa Fe siding.

One of the smallest incorporated towns in Colorado, Prospect Heights provided plenty of trouble. Overworked town marshals didn't stay on the job long. The picture changed after the U. S. Smelter closed and was razed in 1909 and Prohibition closed the saloons in 1916.

Today this separate little municipality, owned and ruled by the Adamic family, buys water from Canon City although Anton Adamic installed a town water system in 1921. As nearly all the thirty-eight presently registered voters are related they run things to suit themselves. It's unlikely this coal town will ever become a ghost while they have things going their way. The ghosts may well be underground, however, for many miles of mine tunnels honeycomb the coal fields around here.

The Canon Reliance Fuel Company opened its Wolf Park mine in the mid 1890's. The surrounding Town of Wolf Park had some thirty company houses, a general store, and a population of about one hundred fifty. At one time, with a shaft of 1,029 feet, this was the deepest coal mine in Colorado, although it was but a few feet deeper than the nearby Royal Gorge mine. An unusual tragedy occurred here when two men sinking an air shaft broke through to a large underground body of water and drowned. The mine was a big producer until it was shut down in 1934. The Cotter Corporation's mill now occupies the site of this one time coal camp.

Late in 1902, the Royal Gorge Coal and Fire Clay Company organized to develop its resources about two and a half miles south of Canon City. The company built houses for its workers but boasted that it paid no scrip to nor demanded any discount of them, indicating an enlightened attitude.

The Rocky Mountain Fuel Company's Nonac (Canon spelled backwards), later the CF & I's #5/mine near Canon City, was the last large coal mine to be opened in Fremont County. It was one of the biggest producers. It ceased operation in 1949[4] when the coal ran out after producing for more than half a century. Its one-time presence was suddenly brought to mind early in December, 1969, when, with a rumble and a roar, a gaping hole forty feet long and forty feet deep appeared just south of Prospect Heights only twelve feet from the Oak Creek road.

Employees of the CF & I hastened to bulldoze material from the old mine dump into this cavein of a section of the main slope extending under parts of the rodeo grounds and Lakeside Cemetery. Old time miners agree that further fall of the old main slope is possible. They recall that a fall of mine entries and rooms damaged Sali's Paradise, a Canon City restaurant run by Gus Salardino of Gold Nugget fame, and other buildings just twenty-one years earlier.

Despite the fact that the value of coal mined in Colorado exceeds the value of gold removed from her mountains, grimy ghost coal camps lack the lustre of romance which pervades weathering ghost gold towns.

Griffith Mine, 1966
This toppling tipple is a reminder of days when small coal mining operations were possible and profitable. *Photo by the author.*

Oil Seep
The dark band at the base of the embankment along Fourmile Creek indicates the seep that led to the development of the Florence oil field. *Photo by the author.*

FOOTNOTES

1. Robert G. Athearn's *Rebel of the Rockies,* p. 32.
2. Not only coal towns were affected, Cripple Creek was crippled, too, in a desperate clash between miners and management. It was during this trouble that Harry Orchard blew up the station at Independence. See Clyde Brion Davis' *The Arkansas* p. 139 ff.
3. Letter to the author from Jack McFall quoting David R. Graham of Coal Creek.
4. The *Canon City Daily Record* of May 6, 1971, reports that the last cut of coal was made 1952.

CHAPTER X

WHEN THE CARS CAME TO CANON CITY

When the rails arrived in Fremont County, newly incorporated Cañon City no longer seemed remote from the States. The city as well as the county grew until the few rutted roads serving the area no longer were adequate. Merchants old and new recognized the desirability of tapping the trade potential of the Wet Mountain and San Luis Valleys as well as South Park. The area's greatest need was money. So many poor had come to settle that few could afford the good twelve dollar men's wool suits advertised in the *Canon City Times*.

Richard Houle was an early user of the new narrow gauge. He may have been one of the many Englishmen who succumbed to the blandishments of Edward Reed of London who spent $3000 of his own money advertising Colorado and distributed thousands of pamphlets issued by Colorado Territory's short lived Board of Immigration.

Born in Barnstable in 1851, Houle had attended public schools and the Agricultural College at Devonshire. When he was twenty-one, he decided to see what life in the new world was like. He arrived in Denver on the Kansas-Pacific and took the D & RG to Pueblo. He had to remain there, using the last of his cash, to wait for the Monday train since the Labran branch didn't run on weekends.

By taking the stage from Labran through Lincoln Park he arrived in Cañon City via the First Street bridge. Near there, the new Territorial Prison stood alone and fenceless facing a swampy field. He soon found a job in a tannery but turned to farming near present Fifteenth Street and East Main six weeks later when the tannery went out of business.

Although the narrow gauge reached only to Labran, improved transportation across the plains sparked a new boom for Cañon City quite different from the one triggered by the gold seekers. There was no rejoicing when a new Mexican dance hall opened in March, 1873. Rather, someone complained in the newspaper that it would "pander to base passion in a disgusting way." The residents preferred to picture their community as a city of culture and refinement. There was even agitation for a public library. However, it seemed more practical to build the town's first public building, the calaboose.

Cañon City fully expected to have rail service soon along the nine miles of graded right of way since Fremont County had gladly voted a fifty thousand dollar bond issue. Unfortunately, this amount was lost to the railroad through a technicality. Palmer, pressed for cash, was forced to use a threat and bribe tactic to assure more support. Much to the city's disappointment, the D & RG demanded an additional fifty thousand dollars to continue the line from Labran.

The people of Fremont County, disenchanted with the D & RG, had held a public meeting in January, 1873, then formally invited the Santa Fe to build along the route first surveyed by the K-P. Unfortunately, the depression that followed the New York bank failures slowed Santa Fe construction to a standstill. A bitter canvass then approved $100,000 for the D & RG but the County Commissioners refused to issue the bonds because there was a majority of only two votes.

In the end, Cañon City alone provided the funds. An issue of $50,000 which carried was supplemented by a gift of $25,000 worth of property adjacent to the right of way. As should have been foreseen, the end of the line was an aggravating distance short of the city limits when the extension was completed. Although then the business section of Cañon City huddled between Second and Fourth Streets on Main, the depot was at Sixteenth and Greenwood on land donated by W. H. Greenwood south of his new addition.

The fuming citizens refused to buy lots around the depot. Wits soon dubbed the D & RG the "Narrow Gouge" in protest at its ten cents a mile fare while admitting that stage coaches were both more expensive and more uncomfortable. When it seemed certain that East Cañon was as far as Palmer intended to take his track, some of the irked souls formed the Canon City and Saguache Railroad to continue the rails to the West. However, as they were unable to do the work required the first year, nothing came of it.

Dick Houle[1] soon decided to desert his farm near the depot for a ranch in the Wet Mountain Valley. In May, 1873, he hitched his team to a wagon and went to Denver to meet his two sisters with their families. Thomas D. and Annie Balman had left England for Ontario, Canada, where two sons, Walter and Thomas G., were born. They went to Chicago to join Eliza and Edwin Chamings whose son, Nicholas, had been born in Fairbury, Illinois, in 1872. These two families, along with Dick's brother George, and John Howard, who would later be Dick's brother-in-law, traveled to Denver together.

After the five day trip down from Denver, the three bachelors went to the Wet Mountain Valley to ranch. The Chamings and Balmans remained on the property Dick had earlier farmed. Ed Chamings, reasonably well-to-do, invested in teams, surrys, a fine stallion, and a stage coach to serve the Cañon City-Rosita trade. He built a good house but the Balmans bought a place near later Hillside. Tom paid $2500 for 160 acres, getting his money back in one year by freighting 100 tons of hay from it to Leadville.

When Palmer finally got around to extending the track nearer to the heart of town, he had work begin on Sunday so that the graders could

116

proceed down River Street. The residents rebelled at that, Sunday or no, compelling him to move a block to the south along Water Street. When the former depot was converted into a railroad boarding house, Annie Balman and Eliza Chamings ran it. By the time this building was razed in 1956, Frank Maynard had long farmed all around it.

The railroad seemed to assure a fine future for Cañon City. James Clelland and partners incorporated the Cañon City Bank in May 1874 for $100,000. Dr. Ferdinand V. Hayden, who had mapped and surveyed Colorado, set up a meteorological observation site in the city that summer to supplement those in operation at Denver, Fairplay, and on the summit of Mt. Lincoln. Governor Samuel H. Elbert appointed Anson Rudd as the first warden of the Territorial Prison when it was turned over to the jurisdiction of the Territory by the Federal Government. However, the Canon City Academy, optimistically established by the Episcopal Church, was able to operate for only a short time.

In the meantime work had gone forward on the wagon roads. The toll road up Grape Creek cut miles from the alternate routes to the Wet Mountain Valley over McCandless Ford to the west or up Hardscrabble Cañon to the east.

Gold dust was still being actively handled in this town of three hundred when twenty-four year old Frederick A. Raynolds opened his Fremont County Bank in a small room off the lobby of McClure House the day it opened in October. Built by William McClure, brother of the builder of the McClure House at Glendale, this McClure House on the site of Rudd's original log cabin had a hundred rooms. It was considered a first class resort for invalids, tourists, and pleasure seekers. When the Panics of 1876 and 1877 swept away McClure's assets before he was able to profit from this investment, he had to leave Cañon City for a couple of years to seek his fortune elsewhere.

Some of the residents moved south across the river. Benjamin Griffin's son helped him build the brick house on Griffin Avenue where six generations of Griffins have lived.

Beautification began on the north side. The Canon City Arbor and Floricultural Society was formed to encourage planting of fruit and shade trees, flowers, grasses, and ornamental or fruit bearing shrubs. Business was suspended for the planting. During two weeks in April, fifteen hundred shade trees alone were planted. George and B. F. Rockafellow planted two hundred of them.

There was so much news that Dr. Isaac E. Thayer started publishing a second paper, *The Avalanche.* It didn't report what Chief Ouray of the Utes thought of all this when he came to town. Indians no longer caused much comment. The people made no to-do over the arrival of the Chief. Large numbers of Utes seldom camped near Cañon City after the removal

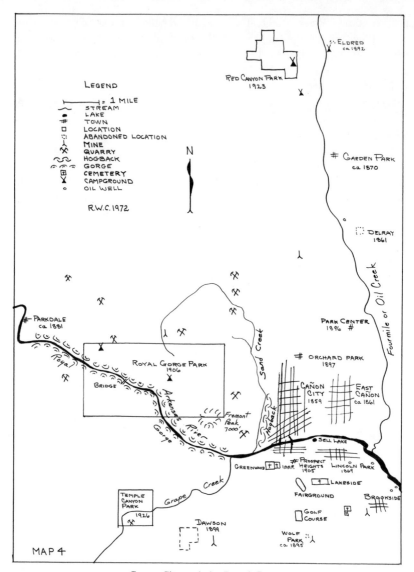

Canon City and the Royal Gorge

The spectacular Royal Gorge, once a barrier to exploration and settlement, is now a scenic attraction visited by thousands annually. Canon City, once the "gate city" to the gold fields, is now the gate to the natural beauty of the Grand Canyon of the Arkansas.

of the agency to the Uncompahgre. However, early in 1874 hungry Utes killed some local cattle. They felt their action was justified. "White man come, deer go. Beef come, we take beef." There was no denying that, unlike the Indian, a white hunter was likely to scare off more game than he killed. The government ordered the agent to issue rations to the hungry Indians at Cañon City and then to see that they returned to Los Pinos.[2]

By 1875, the First Presbyterians were able to build their own church, a board and batten shell twenty-four feet by forty feet lined with building paper. It stood on the site of the present library. Despite an addition two years later it remained rather primitive until a high wind in July 1878 whistled through the cracks and tore the paper lining to strips. The building was properly plastered after that. It served the congregation through 1901 when a handsome new stone edifice was built.

Not everyone in the booming county was prosperous— or pious. When John Newman arrived in 1876 looking for a place to graze his hundred or so horses, Felipe Salazar and Jose Talmage told him they knew just the box canyon he could easily fence. Newman took the Mexicans in his light wagon over the Oak Creek Grade through Rosita toward Gardner. When Newman failed to reappear, searchers found his body where he had camped the first night out. The two men were captured late in July and brought in to the little red calaboose at 416 Rudd.

The town was full of railroad workers who were finally laying the rails into the heart of Cañon City. A large crowd which gathered at Murray's Saloon decided to lynch the guilty men. Morning found Salazar hanging from a beam in an old shed at 603 Rudd. Talmage dangled in a cottonwood grove near the Hot Springs since Cañon City's new trees were too small to serve as gallows.

That same year when Charlie Newland's gang stole horses from Cañon City and Beaver Creek, a posse of prominent men set out in pursuit. They trailed the men to Big Island, a once-well-wooded haven in the Arkansas River near the Kansas border. They hanged the horsethieves and a probably innocent sixteen-year-old boy whom they didn't trust to keep quiet about their unjust justice. They recovered all the horses to return home, their reputations unsullied but their consciences heavy.

Fremont County had housed offenders in the Territorial Prison but now the county built its own jail at a cost of $3500. The commissioners also announced plans for a county poorhouse. The much disliked CCI may have tried to gain favor by deeding land for the first county courthouse.

Catlin donated ten acres of his land on the rise southwest of Cañon City for a cemetery. A typhoid epidemic, resulting from the accepted lack of sanitation of those days, increased the need for burial space. W. N. Davis, thirty-four, had been buried a decade earlier in the corner of one of Catlin's fields. As Greenwood Cemetery, that area now has sections maintained by various lodges, for G.A.R. and Confederate veterans, and for paupers and penitentiary inmates. The most recent addition is Woodpecker Hill which was opened for the unclaimed bodies of prisoners when the original prison section was filled. Twenty-one Catlins have been buried at Greenwood over a ninety-year span. Today the dusty sumac, prickly cactus, and the tawny tan of the native grasses belie the name Greenwood. Without provision for perpetual care, the cemetery long since let nature be the gardener except where proud descendants have cared enough to nurture tiny lawns and scattered trees.

One plot contains four members of the Houle family who died within days of one another. Eighteen seventy six had begun happily for Richard Houle when he went to England to bring back his bride, Elizabeth Howard, in February. But before long, when his brother, George, was taken seriously ill Annie Balman sent for her sister, Eliza Chamings, to come to the ranch to help care for him. Her new baby, Anna, was but six weeks old when Eliza started on her mercy mission. However, Eliza herself was taken sick near McCandless Ford and had to return home. She soon died of typhoid. A few days later George Houle and little Walter Balman, a cripple from birth, died too. Ed Chamings died about ten days after his wife. The once close family was grief stricken.

Annie Balman took the baby Annie Chamings to raise, a cousin took eighteen-month-old Fanny, and the Houles raised the boy, Nicholas. When another sister, Bessie, came from England to take the children back to their grandparents, Annie Balman was so brokenhearted that she wouldn't let any of them go, including Bessie.

The following year another death clouded the Chamings house again. It was then tenanted by one Moynihan, a section boss of the D & RG, an inoffensive and well-meaning man who was constantly bullied by a desperado who worked for him. In fact, Patrick Fitzpatrick terrorized all who worked with him. Moynihan was driven to desperate measures to put a stop to it. He came out of the house one day and simply shot Fitzpatrick as he passed. An appeal reduced Moynihan's sentence from hanging to life. The unhappy association with five deaths gave the house the reputation of being haunted until William McClure bought it to tear it down about 1920.

Meantime, people lived, too. Henry T. Williams, in his book *The Pacific Tourist,* mentions that Cañon City was the next most noted resort then in Colorado after Manitou with its elegant hotels and medicinal baths.

County residents converged on the county seat, where B. F. Rockafellow reigned as the fourth Mayor, to celebrate the centennial of the United States of America on July 4, 1876. There was a thirteen gun salute at daybreak, a balloon ascension, a mile-long parade to the "grounds" which the people complained had no seats and were in "poor condition." Anson Rudd read a brief history of Fremont County after F. A. Raynolds read

FIRST PENITENTIARY
CANON CITY, COLORADO, TERRITORY
BUILT 1869.
DAVID PROSSER, WARDEN.
FIRST PRISONER No. 1 - JOHN SHEPLER, JUNE 13, 1871.
LARCENY - 1 YEAR - FROM GILPIN COUNTY, COLO. TER.
F. HUMMEL.

The Territorial Prison
This modest mansard building soon proved inadequate for its purpose. The grounds
were later walled by the convicts themselves. *Courtesy Florence Pioneer Museum.*

the Declaration of Independence, reaffirmed by those present. Thomas Macon was the orator of the day. The long celebration closed with fireworks following a thirty-eight gun salute at sundown that anticipated Colorado's imminent entrance into the Union.

For all the promotion and optimism, however, Cañon City didn't become the capital when Colorado became a state on the first of August. None the less, the city gained national, if not local, fame in a totally unexpected way that summer.

Ormel W. Lucas, a young graduate of Oberlin College who taught school in Garden Park, some eight miles north of Cañon City on Oil Creek, found some gastroliths one day when he was out hunting. These ancient gizzard stones led to the discovery of agatized fossil bones which he described to one of his former professors. By strange coincidence, Arthur Lakes, another Colorado teacher located a similar deposit near Morrison.

The word dinosaur, if it had yet been coined, meant little to the American public then, despite the first find in New Jersey in 1868 and the subsequent work of Edward Drinker Cope of the Philadelphia Academy of Science and Professor Othniel Charles Marsh of Yale University's Peabody Museum. These men, eminent in the new science of paleontology, once close friends, were bitter rivals by the time bones were found in Colorado. Both had collectors in the field acting with cloak and dagger secrecy.

Cope and Marsh weren't the only rivals in the region. Young Lt. George Montague Wheeler, one of the last of the Army explorers, headed the Geographical Survey of the Territories of the U.S. West of the 100th Meridian. His Army party, working out of Denver, ran into Dr. Hayden's men surveying the same remote wilderness for the Interior Department. The ensuing row between those two touched off a battle in Congress, which failed to see a need for such duplication of effort. In 1874 Marsh had joined those disparaging Wheeler's work. Ironically, it was a Wheeler party in New Mexico the following year that would lead Cope to his greatest discovery.

Marsh was more than annoyed when Lakes sent some of the Morrison bones to Cope as well as to Marsh. Then, when Lucas sent Cope the bones he later identified as *Camarasaurus supremus,* larger than any other land animal previously described, Marsh was stung. An egoist capable of unscrupulous duplicity, he tried to get bones from the Lucas quarry by offering more money, but Lucas held fast to his agreement with Cope.

Both Cope and Marsh came to Cañon City to study the findings and were visited by Dr. Hayden, with whom Cope had previously worked. Cope commented that Cañon City was a "new and rather rough town of small size."

A. M. Cassiday gave Cope the exclusive privilege of excavating fossil bones from his oil tract on Fourmile Creek with the express statement that he did not desire nor demand any compensation in return. Cope's Quarry #1 was five hundred yards west of the small conical hill known as "The Nipple." His Quarry #2 was almost at the crest of the escarpment at the west boundary of Garden Park. This, or another Cope quarry, was reworked in 1901 by J. B. Hatcher for the Carnegie Museum.

These quarries were a short distance north of one worked for several years by M. P. Felch who lived near by. Felch recovered a *Brontosaurus excelsus* fifty-three feet long for Marsh in 1883. Although these finds seemed to cause little stir in the city, the editor of *The Cañon City Record* reported in August that he had made three trips that week to the "bone yard" in Garden Park although the severe rains had played havoc with the road. This quarry, later known as the Marsh-Hatcher quarry, yielded *Diplodocus longus Marsh, Haplocanthosaurus priscus Hatcher,* and *Haplocanthosaurus utterbacki Hatcher,* excavated at a much lower geological level than Cope's finds. Seven miles of hills along Fourmile, rich in fossils, are known as the Museum Range.

The quarries were far from exhausted when both Cope and Marsh began to receive more bones than they could describe from Colorado and elsewhere. Each man made ludicrous errors in his haste to be the first to publish scientific descriptions of his finds. For example, when one of Cope's colleagues restored *Camarasaurus,* its length startled scientific circles since he had mistakenly included several extra vertebrae of other individuals found near it.

A bone or two in the Canon City Municipal Museum along with arrowheads and hand pieces found near the caves and shelters close to Fourmile Creek are all that were kept locally to show the prehistoric life of the area.

A monument some ten miles north of the city on the west side of the dirt road rather incompletely reveals the importance of the finds in the vicinity. It shows in relief the five types of dinosaurs discovered within a two mile radius of the spot. This part of the plaque was designed by Mrs. Lavona Martinez, later finance officer for Cañon City. Another marker along this road indicates the location of our nation's second oil well.

Only one complete dinosaur skeleton remains in Colorado. There is a *Stegosaurus* at the Colorado Museum of Natural History in Denver. Museums in the East display the *Tyrannosaurus,* the *Brontosaurus,* the *Diplodocus,* and the *Ceratosaurus.* Old bones intrigued few residents when there was oil, coal, gold, and silver to be had, or railways to be built.

With Rosita booming in 1877, James Clelland joined Augustus Macon and B. F. Rockafellow in organizing the Cañon City, Wet Mountain, and Rosita Railway Company to connect Rosita with the D & RG and thus make Cañon City the focal point for shipping. However, Cañon City's citizens were disappointed when men in the new mining camps succeeded in carving Custer County from the southern section of Fremont County even if it did leave Fremont larger than the State of Rhode Island.

The then popular author, Helen Hunt Jackson, wrote that Cañon City had a "wide-awake look," several good shops, and three tolerable hotels. There were still Indians about, now more a nuisance than a threat.

Soda Spring remained a popular spot. Public spirited citizens built a little rustic pavilion over the stone catch basin and provided a hitch rack in front for those who came by carriage.

The CC, WM & R evidently died aborning since the Wet Mountain Valley Railroad was formed the following year by William B. Strong and other Santa Fe men. It was to connect their newly incorporated Pueblo and Arkansas Valley Railroad with Silver Cliff and Rosita by way of Copper Gulch. A month later, Palmer associates organized the Rosita and Silver Cliff Railway to reach those points via Grape Creek and also via Texas Creek.

Cañon City was a busy county seat with five hundred residents in 1878. Stages to Fairplay, South Park, Ula, Rosita, and the Wet Mountain Valley contributed plenty of action. The Colorado Stage and Express left Cañon City at seven-thirty a.m. daily arriving in Silver Cliff at three p.m. the same day. Long trains of wagons brought ore or bullion to be shipped or to be processed at the Mallett Reduction and Sampling Works. Large wagon yards accommodated the wagons and teams between trips.

American Mining and Smelting Company had water wheels providing power for its ore smelter on South Ninth Street on the north bank of the Arkansas. This mill handled Leadville ores until the turn of the century. In those less ecology-minded times the slag was conveniently dumped into the river. Anson Rudd, Henry Harrison, Warren Fowler, and others formed The Cañon City Hydraulic and Irrigation Ditch Company[3] to construct, maintain, and repair the ditch earlier known as The Cañon City and Four Mile Ditch. The new company's six mile ditch provided the town with water and irrigated two thousand acres of land to the east in which Harrison had invested.

There was opportunity for relaxation as well as work. J. P. Ring ran the bath house for health seekers at the Hot Springs owned by the hated CCI. The Rings were still managing the dozen tubs when Dr. J. L. Prentiss came to town. He eyed the location and envisioned Cañon City as a spa to compare with the Hot Springs in Virginia.

In addition to doctoring, Prentiss was the proprietor of a book and stationery store. As the town grew, so did his investments. The 1881 *Colorado Business Directory* lists him as one of four physicians. There were also J. L. Prentiss Brothers, drugs, and J. L. Prentiss and G. R. Shaeffer, jewelry. Shaeffer, once a diamond salesman for Tiffany and Company in New York,[4] also engaged in the buying and selling of real estate. Prentiss still had to wait to see any development at the Hot Springs until a new hotel with cottages was completed and an addition made to the bathhouses "for the accommodation of invalids and tourists."

The first big top show to appear in town was W. W. Cole's New York and New Orleans Circus and Menagerie. It arrived in the summer of 1879 while Eddie Foy, the great comedian, was playing at the Opera House. Holidays called for parties or dances and special attractions at the Theater Comique.

Clelland, Mulock, Shaeffer, William E. Johnson and his brother Wilbur, James H. Peabody, and others formed The Canon City Water Company to take water from the Arkansas within five miles of the Hot Springs to furnish to the expanding community. Peabody, Clelland's bookkeeper, then twenty-five, who had recently married the boss's daughter, Frances, became a partner in Clelland's clothing store. Twenty-two-year-old William Johnson had come to town to try his hand at real estate.

Levi Haley and Harry Breton began work on a narrow gauge freight railroad to the Wet Mountain Valley despite advice to the contrary. They planned to put it close to Grape Creek, a boisterous and treacherous stream that had earlier washed out a new wagon road before it could be used, but abandoned it after some engineering work was done. Heedless of the risk, the D & RG began building along this same route in 1881. Workers at a construction camp near a side canyon discovered there a natural amphitheater one hundred feet across and fifty feet deep in a granite cliff. Called The Temple, it looked like a vast stage with flats and flies. As work progressed, the populace deplored the despoiling of the vine festooned canyon but accepted the fact that "the beautiful must fall before the useful."

Although G. R. Cassidy and G. R. Shaeffer had located claims along Grape Creek as early as 1871, most of the claims in the Grape Creek Mining District were filed in the early 1880's concentrated in the Green Gulch and Horseshoe Camp areas. None of these proved to be notably rich although in 1883, the Gem was considered the most important property in the county. The greatest portion of bullion output for the previous two years had been shipped from there.

The railroad made working the CC & I's mine of magnetic ore feasible. In 1882, it shipped eight hundred one tons to the Pueblo plant. Stations at Marsh, about ten miles from Cañon City, Soda Springs, about ten miles farther on in Fremont County, Blackburn, Govetown (earlier called Dora City), and Westcliffe in Custer County, served other mines. However, the nature of the terrain made the thirty-one and a half miles of narrow gauge expensive to maintain while the mines generated too little traffic to make the line a paying proposition.

The D & RG had followed the accepted practice of building on the

Grape Creek
Spikes and bits of rail can still be found along the creek bed where once the narrow
gauge railroad climbed the canyon to Westcliffe. *Photo by the author.*

drainage grade, blithely disregarding the fact that Grape Creek drops nearly twenty-three hundred feet in twenty-eight miles in an area subject to cloudbursts. The narrow gauge track crossed the creek thirty-five times in twenty-six miles. The rails never did reach booming Silver Cliff. Palmer typically ended the track outside the established town. This time the terminus was the ranch property of Dr. Bell, Palmer's long time friend and business associate, where Westcliffe soon outshone Silver Cliff, a mile and a half farther east.[5]

The first excursion train carried two hundred passengers to Westcliffe on May 11, 1881. On August 20th, a series of cloudbursts demolished all but two of the bridges and washed out eighteen miles of track. Workmen on a gravity car raced down the grade to warn the mixed train on the way up from Cañon City. The engineer backed the train to higher ground. All aboard walked the five miles back to Cañon City. No one was hurt, but the train couldn't be rescued for a month. The line reopened in October after much labor and expense.

In 1884 a spring flood, as predicted, washed out sections leaving a passenger car and a mail car stranded with a half dozen freight cars. The track had to be rebuilt to salvage the train.

The first annual report of the state railroad commissioner, covering the year ending June 30, 1885, reveals that the Grape Creek branch was dangerously out of repair, especially the section between a point three miles south of Canon Junction and to within two miles of Marsh Station. The high water of that spring had caused a condition which permitted Engine #74 to go over a precipice on the ninth of May. W. B. Felker, the commissioner, wrote to William S. Jackson, receiver for the D & RG, on the twenty-third of June to point out that at the scene of the disaster the road bed was so narrow the end of the cross-ties extended twelve inches over the precipice and that he considered it criminally negligent to permit a train to pass over the road, especially when an expenditure of five hundred dollars for construction could prevent a recurrence. The repair was made. Felker considered then that the road was in better condition than at any time since its construction.

But fires and litigation were closing the still producing mines while the remaining ones provided too little revenue for the foundering D & RG. An 1888 flood put the line out of commission for two months. The broken and twisted track was never replaced after a cloudburst the following August. The railroad's usefulness was over. Blackburn served as the center for the dismantling operation. When that was finished so was the town.

Other towns had withered away when the railroad was built. Titusville, a town of two hundred fifty, began to fade soon after the trains began running. It had been a meal stop on the daily stage that plodded up the Oak Creek Grade, a road so steep and winding that freight horses wore

127

bells to warn of their approach. Titusville was soon no more than a cluster of dilapidated buildings on land that became the Al Griffin ranch. Yorkville, a settlement a half mile to the north, and Galena, two and a half miles to the south near the Custer County line, survived a while longer before being deserted.

When Silver Cliff showed signs of slumping, the large and elegant St. Cloud Hotel,[6] originally built as the Powell House, was torn down. All the dimension lumber and cut rock was hauled down the Oak Creek Grade to Cañon City. The St. Cloud was rebuilt in 1888 at 631 Main Street, at that time outside the city proper, and advertised as the "health seeker's resort." It still does business as the Canon Hotel.

By the time the railroad was abandoned, there was a new wagon road that followed the Indian trail across Grape Creek. It traversed the so-called Indian burial ground where once were many cairns of sedimentary rock which were periodically strewn with evergreen boughs by the Utes. Some say they indicated graves of Utes killed in a running battle with the U.S. Dragoons following the massacre at El Pueblo. According to others, the place was the scene of the bloody battle, between Utes and Arapahoes. The battle extended from Brewster Spring to Copper Gulch. Yet another version[7] has it that Lucien Maxwell's daughter, Sylvina, eloped with her Spanish lover and that they were captured by Apaches. After several months, Sylvina escaped from Chief Little River only to be taken prisoner by Lame Wolf during a fight with the Utes. The rocks were heaped over the Utes who fell in this fight. As for Sylvina, she was finally ransomed but died after returning home to tell her tragic story. The mounds were soon desecrated when the wagon road made them accessible to souvenir hunters. Whatever they commemorated, there is scarcely a trace of them left today. Modern vandals defaced the marker put there when the park was improved during the Depression by the Civilian Conservation Corps.

Temple Canyon was a popular picnic site in the 1890's for Canon City residents who reached it via a foot bridge across Grape Creek. An Act of Congress granted Temple Canyon Park to Canon City in 1912. However, as late as 1937, the government still was waiting payment of eight hundred dollars for it. During the Depression, the WPA spent $118,348 to construct roads, trails, lookout points and recreational areas there, providing useful work for the men living at Kenwood. Both the park and the road were neglected during World War II. Only recently has Canon City regraded the gravel road and rehabilitated the facilities.

Although the Temple itself has gathered any number of appropriate legends, it is still unspoiled by tourists. It is well worth the strenuous climb down and back along the trail from Temple Canyon Park about five miles southwest of Canon City. However the bridge is gone and Grape Creek cannot be crossed there when the water is high. The creek itself is

Temple Canyon
The size of this natural stage-like formation can be judged by the small figures
climbing up to the opening. *Courtesy C. Arthur Frederickson.*

photogenic, and railroad buffs can discern traces of old track along it.

Even before work started on the railroad up Grape Creek, conditions had been ripening for a spectacular war[8] between the locally financed D & RG and the Santa Fe, strongly backed by Easterners. Cañon City men sided with the Santa Fe. They were bitter, convinced that they had suffered a serious setback when handsome, mustachioed Palmer, again choosing to build south, had apparently left them at a dead end after they had furnished funds to get his tracks to Cañon City. B. F. Rockafellow, James Clelland, and Frederick A. Raynolds with Ebenezer T. Alling had formed the Cañon City and San Juan Railway Company in February, 1877 to carry on where Palmer left off. It was actually set up for the Santa Fe, which took it over through its Pueblo and Arkansas Valley Railroad. The CC & SJ Railway was reincorporated to parallel with standard gauge all existing branches of the narrow gauge D & RG. This was an attempt to outmaneuver the D & RG and build through the Royal Gorge.

Palmer seemed unconcerned. He was certain that the route through the gorge was the only feasible one and that his original federal charter specified construction up the Grand Canyon of the Arkansas which entitled him to it whenever he wished to build. However, the Palmer group soon came up with an elaborate scheme for an Alamosa, San Juan, and Pacific Railway to by-pass the gorge in case the Santa Fe got the upper hand there. Colorado Springs associates of Palmer's set up the Upper Arkansas, San Juan and Pacific Railway Company to reach Leadville from the end of the D & RG in Cañon City.

Palmer, forced to find funds on his own, was in difficulty. Even Alling, president of the CC & SJ, saw a better opportunity in Ouray where he went to operate a store to serve the silver seekers in the San Juans. Henry Ripley, editor of the second *Cañon City Times* which had changed owners many times, complained that he couldn't live on "corn, bear meat, and moldy loaves" offered in lieu of cash for subscriptions and advertisements. He moved his paper to Ouray also. Thayer's *Avalanche* became the *Fremont County Record*.

Trade took a turn when a new rush to California Gulch followed the discovery of lead carbonates. Crumbling Oro City became Leadville and rapidly grew to be second to Denver in population.

Cañon City rejoiced when the D & RG was elbowed out of Raton Pass by its hefty rival. Palmer then turned his sights again toward the western route. Both he and the Santa Fe meant to secure the right of way where there was hardly room for one. Stinging from his defeat at Raton, Palmer was determined to keep the Santa Fe out of the narrow gorge.

The story of the ensuing Royal Gorge War reads like a melodrama. In brief, when the D & RG readied a work train in Pueblo to send to Cañon City, the Santa Fe decoded the secret dispatches and sent its construction official to overtake it. He arrived behind lathered horses at dawn just ahead of the train. Both companies rushed grading crews and fighting men into the gorge. With no Interstate Commerce Commission then for appeal, Palmer went to the courts. There were pleas and reversals and indecisive decisions. Both sides showed contempt for court injunctions by continuing their commando-like tactics.

Hard up for cash and pressed by bondholders, in 1878 Palmer was finally forced to postpone construction and to lease his whole D & RG to the Santa Fe for thirty years.

No sooner had he signed the lease than Leadville boomed. Then the rush to Gunnison began. Prospectors had learned that the heavy black sand which had been an annoyance to the placer miners was full of lead and silver. Colorado, once a land of gold, became a silver state.

FOOTNOTES

1. Judith A. Briscoe recounts the Houle and Chamings story in her unpublished paper, *Early Fremont County*. Interviews with Mrs. Briscoe, daughter of Nicholas Chamings, added details.
2. There is information about the Utes in the area scattered throughout Rockafellow's chapter on Fremont County in the *History of the Arkansas Valley*.
3. Colorado State Archives and Record Center.
4. Interview with Fred E. Riede, July 24, 1969.
5. The most comprehensive account of the Grape Creek railroad seems to be Morris Cafky's "Railroad That Couldn't Make Up Its Mind," *Trains, the Magazine of Railroading*, 26:38-46, August, 1966.
6. G. D. Sowers, Proprietor, advertised Canon City's McClure House as "the only first class hotel in the city," in The Denver & Rio Grande *Official Guide*, [1888.]
7. Janet Sterling offers this imaginative account in her *Legends of the Royal Gorge Region*, p. 29.
8. Glenn Danford Bradley in his *The Story of the Santa Fe* gives an excellent account of this, pp. 155-203.

Soda Spring

Convict stonemasons built new shelters about 1900 to replace the rustic arbors over the Soda and Iron Springs. *Courtesy Katherine Malone.*

Sell's Island

At the turn of the century new orchards graced the popular fruit farm and pleasure resort. *Courtesy Katherine Malone.*

CHAPTER XI

TIE HACKS AND TYCOONS

Transportation of heavy pigs of lead and silver was expensive, killing work for mules and men. With the boom, as Palmer was able to raise more millions on Wall Street than he needed he renewed his efforts to oust the Santa Fe from his right of way, but the court dallied while the lawyers sparred. In the meantime, the gorge itself was filled with forts and snipers. The Santa Fe put a price on the head of James R. DeRemer, the leader of Palmer's stalwarts whose favorite tactic was rolling boulders over the edge of the gorge onto the Santa Fe work parties. The chunks of disintegrated granite made a frightful noise as they ricocheted from wall to wall like bullets. It was nerve shattering but fortunately not deadly.

DeRemer avoided capture and successfully held the Santa Fe to his boundary at the Twenty-Mile Post which marked the end of the right of way through the narrowest part of the defile awarded to the Santa Fe by an earlier court decision. After oscillating between courts and forts, the dispute finally went to arbitration and both lines signed a peace treaty in February, 1880. The D & RG, by then under the thumb of Jay Gould, paid the Santa Fe $1,400,000 for the track it had laid in the Royal Gorge.

Once the Royal Gorge War was resolved, day and night shifts worked to complete the line to Leadville. Built with mule and horse power, plows and scrapers, hand tools and dynamite, the narrow gauge reached Leadville in September, 1880, quite an achievement.

Many men hied to the hills to cut and trim ties with cross cut saw and broad axe. The first ties, flattened only on top and bottom, of green untreated pine or spruce lasted only five or six years. They were skidded down the slopes to where teams could haul them to the grade. The demand for ties and charcoal denuded the slopes. The kilns at Texas Creek, Hayden Creek, Cotopaxi, and Howard furnished the charcoal needed by the smelters.

Not only General Palmer but ex-President U. S. Grant rode the first train to reach the headwaters of the Arkansas. They stopped to admire a unique and brilliant bit of railroad engineering, the hanging bridge that supported the tracks parallel to the river over the water in the Royal Gorge where the walls are too close to permit more than the river to pass. This spot was a special stopping place for viewing the gorge until, after eighty years, passenger cars were discontinued on that route on July 27, 1967.

Until the railroad reached Leadville, traffic piled up on the poor roads that circumvented the gorge. In February, 1880, for instance, a freighter needed eight days to reach Buena Vista from Pueblo because of ice, snow, and traffic. After making his way up Grape Creek and through Copper Gulch one had to wait two hours before he could break into the traffic on the road along Texas Creek.

With the increase of travel along the river, the State Legislature clarified a long disputed point by decreeing that the name of the river should be pronounced Arkan*saw* within the State instead of Ar*kansas* as was the custom to the east.

Twenty-four year old Theodore Marsh Harding was among the newcomers who flocked to Cañon City. His widowed mother brought him from Ohio for his health which rapidly improved. T. M.'s married brother, Lebbeus L., soon joined him to open a hardware store.

When Henry Harrison married Mary Frank, a railroad strike prevented their taking a wedding trip to Denver.[1] They had to be content with a buggy ride to Lincoln Park across the river instead. Despite such labor disputes and railroad wars, Cañon City had her share of would-be railroad tycoons.

In 1880, Clelland, treasurer of the Canon City Loan Company since 1878, his son-in-law Peabody, and a number of others, organized the Canon City and Western Railroad Company. It expected to reach Leadville by going up Oil Creek and the Platte River over much the same route proposed by the earlier Canon City, Oil Creek and Fairplay Railroad. James McCandless and Ira Mulock were among those who had an interest in this operation. This line did not materialize although signs of grading can be discerned along Fourmile Creek.

The Colorado Boot and Shoe Company, one of Cañon City's larger industries then, employed forty convicts to manufacture its products at the penitentiary. Convicts also kept busy burning lime, quarrying stone, and making bricks.

Cañon City had a population of some two to three thousand when young T. M. Harding was elected to the Board of Trustees. George Rockafellow and many others recognized that the town needed a proper school building. They made plans to build a two-story building to be furnished with patent seats instead of benches. In 1879, bonds were voted for construction at Ninth and River Streets. However, the D & RG eyed that location for its depot when it would build into town from the outskirts.

The school lots were exchanged for those at Seventh and Macon. The new Public School, built of prison-made bricks, opened in 1880. It was considered one of the finest school buildings in Colorado although it had neither plumbing nor central heating. Each room had its own coal stove. When a three year high school was started the following year, one of its interesting regulations was that a pupil could be expelled for wearing a gun to class.

This building, enlarged and named Washington School, was in use until 1950. Seven years later it was torn down to make way for Fremont County's present handsome courthouse. The bell, from the tower added in 1888, was moved to the grounds of the Municipal Building.

Although the McClure House had been Cañon City's leading hotel since it opened, it did not make money fast enough to get its builder out of debt. William McClure returned to Cañon City to form, with his brother, the McClure House Investment Company to purchase, lease, and maintain the hotel. Mrs. M. M. Sheets was the leasor. She bought furniture in Denver, setting it off with red carpeting and rich draperies. She made the McClure House famous throughout the State. William McClure was still struggling to recoup his fortune when his wife, Elizabeth, died in 1881.

The Canon City Water Company's water works which included iron pipe on the principal streets and a reservoir on the hogback for fighting fires, was ready that January. With the completion of this facility, Cañon City's second great building boom began. An additional fire precaution was made available when the First Presbyterians agreed to let the fire department use their fine bell, donated by a New York woman, to sound alarms. The bell, much too heavy for their frail steeple, was housed in a separate tower. In exchange for use of the bell, the fire department agreed to move and repair the tower and cupola, build a fence, and paint the church.

By this time the Udell brothers had started their "fresh, spicy sheet," the *Canon City Reporter*. The *Fremont County Record* became the *Canon City Weekly Record* in an effort to meet the competition.

Fremont County issued bonds for thirty thousand dollars to build a fine red stone courthouse on Macon near First. It and the Masonic Temple were dedicated the same day. However, the classic courthouse, complete with clock in the tower, lasted only five years. Built on unstable soil, it had to be torn down and was rebuilt on sounder ground at Macon and Fourth, at a cost of ten thousand dollars

When the Courthouse was vacated an 1881 letter came to light, inquiring of Huerfano County what to do with the body of a Mexican found frozen to death. Despite Cañon City's cultural and pious pretensions, it remained prejudiced. Its citizens were quick to assume that any Mexican must be the responsibility of some other county. It was at this time that the Spanish tilde in Cañon began to be used less and less frequently.

F. A. Raynolds, slightly grayhaired at thirty, president of the First National Bank of Leadville, was the youngest national bank president in the United States. He had established banks in Rosita, Silver Cliff, Buena Vista, Alpine, and Saguache as well. Although this pillar of the Presbyterian Church was cool, decided, and sharp at a bargain, he never took mean advantage to get ahead. He soon disposed of all but the Fremont County Bank, concentrating his capital there.

Cañon City was booming. The town's young business leaders recognized a variety of opportunities. Raynolds, with Harrison, J. F. Campbell, James H. Peabody, and some others organized The Canon City Land and Improvement Company to deal in real estate. Raynolds, Campbell, and Peabody, with Anson Rudd, Dr. Prentiss, and W. R. Fowler organized the Colorado Collegiate and Military Institute in June, 1881, to provide some of the culture the citizens craved.

This institution was to be capable of granting degrees that are usually conferred by college and universities in the United States. The county's leading families enrolled their children. By the time the impressive two-story brick building at Seventh and Pike was dedicated in the fall of 1882, Frank Prentiss became cadet captain and Peter Mulock cadet lieutenant of Company B.

A couple of years later the school was reorganized as the Grand Army Collegiate and Military Institute when General E. K. Stimson was persuaded to be president. The capital stock increased from five thousand to twenty thousand dollars. This pretentious institution charged five hundred dollars for forty weeks' instruction. It was open to cadets of both sexes, at least six years old, who could speak, read, and write English, had some knowledge of math, would abstain from consuming alcohol on the premises, and had parents who could afford the fee. The school day lasted from five a.m. to ten p.m. The school's fame was short-lived.

Alling had returned to Cañon City by May, 1882. With Peabody and Edwin Lobach, he incorporated The Land Investment and Coal and Oil Mining Company. David Peabody was president when the following month the corporation increased its capital stock to one million dollars.

By this time Ira Mulock and his brother Joshua had eight thousand head of cattle. They had cash to lend besides. They established Mulock Brothers and Company as bankers in an adobe building on the north side of the 200 block on Main Street. They too looked for opportunities. They joined Lyman Robison and others in 1884 to organize The South Park Land and Cattle Company, capitalized for $750,000. Two years later, Ira Mulock became president of the Exchange Bank, replacing W. E. Robertson. It was then that Mulock invited his son-in-law, A. R. Gumaer, to come West and function as cashier. The Exchange had earlier bought out young William Johnson's banking house established shortly after his successful sortie into Cañon City real estate.

The building boom brought many opportunities for lending. Westlake, Arlett and Company was running the four-story mill originally built by J. M. Ficke. As smelting activity in Cañon City increased new equipment was installed. The Colorado Coal and Iron Company began to develop iron mines up Grape Creek and at Orient over the crest of the Sangre de

Robison Mansion

Built by Lyman Robison, mining magnate, in 1886, this handsome house has been refurbished and is preserved as a house museum. *Canon City Illustrated, 1905.*

Cristos. The Hot Springs addition along Riverside Avenue was platted near where Mrs. Ring ran the bathhouse.

With the boom continuing, and population reaching two thousand, prospects looked good for the organization of the Canon City Improvement Company by Alling, Gumaer, Shaeffer, B. F. Rockafellow, and W. R. Harp. Capitalized at $100,000, it proposed to develop real estate and to build a ditch from the river at Ninth Street to serve the north side.

There was much interest in new irrigation methods at this time. John Gravestock, the Englishman who had farmed in Cañon City since 1868, experimented with sub-irrigation, creating a stir by thus reviving squash and grapes nearly dead of drought.

In April, 1883, The Royal Gorge Smelting Company, of which Gumaer was president and W. R. Harp vice-president, began construction of a smelter with the capacity of seventy-five tons in twenty-four hours. This plant was at the foot of Ninth Street near the D & RG depot.[2] The American Lead and Zinc Company plant on Smelter Hill in South Canon drew so many families with children that a new school had to be built there in 1885. It accommodated pupils from outside the district for seventy-five cents a week tuition.

Despite high hopes, trade languished in Canon City the following year, as it did throughout the nation when Wall Street faltered and banks failed. According to some stories, a group of merchants paid a couple of Leadville ne'er do wells two hundred dollars to dig an eighteen foot hole on the western shoulder of Pikes Peak and to produce ore allegedly found there.[3] All was in order for a new gold rush when a committee sent to "Suckerville" by skeptics burst the Mount Pisgah bubble and named the claim "Teller Placer." Before this revelation of the great Mount Pisgah hoax, some five thousand people poured into Canon City to the joy of the guilty merchants.

Tourists arrived from both directions by rail. The awe-inspiring Royal Gorge brought forth descriptions such as the "deep wrinkle in the dread frown of nature" from literary ladies like Alice Polk Hill. Alice Hill was as deeply impressed with the elegant accommodations at the McClure House where she had been furnished a private parlor without extra cost. She felt that Canon City made excellent provision for tourists and convicts. She described urchins selling soda water for five cents a glass and invalids lolling in the rustic arbor near the mineral spring where they drank the water that was good for "chronic, cutaneous, and blood diseases." One of the high points of her stay was a trip to Talbott Hill to see where Cope and Marsh had exhumed the bones of animals of enormous size.

Tall, vibrant, twenty-seven-year-old Joseph H. Maupin arrived in town about this time. He had practiced law for five years in Huerfano County after putting himself through school and then the State University of

138

Missouri. The August morning after he hung up his shingle in Canon City, he opened his newspaper to read of the lynching of Ed Watkins[4] the night before. As he read a rancher came into his office to ask if he was a lawyer. He was soon retained in the Watkins case, a sensational one that involved some of the most prominent names in the cattle business.

That started Maupin off on a successful career as a jury lawyer. With his towering forehead, deepset blue-gray eyes, generous mouth, and splendid six-foot-two physique, he could sway a jury with humor, pathos, or infectious earnestness. Although he was a Democrat in strongly Republican Canon City, this "Tall Cottonwood of the Arkansas" became mayor in 1888, the same year that he married Lily J. McClure, daughter of John McClure who had died three years earlier.

Sixteen-year-old Elwood C. "Woody" Higgins got his first job driving the sprinkling wagon all day up and down Main Street which was kept rutted and dusty by the heavy freight wagons serving Leadville's booming population.

Young Dall DeWeese brought his family from Glenwood Springs where he had raised Galloway cattle and had established the first orchard on the western slope. Son of a well-known Ohio horticulturalist and architect, he was impressed with the agricultural aspects of Fremont County. He bought land south of the Arkansas to establish the Rocky Mountain Nurseries, the first in the State, on one hundred sixty acres where he devoted twenty acres to experimentation. In 1886, he conceived, planned, and built an extension of the Lincoln Park Crooked Ditch. Long planned Lincoln Park was finally platted.

C. J. Frederickson sold the land where A. H. Danforth had platted another new addition, Cañon Gardens, near the end of Main Street for the Colorado Coal and Iron Company. The Prospect (later Fourth) Street School was built with brick from Catlin's kiln.

After years of talk, Canon City's public library got its struggling start when leading ladies of the town pressed the cause of culture. The Canon Ladies Library Association held bazaars and socials of all sorts until they raised enough money to buy a small building at 505 Main Street. Mrs. J. F. Campbell, whose husband was cashier of the Fremont County Bank, went from door to door with a baby buggy gathering donated volumes which members could borrow by paying twenty-five cents for a card.

Like much of Colorado, Canon City was often faced with the problem of the respiratory sick. There was a stigma attached to the highly contagious consumption now recognized as tuberculosis. All too often sensitive family members pretended the ailing merely had a common cold. The hospitals that then existed in Colorado refused to take consumptives. Newspapers avoided all mention of consumption if possible. The attitude seemed to be that if everyone ignored it, it would go away.

Eastern doctors were convinced that the cure would be found in the sunny mountain air. Sometimes rest and a balanced diet made the change in climate seem responsible for arresting a case. Othertimes, the patient would be too far along to respond to treatment of any kind. The delightful climate and both hot and cold mineral springs gave Canon City peculiar advantages as a health resort. It fast became a refuge for invalids at a time when a third of all Colorado settlers were health seekers.

Lyman Robison moved to Canon City with his wife and young son after making his fortune in Leadville. He created a stir in 1886 when he built a handsome mansard mansion at First and Riverside on the road to the Hot Springs.[5] Here the wealthy Robisons entertained many of the political, business, and social notables of the day. Their New Year's Day open house became a tradition.

Robison had sold the Colonel Sellers mine in Leadville, and invested in the Doctor mine in Cripple Creek which he also sold for a large sum. He invested in many of the local enterprises and once owned much of Canon City's Main Street where he built the Apex and Annex blocks.

After the death of his parents, David Robison moved into the mansion with his family. The family fortune was pretty well gone by the time David and his wife died. The third generation left the area. The house remained vacant for several years while the grass grew high behind the black iron fence bounding the ample grounds. Rescued in the nick of time, refurbished and refurnished, it is today a privately operated museum.

Plans for an elegant new hotel at the Hot Springs were probably already revealed when Robison built. Palmer's CCI Company had snatched up the area around the springs at the very mouth of the Cañon, a picturesque spot enclosed by a variety of rocky formations. A swinging bridge across the Arkansas accommodated guests arriving by train to benefit from waters advertised as alleviating "rheumatism, catarrh, tropidity of the liver, cutaneous diseases and all scrofulous affections."

Once they had the library functioning, Canon City's high-minded ladies got together to organize Friends in Council, one of the earliest women's clubs in the State, for their further self-improvement and cultural benefit. Still in existence, it has been an important force for improvement in the town. It provided traveling libraries for the coal camps, promoted the establishment of a park at Eighth and River Streets, and led in uniting other clubs to obtain the Rudd cabin for the city.

An overflow of homesteaders from Kansas and Nebraska streamed into Colorado. A few years of ample rainfall fooled folk into accepting the theory that cultivation of land increased rainfull. They had no doubt that the industrious husbandman had caused the rain belt to move West. Cañon City continued to grow.

The Canon City Smelter turned out one hundred forty bars of bullion every twenty-four hours. An electric plant and a telephone exchange were added to the city's amenities. There was a seamier side too that included murders and lynchings. It was about this time that Witherill's moustache went on display for all the visitors to see. Fremont County's cattle business was at its height while rustlers and wrongdoers kept the ranchers riled up.

In 1888, Frank B. Sheafer, dark, dashing, and handsome, arrived from Pitkin County where he had published the *Mining News*. Although the previous decade had seen a number of short-lived newspapers in Canon City, he successfully published the *Canon City Clipper* for several years in competition with the *Reporter* and the *Record,* employing as many as eighteen men.

Marriage hadn't settled Sheafer very much nor did the death of his baby daughter. But the subsequent deaths of four more children did. When his six-year-old son died, he lost all interest in his work and moved away.[6] The *Clipper* continued under other management until 1905, then became *The Cannon* which lasted until 1912.

Leb Harding was as much interested in real estate as in hardware. In addition he developed a patentable way of printing the words to go with the music on rolls for player pianos.[7] He offered fifty dollar lots in Harding's First Addition northeast of the city. Rudd's Addition also expanded the residential area. As interest in orchards and health widened, B. F. Rockafellow and others, including the Fruitmere Health and Home Company, platted the Fruitmere Subdivision.

Colonel and Mrs. F. E. Graydene-Smith built one of the more impressive houses at 2650 East Main Street. They added a tower later as a playhouse for son Vincent. The Colonel, a West Pointer, retired from the army with tuberculosis from which he died early in the 1900's. His widow Mabel continued to live in the mansion until her death in about 1932. One of the founders of the Dickens Club, she was a leading social light of the town. Her elegant coming-out party for Vincent was one of her more spectacular soirées.

The city also grew to the south. Thomas Ripley laid out the Town of Ripley as a suburb, where The Florence Oil and Refining Company platted an addition.

Isaac D. Williams, born in Wales in 1877, came to Fremont County in 1888 with his father who was perhaps typical of the many Welsh miners coming to work Colorado's mines. Father and son found employment at the Prentiss Mine, owned by Dr. J. L. Prentiss, and located just beyond present Lakeside Cemetery. When Ike was twelve, he moved to the #5 Mine at Prospect Heights where, as a nipper helping the mule driver, he worked a full ten hour day. Men who dug the coal got 68¢ a ton which averaged out to $2.75 for a day's work

Ike married in Williamsburg in 1899. After a wedding dinner at Pennington's in Canon City, the guests danced all night at the Williamsburg Hall. The Williamses moved to Lincoln Park in 1910. There they built the house where they lived for the next thirty-three years. By 1917, Ike was hoist engineer at the Bear Gulch mine when in turn his son, John I., started work in the mine— but not until he was seventeen. John began as a slate picker, blacksmith's helper, and similar jobs, for $1.15 per ten hour day. He earned enough to buy a bicycle so he would no longer have to walk seven miles to work from his home in Lincoln Park. John I. didn't stick to mining as his father and grandfather had. He prospered above ground and became a Municipal Judge in Canon City.

Eighteen-ninety saw progress at the pentitentiary, too. No longer would executions be public affairs. Only the authorities and official witnesses would see the doomed soul pay the highest price for his crime. An ingenious hanging machine, invented by a convict, replaced the simple gallows. When the condemned, hooded, noosed, and bound, stepped on a platform his weight released a lever. This drew the plug from a water bucket. As the water drained, it permitted a three hundred pound weight to fall, jerking the victim into the air. This do-it-yourself hanging machine was considered humane because the second jerk as the victim came down would surely do him in if the first jerk failed! However, it sometimes merely strangled him. In 1896, Peter Augusta's heart continued to beat for seven minutes after his hanging. This Rube Goldberg device, last used in 1933, took the lives of forty-five murderers before it was replaced by the gas chamber.

Records fail to show precisely when Mulock's bank failed. Perhaps it was after he and Gumaer made unwise loans to compete with the newly established First National Bank which had opened with James Peabody as president three or four doors up from the McClure House. Whatever the reason for the failure, Ira and his three boys were ever after held in scorn since they all held important positions in the bank.

Some, who felt that the Mulocks had knowingly stolen their friends' money, suggested a necktie party. Most of Mulock's cattlemen neighbors had invested in the bank or had funds on deposit. George H. Green, who had settled on Fourmile, sold his 63 Ranch in South Park and banked several thousand dollars. When the showdown came, Green was the only one paid in full. According to one oft-repeated story, he stuck his Winchester between Gumaer's eyes and said, "I came in here with fifty thousand dollars and I'm leaving with the same amount." He did.

Fred Riede, the baker, lost two thousand dollars, a blow to a small businessman. One irate woman waited until Mulock emerged from the bank at lunch time and blew a strawful of red pepper in his face to express her feelings.

The Mulocks left town. Parker fled to Old Mexico, Ed went to work for the prominent Park County rancher, Sam Hartsel, for twenty-five dollars a month, and Pete drove an ore wagon in Leadville. Ira, crushed by the resentment that built up against the family, died of a broken heart in 1893. Most of the IM cowboys found themselves in an awkward position and left. The public's suspicions of Gumaer weren't abated when his Boston Land and Cattle Company came up owning the IM outfit and Eddy's VVM.

When the railroad washed out of Grape Creek at the end of the decade, the Grape Creek Division of the Arkansas River Wagon Road again became a busy thoroughfare. The toll rates were fifty cents for a wagon or carriage with one span or yoke; fifty cents additional for each additional pair of animals; twenty-five cents for a horse and buggy; fifteen cents for a single horse. Cattle cost three cents a head. It was typical of the wagon roads to the West which had opened that part of the County to settlement and trade.

Despite human and natural disasters, Canon City continued to bloom and would boom again.

FOOTNOTES

1. Interview with Mrs. Ida Harrison Hawthorne, July 23, 1969.
2. Accounts do not make clear if this was near or replaced the earlier American Mining and Smelting Company mill.
3. See David Lavender's "How to Salt a Gold Mine" for details; also contemporary accounts in Colorado Springs *Weekly Gazette,* May 3, 1884, p. 1.
4. For details see Chapter XIII.
5. Mabel Hall's booklet, *Stella Hayden Balman; a "Rush to the Rockies" Centennial Story,* mentions this in connection with Stella's birth at that time. Unfortunately, much of Mrs. Hall's story is marred by inaccuracies.
6. Elma Dill Russell Spencer, *Green Russell and Gold,* p. 33A.
7. Interview with Marie Rogers Altpeter, a niece, August 4, 1969.

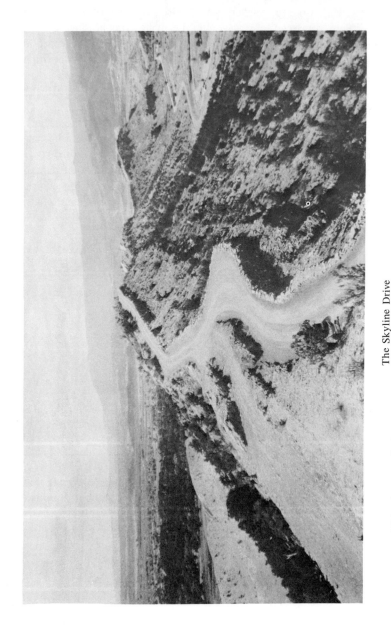

The Skyline Drive

This view was included in the memorial to Congress proposing National Park status for the Royal Gorge and Canon City's other outlying parks. *Courtesy C. Arthur Frederickson.*

CHAPTER XII

CANON'S NIFTY NINETIES

With the rise of silver mining in Leadville came the realization that silver had been discarded as currency by what came to be called the Crime of 1873, the act to demonetize silver and establish the gold dollar as standard. Free coinage of silver became the major political issue of the times.

The Bland-Allison Bill, passed over President Hayes' veto, provided for the purchase by the government of not less than two million nor more than four million dollars worth of silver per month to be coined into dollars. Passage of this bill made possible Colorado's continued growth as a silver state, and a new stampede started when N. C. Creede found rich silver ore in the San Juans.

The Sherman Silver Act, passed in July, 1890, repealed the Bland-Allison Bill. This measure provided for the purchase by the U. S. Treasury of four and one-half million ounces of silver bullion per month and the issuance of treasury notes redeemable in either gold or silver. This was considered a half-way measure since it left the legal ratio of metals at sixteen to one. The price of silver continued to drop.

Meanwhile, Canon City prospered as Leadville prospered. The D & RG converted to standard gauge by adding a third rail along its grade. With prospects bright, the Benedictine Sisters of Chicago opened Mount St. Scholastica's Academy as a girls' school in the three story brick building that had been empty since the Grand Army Collegiate and Military Institute folded.

M. M. Engleman, who had established a general store before 1870, was one of Canon City's leading merchants. His son, John Dyke and his wife, the former Genevieve Patton, became the proud parents of a daughter, Jennadean, in October, 1890. Although the Dyke Englemans would achieve varying degrees of success as vaudeville careerists, this little girl would grow up to bring fame to Canon City as Bird Millman. Her parents included her in their act when she was a small child. She later became a vaudeville headliner and also appeared in "the greatest show on earth." After triumphant tours abroad, she performed a high wire act above Broadway in New York for the Liberty Bond drives of World War I. This stunt sold more than a million dollars worth of bonds for the United States.

Although Bird also appeared in the Zeigfield Follies and other shows, she was greatest in the circus. Everything stopped for her dramatic entrance in her white Rolls Royce manned by a chauffer and a footman in white livery. She enthralled the audience with twelve minutes of skillful and beautiful ballet on the high wire.

In the mid-twenties, Bird Millman married for the third time, then lived a life of ease with Joseph O'Day, a wealthy Bostonian, until he died in 1930. As she was crushed by his death she sought seclusion in Canon City. Her generosity, poor investments, and long illness left her in straitened circumstances. She died there in 1940 and was buried in Lakeside Cemetery as Jennadean Engleman O'Day. Her legendary life as "The World's Greatest Wire Artist" is remembered by the Canon City Municipal Museum and the Bird Millman Tent of Circus Fans of America.

Bob Womack's seemingly freak 1891 find of Cripple Creek ore assaying at $250 a ton was the beginning of a bright new decade for Canon City. South Canon grew with another Harding Addition, and the Smelter Addition platted by the American Zinc Lead Company.

In the fall, Dr. J. L. Prentiss, who had a drug store and stationery store in addition to his practice, signed, with William B. White and others, articles of incorporation for the Canon City and Cripple Creek Toll Road Company to build and maintain a toll road from the north end of Garden Park up Fourmile and Wilson Creeks to the intersection with the west line of what was known as the Raynolds Cattle Company ranch. This road was a going concern before Florence opened her free road to the gold field the following year.

Charles E. Canterbury, a rancher, freighter and stage coach driver, was the general manager. For eight years he was also tollkeeper at the lower gate about fifteen miles north of Canon City. Here traces of foundation stones and charcoal kilns can still be seen. W. O. Higgins manned the upper gate, three miles farther on.

There was a Half-Way House at Eldred where Eric Freek had settled in 1887 after immigrating from Sweden. Freek served as postmaster at Eldred for fifteen years and also sold tobacco and cigars. His son, Eric, one of eleven children, moved part of the old toll gatehouse to his ranch to make a living and dining room.

This toll road successfully competed with the F & CC for a time by investing two thousand dollars in turnouts to accommodate the larger wagons. When it ceased to be profitable, the county bought the right-of-way to make a free road of it. Commonly called the Shelf Road, this hair-raising route traversed hillsides fifty to two hundred fifty feet above a gurgling stream. Woody H. Higgins and Dave Wood were among the intrepid drivers who maneuvered four and six horse stages as well as ore wagons up grades and around elbow curves on a road so narrow that often one wheel went off the road. Only momentum and the driver's skill prevented a spectacular spill. Today it's passable for four-wheel drive vehicles but is not recommended for lily-livered drivers.

William Bainbridge White was among those who incorporated the toll road company. He was a well-traveled West Virginian who had been to

Australia and California before arriving in California Gulch about 1861 where he became president of the all-important ditch company. When the easy gold in the gulch was gone and the mining frenzy faded temporarily, he took up a homestead in Park County. About 1890, at seventy-seven, he moved to Canon City where he remained until his death in 1899.[1]

B. F. Rockafellow tried another railroad scheme in 1892. He and his partners formed the Cañon City and Cripple Creek Railway Company to build up Fourmile Creek to Cripple Creek and to provide a spur to Florence. Although some construction along the right of way can still be seen from the Garden Park road, little was done before the depression and the completion of the F & CC put a crimp in the plans. Other investors formed the Canon City and Cripple Creek Gold Belt Railway in 1895 to accomplish the same purpose— with much the same result.

Canon City not only boomed as a supply point during the mining excitement, but grew in fame as a sanitarium and health resort. The city could claim that malaria, the bane of many river bottoms, was never found there. With the building of accommodations for the ailing, including the long ignored "consumptive," health seeking almost became a status symbol. However, until there was an actual hospital, doctors performed any necessary surgery on the kitchen table.

By 1893, Dr. Prentiss was on the way to his dream. He had acquired the Hot Springs Hotel which he either enlarged or rebuilt, promoting it as the Royal Gorge Hot Springs Hotel.

The long frame structure of two stories, with dormers on a third, had a porch along its length overlooking the tree shaded river. The small plunge was popular with the younger set in Canon City. The baths were equally popular with invalids. It was a fashionable resort during the 1890's, judging from the names appearing on the register which is now in the Cañon City Municipal Museum. The D & RG stopped at a small rustic station reached by the hanging bridge across the river. Hacks from the hotel ran a regular route every hour and a half to take guests into town if they wished to go.

Guy U. Hardy was a health seeker at twenty-three. He had completed two years of college and was qualified to teach but there were no jobs open. He was still taking a turpentine base concoction for T. B. when he became a reporter for the *Canon City Record*. By 1895, he had bought out the editor, A. R. Frisbee, for three thousand dollars.

Hardy paid his one employee eight dollars and fifty cents a week and paid twenty-five dollars a month for rent. He slowly built the paper into a substantial sheet. He added a daily *Record* in 1906 while continuing the weekly. The *Daily Record* is still going strong but the weekly which had survived under subsequent Hardys was suspended in 1969 one day short of its ninety-second anniversary. The daily could no longer sustain the increasing loss chalked up by the weekly.

As Canon City rode on the crest of the silver boom about her, she strove to revive her image as a gate city. The 1893 *Colorado Business Directory* carried the following long and flowery description of "The Silver Gate City of Colorado."

Beautifully located, its "gate" being the high colored back-comb rocks, opposite the Hot Springs, the real entrance to the Royal Gorge of the Arkansas river, that here debouches from the mountains plainsward, with the wealth of Leadville, Aspen, Monarch, Gunnison, Cleora, Bonanza, Summit, Creede, San Juan, Silver Cliff, Rosita and Basic [sic] mining districts, that dazzle the world with their exhibitions of fabulous wealth; and now comes Cripple Creek gold district via the Oil Creek Toll Road to the lap of Cañon, from which place Dave Woods' line of four and six-horse Concord coaches runs daily to Fremont and Lawrence, connecting here with railroad trains. The best elements of wealth of the continent seem to be concentrated about Cañon City, for besides precious minerals, coming through her "gate" from the heights of the continental divide for one hundred and fifty miles of its length, and as many more miles of its "spurs, dips and angles;" the baser metals, copper, zinc, nickle and iron, with cement, fire-clay, extensive brick yards, building stone quarries and plastic clays and lime-belt, eight miles long; alabaster, and gypsum belt ten miles in length; true petroleum basin yielding near two thousand barrels per day, the supply of five States, and the famous Cañon City coal fields, from which about a half million tons are annually mined, are all within the borders of Fremont county, of which this, the Silver Gate City, is the county seat.

From the State ditch on the mountain side, just west of town, there is one hundred and twenty-five foot fall, a magnificent water power from which the State can furnish any amount of hydraulic power. The Cañon Roller Process Flouring Mills only utilize ten feet of the immense water power of this place. Of the mineral springs here, Oscar Lowe, chemist of Wheeler exploring expedition, stated in his official report, published by the interior department as follows: "Of all the mineral waters of the West I have analyzed, I find those of Cañon City the best." This feature being worthy of especial mention in such a thoroughly sheltered locality, that acknowledges no peer for healthfulness, and that already possesses advantages of civilization in enterprising cultivated population of four thousand souls. Mrs. Dean Hart, in her trite advice to a friend concerning the use of this water, said: "It will do you good from the crown of your head to the sole of your shoes." This city and its suburbs abound in cosy houses, embowered in vines, with fruit trees, flowers and shrubs, vegetables and alfalfa fields, all naturally and easily grown, that with age a Rochester or Los Angeles cannot excel. Having also two railroads, one the main line of

Denver & Rio Grande and terminal branch of Santa Fé. Seven churches showing larger attendance according to population, than can be seen elsewhere in the West, and lodges 'twould seem of all order and degrees. Two large public schools, having twelve grades presided over by as able teachers as can be secured in the land. Two substantial banks, the American zinc-lead smelting works, canning works, roller process flouring mills, extensive mercantile houses, Cripple Creek stage line and large livery establishment, good hotels, furnishing better accommodations for less money than is often found. Cañon buildings are mainly brick, lighted by electricity, supplied with water works, good sewerage, telephone and telegraphic connection with coal mining towns as well as all the principal places of the State. Here the beginning has scarcely commenced in development; come and see, mayhap you will be glad to join us in shaping the future of Cañon, the Silver Gate City. Telephone, electric light, water works, excellent churches and schools. Population, 4,000.

The local papers advertised DeWeese's Rocky Mountain Nursery offering 200,000 fruit trees, 500,000 shade trees, and 300,000 ornamental shrubs or small fruits. A report of the Canon Ladies' Library Association's annual tea noted that the president's address included the statement that "Two hundred and fifty dollars is not too much to put into books and periodicals annually."

The *Record* also quoted from the celebrated humorist, Bill Nye. "Cañon City is romantically situated at the entrance to Grand Cañon. It has everything that heart could wish except more tourists. Hot and cold springs with or without mineral in them are ready for the invalid who craves a new kind of water to sozzle in. There is one spring which was famous for its healing powers centuries ago, and the Indians came from all over North America to bathe in it and show off their new clothes. The proprietor wishes me to say that since then the springs have been entirely refitted with fresh towels, combs, brushes and soap. The change is noticeable and agreeable." The editor wonders how Nye could describe this and write the rest of his article about Canon City when he had never been known to visit it.

Despite the boom, St. Scholastica's found going rough. The struggling school faced hard times compounded by settling earth threatening to damage its commodious quarters. In 1893, the brick building was destroyed by nearby blasting for the construction of the Kansas-Colorado Irrigation Ditch. Two years later the Sisters persuaded the State Legislature to pass a bill partially repaying them for the devastated building.

The Sisters' persistence must have impressed the Bishop of Colorado for he invited the Benedictine Fathers of St. Vincent Archabbey in Pennsylvania to take over the Fremont County missions with their debt of nine thousand dollars. The County's Roman Catholics had had a struggle ever since the town company had donated two blocks of land to Father J. P. Machebeuf for a Catholic Church[2] and College in 1861. The few Catholic families had to be satisfied with irregular visits of mission priests until 1883. Not until two years after that was there a regular place for them to worship. Then the priest who served St. Michael's also served the missions at Rockvale and Williamsburg.

The early struggle of the new parish had resulted in greater acquisition of debt than of membership when the Bishop felt it best to turn to the Benedictines who had already served in Breckenridge. The rectory in Canon City became St. Leander's Priory, headquarters for all Benedictines in Colorado. They did reduce the debt but they also found progress slow. In 1903, they elected to move the Priory to East Pueblo to found a school there.

Meantime, St. Scholastica's was back in business by 1897 with a new building. The school became St. Scholastica of the Royal Gorge when construction of the bridge over the gorge brought new glory to the area. Now simply St. Scholastica Academy, it has greatly enlarged facilities. Today it is very much a going concern as a girls' boarding and day high school.

County families who did not choose to send their children to boarding school often acquired homes in Canon City so that their children could attend public school. Many elaborate and ornate houses were built. Jeff Tong built a fine brick home in town for this purpose. The family hitched up the buckboard or surrey to spend weekends and vacations at the ranch. However, despite Canon City's craving for culture, few took advantage of the higher education offered. The eight who graduated from Cañon City High School in 1895 comprised the largest class in five years.

The repeal of the Sherman Silver Act in 1893 and the closing of the mints in India to the coinage of silver sent most of the State into a depression. Leadville was quiet for the first time since 1876. Although Canon City's silver gate slammed shut, the gold gate stood ajar. Because the Cripple Creek gold mines kept busy, Fremont County remained relatively prosperous despite the strike in January, 1894, called at the instigation of agitators. This temporarily upset the Cañon City economy when it tied up the entire Cripple Creek District but both were busy again as soon as the strike ended.

The stage also continued to run daily to Silver Cliff. A dollar fifty for the four hour trip, two dollars round trip. However, as Silver Cliff dwindled, Canon City continued to grow.

There were acres of fruit trees in Lincoln Terrace and at Sell's Island Fruit Farm and Pleasure Resort. In 1870, Ernest Sell had homesteaded on the river bottom just north of present Pump Hill. One of the Arkansas' many floods cut a channel through Sell's property. Later, when the channel

150

shifted again, a three acre lake remained. This suited Sell. He developed a resort which became popular for picnics, moonlight boating, swimming, and ice skating. He built a dance floor near the edge of the lake and later a cinder track around it. The high school used this for track meets. Ernest, junior, and his brother, Charles, ran the place until the 1920's and sold out about 1931.

By 1896, Dall DeWeese had bought up nineteen decrees for water rights and was ready to irrigate twelve hundred more acres on which he had acquired options in Lincoln Park. He persuaded W. H. Dye of Ohio to invest in a ditch he planned from Grape Creek. Dye sent his son, C. R. C. Dye, to Canon City to represent his interest. DeWeese operated the Rocky Mountain Nurseries, the Lincoln Park Orchards and Fruit Lands, and a speed track with Dye. However, Dye refused to put up additional money when he realized that Grape Creek didn't carry enough water to supply the fruits and flowers that wouldn't flourish without it. Normal and dry years had proven the fallacy of the cultivated rain belt theory. C. R. C. Dye continued to live at Hillhurst, his imposing home at the top of the Ninth Street hill in South Canon. DeWeese went on alone to plan a reservoir at the head of Grape Creek but it was several years before he attained this goal.

Other land was opened to agriculture when William H. McClure and James J. Cone platted the Fruitland Subdivision, then with S. H. Atwater developed Park Center and Orchard Park in 1896 and 1897. Soon two thousand acres were planted to fruit. No harvest season was complete without a display of apples, pears, plums, peaches, grapes, and other small fruits at the Opera House during Fruit Day each fall. This celebration included a variety of events such as the popular hose cart races between neighboring volunteer fire company teams.

Lack of effective equipment often prevented these volunteers from being as competent as they were competitive. The disastrous Cripple Creek fire of 1896 raged out of control to fan the fortunes of a few. Among them was D. E. Gibson who sold lumber and building supplies there after the blaze. He acquired the R. W. English Lumber Company. Later he built an imposing mansion at 907 Greenwood.

The Iron Duke Spring, flowing at waist level and the Little Ute Soda Spring, bubbling from the ground, continued to be freely available to all who frequented the pavilions at the west end of town. A curious eccentric known as Doc Twilight inhabited a nearby shanty made of a rainbow array of tin. He not only drank the water but washed his feet in the handy Soda Spring. He usually showed up every morning at Sam Stinemeyer's barber shop carrying medicine of his own manufacture to sell. He and Sam thought the day poorly started unless they could cuss at each other over religion, politics, or whatever controversy was in the news.[3]

151

Sam Stinemeyer, associated with General Palmer during the Civil War, went to Silver Cliff in 1879 to operate a barber shop. He moved his family to Canon City when the silver town declined. His son, Ed, opened a law office in Canon City after earning a law degree at the University of Michigan in 1898. The young lawyer's first criminal assignment was to help Maupin defend a murderer. Maupin was then a great success as a trial lawyer despite a rather spectacular capacity for drink. He built a fine building at the southwest corner of Fifth and Macon which accommodated the post office at the turn of the century.

Ed Stinemeyer went on to earn high honors in the Colorado and American Bar Associations. He was county attorney for many years and deputy district attorney for the Eleventh Judicial District from 1913 to 1917. He handled much of the grand jury investigation for the Chandler murder trial resulting from the 1914 coal strike.[4]

The Canon City and Cripple Creek Railroad Company was formed to acquire the Canon City and Cripple Gold Belt Railway as well as the earlier Canon City and Cripple Creek Railway Company incorporated by Rockafellow. This new company completed seven miles of track connecting Canon City with the F & CC at Oro Junta. Although it entertained ideas of more extensive construction, the railroad was but a spur of the narrow gauge F & CC. However, a large quantity of coal and produce was shipped to the District over this line. Before long the F & CC moved its shops to Canon City, much to the annoyance of the residents of Florence.

The New Jersey Zinc Company opened an experimental plant in 1898 to see if a new process could produce zinc oxide for the paint and rubber trade. Although the American Zinc Lead Company earlier had a plant in Canon City, it had never successfully produced zinc oxide.

The new plant was built in part through the efforts of G. R. Shaeffer, the jeweler. His boyhood friend, August Heckscher of Pennsylvania, who had made a mint in coal and zinc, got the idea that they'd make another fortune by investing in Mormon property in Salt Lake. Shaeffer left Canon City for Utah. Heckscher put plenty of money into the scheme but neither got much out. Shaeffer returned to his Canon City interests.

In the meantime, Leadville was about to go broke. The ore they were getting there had so much zinc in it that the Leadville furnace kept freezing up. The refractory ore was put aside and the companies were being sued because the piled up ore kept falling down on buildings.

Heckscher's Lehigh Zinc and Iron Company had consolidated with others in 1897 to become the New Jersey Zinc Company with Heckscher the general manager. Shaeffer sent some of the Leadville ore to him to see what he could do with it. W. C. Wetherell and his brother had invented the Wetherell Magnetic Separator that could take out zinc by magnetic separation and flotation. When it appeared that this process could turn the trick, the New Jersey Zinc Company built the experimental mill. Since the method proved successful the company made plans to obtain water from the Greenhorn Range for a full plant. This was accomplished before 1902.

Once in operation as the Empire Zinc Company, the new mill bought Leadville's discarded ore for 25 to 50 cents a ton, or, occasionally, got it for nothing. Soon there were thousands of tons of ore on the ground in Canon City, brought in at the rate of a hundred tons a day. More was shipped in from Hanover, near Silver City, New Mexico.

Empire Zinc built a smelter in 1918 to roast the zinc concentrates and tore down the old mill about 1925 or 1927. The new smelter was put into operation by Frederick E. Riede. It reached the peak of its operation in the mid-twenties, employing four hundred people. It closed down for awhile in the 1930's, never returning to its former production.

Canon City ended the century with a new flurry of gold excitement. Reports of a very rich gold strike to the southwest lured practically everyone in town out to stake a claim. A tent city grew up overnight. The Greenhorn Mining Company platted Dawson City in June, 1899. A large boarding and rooming house housed some, but most mining hopefuls commuted from Canon City. The one producing mine with fairly rich ore petered out all too soon. Other mines nearby never paid because the ore was poor.

In 1901, the Joker Mining and Milling Company with a 500 foot tunnel gave George R. Dalton a contract to extend it another 100 feet at $10 a foot when their test showed a return of $69 per ton in gold and copper, mostly copper. There was some prospecting in this area later. As late as 1930 a mining company had a crew working old claims but no paying vein was found. Today, traces of the workings of the Copper King Mine can be seen near the deserted town of Dawson, as can the old wagon road to the camp, not far south of the present Temple Canyon Road.

There seemed no reason why Canon City shouldn't face the twentieth century with optimism.

FOOTNOTES

1. Interview with Elwood G. White, July 28, 1969.
2. The Reverend Justin McKernan's *Historical Review of St. Michael's Church, Canon City, Colorado, 1880-1945,* includes information on earlier Roman Catholic activity in Fremont County.
3. Interview with T. Lee Witcher, July 30, 1968.
4. Ed Stinemeyer died in 1967 at ninety-one, active to the last. One of his sons who practiced with him was killed tragically in an auto accident two years later.

The Royal Gorge Bridge Under Construction
In 1927, Canon City leased a portion of the Royal Gorge Park to Lon P. Piper who
fulfilled his dream of seeing the world's highest suspension bridge span the Gorge.
Courtesy C. Arthur Frederickson.

CHAPTER XIII

CANON'S NEXT HALF-CENTURY

On the cold, dark night of January 22, 1900, Thomas Reynolds, Kidd Wallace, C. E. Wagner, and Antoine Wood killed William C. Rooney, the night captain at the penitentiary. Then they threw soapy water on the generator belt to plunge the place in darkness, and the four escaped with a pre-planned pipe ladder and ropes over the walls. The men evaded police and posses for four bitter days and nights.

One, hatless, stopped in Florence to beg for a hat. Mrs. Cronk obliged, then notified police. The lawmen held their fire for fear of hitting innocent by-standers when they found two men hiding at the rear of a store in the dark. The men broke and ran. Reynolds tangled with some barbed wire and was captured. The police took him to city jail then sent a message to Warden Hoyt at Canon City while the town seethed with armed men looking for his companion, Wagner.

Although Reynolds wasn't handcuffed, he was tied by ropes with a noose around his neck when three heavily armed guards took him to Canon City about 9:30 that evening. He seemed very anxious to return to the protection of the pen, with good cause, judging from the temper of the men who swore vengeance for Rooney's death.

Reynolds never made it. A posse in Canon City intercepted the guards as the wagon reached the First Street bridge, took charge of Reynolds, and hanged him from a pole at First and Main near where Witherill had dangled in 1888.

Wagner was apprehended in Pueblo and kept in jail there until it was safe to return him. The other two were captured on Garden Ranch and smuggled back to the prison, hidden under hay in a wagon.

Despite such occasional excitement, Canon City homes, according to contemporary reports, bespoke culture and contentment like old communities in the East.[1] The busy ladies of the library association approached Andrew Carnegie for a grant, held a campaign for funds, then bought two lots in the 500 block of Macon, the location of the frame Presbyterian Church, for $3500. They sold the building to the prison for $140 to be razed for salvage. Impressed with the ladies' efforts, Carnegie sent a check for $10,000 for a new building. This was ready for occupancy December 15, 1902. The following April the association turned the property over to a new library board. The Public Library was considered the most popular institution in town next to the post office.

The United Presbyterians newly organized congregation also moved to its new sanctuary at Ninth and River Streets. Churches of a variety of faiths created so much church news that the Evangelical Churches and Societies of Canon City published a four-page paper, *The Messenger.* C. J. Frederickson served as business manager (he also had an interest in *The Canon City Times)* when he wasn't pursuing his dream of bringing in another gusher.

Canon City at last had a hospital when Dr. Levi B. Ward established a small one at Sixth and Macon. His practice soon warranted an addition to it but he unfortunately died shortly after it was completed. Dr. C. H. Graves purchased the property in 1903.

Young Dr. Warren D. Howe came to Canon City to practice about 1897. In 1900 he built a hospital-house combination at 902 Greenwood for the treatment of tuberculosis and other respiratory ailments. Although the young Howes were popular additions to picnic parties and the doctor was an appreciated cello player in amateur string quartets, he didn't remain in Canon City long. His father convinced him to give up medicine to return to Chicago and help in the family business. In 1903, the Howes sold their hospital as a private dwelling, then took their two babies back East, leaving the field to Dr. Graves.

By this time the ladies were cooking with gas. The Canon City Gas Company laid lines in 1901 and 1902 from a brick plant at Fifteenth and River, where the company manufactured gas until natural gas was available in 1947.

As home chores lessened, Canon's women, like those throughout the country, busied themselves more and more in outside activities. Mrs. T. M. Harding, president of the Colorado Federation of Women's Clubs, inaugurated the Scholarship Committee. The Federation's scholarship fund was established with three subscriptions totaling ninety dollars at the annual meeting held in Cripple Creek and Victor. Since then many thousands of dollars have been loaned to help worthy girls through college.

Women were active in other clubs in addition to Friends in Council and the Canon City Women's Club. The twenty members of The Alliance Club, "of intellectual ability," devoted their leisure time to reading and study. The Dickens Club was even more exclusive with twelve members, all Dickens devotees. Young business women, probably graduates of Dodds' Commercial College then flourishing in Canon City, formed the Progress Club. Organization of the Wednesday Musical Club did much to raise the musical taste of the town as it studied classic and contemporary composers.[2] Mrs. F. A. Raynolds of the Board of Education commended Canon City's women's organizations for their tone, culture, and good hard work. She concurred with Miss Ida T. White, County Superintendent of Schools, who claimed that Fremont County demanded the best in education. As evidence she cited the $25 per pupil spent for educational purposes in 1904.[3]

The American Zinc Lead Works, employing sixty men, was Canon City's largest industry at the turn of the century. It produced the biggest payroll in the tree-shaded town of 7,500 population. Seasonal activity at the Pickle and Cider Works required the services of some sixty women. The nurseries employed the next largest number. In addition to the usual services, two small cigar factories, rock, marble and silica quarries, brick yards, and a flouring mill provided employment.

Catlin and others had early brick yards south of the Arkansas. In 1893, W. H. Trout started operation at his Canon City Brick and Tile Company situated at Sixteenth, north of Main, near the site of the original D & RG depot. Trout soon had some twenty-five men producing two million pressed building bricks a year. Wagons hauled the shale and clay from pits south of the Indian Burial Ground not far from short-lived Dawson City.

It was while working near Dawson that Ernest F. Jewett found fire clay about a half mile from his claim, a discovery that led to his establishing, with James H. Horney and E. C. Hiatt, the Diamond Fire Brick Company plant on South Ninth Street.

The continued success of the area's orchards inspired more elaborate celebration of Fruit Days to promote the produce of trees, bushes, and vines. High school girls offered free samples of the fruits displayed on stands along the sidewalks. Later the celebration moved to the circus lot north of town where races were added until it became as fancy as a county fair.

Canon City entered the motor age in the summer of 1901. Dr. Frank L. Bartlett, a metallurgist of world renown, connected with the U. S. Smelter, ordered the thirteenth Oldsmobile made.[4] He had it shipped to him by express and thus became the first owner of an internal combustion motor car in Colorado. Only steam and electric autos had been owned here earlier.

After Bartlett assembled his one cylinder, four horsepower car, he took it to a sixty acre field back of the smelter to practice driving. When he had mastered the monster, he started to town. All went well until he met a woman driving a horse and buggy. The horse took fright, the buggy tipped over, and Bartlett had damages to pay.

Bartlett learned his lesson. He had the sheriff completely clear Main Street before he drove up and down giving free rides in the newfangled contraption to all who wanted to risk it.

Dr. G. H. Kellenberger, the dentist, soon owned a curved-dash Olds. By 1905, there were eight locally owned cars in Fremont County, considered "great country for automobiling."[5] With the arrival of such modern conveyances, Canon City wanted to be as up-to-date as any place. The huge shade trees that arched over wide Main Street soon fell in the name of progress, although the town had earlier boasted as being "embowered in umbrageous foliage."

In 1902, DeWeese was able at last to superintend construction of the DeWeese Ditch and Reservoir. When the project was completed, he sold land to 287 families at $250 to $300 an acre, watered, fenced, and planted to trees. Orchard Park and Park Center also offered additional tracts for small orchards. As DeWeese's Rocky Mountain Nurseries grew into building sites, Rockafellow's Fruitmere Orchard and Vineyards rose to prominence. Fruitmere's 1901 schoolhouse was used until 1910 when the new school building, also named for Henry Harrison, opened. The old schoolhouse was later sold to the City of East Canon for $450 to be used for the East Canon Town Hall. What had been Fruitmere is still part of East Canon, fiercely independent of Canon City proper.

Today, DeWeese Reservoir in Custer County, a monument to an amateur engineer's imagination and persistence, provides recreation as well as water. There are picnic grounds on the east shore. Other fair weather picnic spots are located on the Oak Creek Grade, one of the most scenic ways to reach the reservoir, the beauty of the Wet Mountain Valley, and the mountain route to Lake Isabel.

Guy Hardy with his *Canon City Record* actively supported Mayor James H. Peabody, as candidate for Governor. Thanks to Hardy's support, fifty year old Peabody, President of the First National Bank, became the only citizen of Canon City to make it. Maupin had run as a Democrat in 1892 but had been beaten. Hinsdale had long left the city before he aspired to the office.

The socially prominent Peabody family was well liked. Canon City hailed as its most elegant party that given when Jessie Peabody married Lt. Cuthbert Stearns. Attended by Stearns' West Point classmates, it was considered a smash by the young ladies. The Peabody house at 403 River Street, now part of the Cadaleen Motel, was built by the Clellands in the 1880's. It had a fireplace in every room, including the twin grand parlors. Peabody replaced a large bay window with a privacy protecting high window of French design after a would-be assassin fired at him.

Peabody was inaugurated during the labor trouble. He called the militia into the field at Cripple Creek to stop the battle between mine owners and union factions. He was much critized for this. Although his administration was a stormy one, the Republicans nominated him for a second term against Alva Adams who had been Governor earlier.

Charges of fraud and corruption which followed the election gave Colorado the unique distinction of having three different governors in one twenty-four hour period. Adams was inaugurated in January, then unseated in March when Peabody, his health impaired by the tribulations of his turbulent term, was declared the winner. Peabody took the oath of office on March 17, 1905, with the understanding that he would resign immediately to permit his Lieutenant Governor, Jess F. McDonald, to take his place. McDonald subsequently served until 1907. When Peabody died in

1917 he was buried in Canon City with Masonic honors.

There was plenty of space for boys to roam around Canon City when T. Lee Witcher and his cousin, John Merit, were young. They used to run with Ed Cassedy and Clifford Tice. The four often hunted horned toads to sell to Sing Lee, who still wore a queue, proprietor of one of the two Chinese laundries. One day they found more than toads on the west side of the hogback near where stone had been taken out for a church. When they brushed dirt off a rough, dried-out box they discovered a black-haired skull. It gave them delicious shivers and dreams of turning the skull into dollars by selling it to Henry N. Beecher who bought Indian relics at his drug store.

Beecher refused to buy. It was no Indian skull, but a negro's. The boys took it to the Cassedys' workshop. They were fooling with it one day when Mr. Cassedy came in and caught them with it. As he heard their story, he recalled that a furious mob had lynched a negro who had ravished a white woman. Judge Lynch was a long time leaving Fremont County.

Perhaps such tales of illegal law prompted T. Lee Witcher to go to the University of Colorado Law School after graduating from Illinois Wesleyan. He married Hazel Coates and was admitted to the Bar in 1909. The following year he moved into Maupin's new building on North Fifth Street where his office remained for nearly sixty years. During his long and distinquished career he served as city and county attorney, district attorney (from 1917 to 1925), and mayor of Canon City (from 1925 to 1931).

As district attorney, T. Lee often prosecuted Prohibition violaters defended by Maupin. On one memorable occasion, Maupin, well known for his thirst, gulped down the whiskey offered in evidence, leaving the case in a state of permanent adjournment.

About 1905 convict labor built the two and half mile Skyline Drive that rides the hogback behind the penitentiary. The two-way gravel road on the crest of a Dakota sandstone ridge six hundred feet above the land below was soon considered a perfect Sunday afternoon drive. If you didn't have your own rig, W. A. Garton would take you by carriage for twenty-five cents a round trip. As late as 1910, it had not been conquered by car.

Today, it's a paved one-way road approached from a more recent entrance off Highway 50. Entirely safe for sane drivers, it is well worth the few minutes of a tourist's time that it takes to travel the loop and reenter Canon City.

Convict labor also began construction of a ditch with three tunnels beneath the ridge for an ambitious irrigation system to serve the growing section east of Canon City. The project was abandoned when the money gave out before completion. Later, businessmen and civic leaders saw the possibility of a scenic drive along that three mile right of way. Again prison labor was enlisted to fill the ditch and level a road. It was open by day but fenced at night to keep deer from using it as a path from the mountains to the gardens in town.

Entered on Canal Street off Highway 50 west of town, about a quarter of a mile beyond the Southern Colorado Power Plant, this dead end Tunnel Drive skirts a section of Fremont Peak to end near the edge of the Arkansas at the east entrance of the Royal Gorge. It overlooks the site of the Hot Springs Hotel, commercial gardens, and homes.

The thought of that drive must have soon been too much for some of the prisoners. When Mrs. John Cleghorn, the warden's wife, went inside the walls to visit the women's ward, her usual morning smile was rebuffed as the guard refused to let her in. Before she could convince him that the warden's wife had special visiting privileges, another officer offered to take her back to the front gate.

En route, Mrs. Cleghorn noticed a striped shirt under his uniform. The guard thrust a long, sharp knife close to her side. Arriving at Cellhouse 3, Mrs. Cleghorn found one of the real guards stripped to his underwear and the prison physician, Dr. T. D. Palmer, standing in his longhandles minus his pinch-nose glasses while another prisoner squinted through the heavy lenses trying to resemble him.

Kerch Kuykendall, James Armstrong, Tom Fallon, Thomas Fisher, Cuaz Cardona, and Robert Kane, or Cain, held two guards and the prison pharmacist hostage with Mrs. Cleghorn and Dr. Palmer. Kuykendall, a former miner, informed them that he had enough explosives to blow up the prison if their plans went awry. As a last precaution, the convicts locked up Officer Peabody, son of the Governor; Guard Cleghorn, the warden's nephew; and the pharmacist. They herded Mrs. Cleghorn across the open court.

As the guards watched from the walls, afraid of hurting the warden's wife if they fired, Kuykendall coolly stuck some dynamite under the heavy steel door and lit the fuse. When the explosion tore off the door the men rushed their hostage through. The second door was unlocked. After the third door got the dynamite treatment the convicts hustled out. Mrs. Cleghorn fell in a faint about halfway across the ten acre field separating the prison from the D & RG tracks. The cons panicked as the sirens began to wail. They abandoned their hostage. Shots rang out as townspeople with a variety of weapons joined the manhunt.

Kuykendall went down with a bullet through his head. Will Cleghorn, the warden's son, felled Armstrong who was still alive when they bore him back to prison. Cordona and Kane stole a team from a wagon, hopped on one of the horses, and headed across the bridge. A citizen sent a bullet through Cordona's foot and on through the horse. Freeing themselves from the falling animal, the fugitives comandeered a small wagon for their getaway. At this point, Dall DeWeese showed his prowess as a hunter. He and H. J. Evans, both mounted, set off in hot pursuit. They chased the men for four miles, finally capturing them near Brookside.

J. B. Lantz, not such a great hunter, also gained renown that day. He almost ran over Fisher hiding in the tall weeds. Lantz, but ten feet from him, called on him to surrender. Fisher jumped up to run. Lantz aimed his gun, shot, and missed. Determined to get his man, he ran after Fisher, aimed, and missed again. Fisher stopped, threw up his hands, and yelled, "Don't shoot anymore! You might hit me! "

Few men, the witnessing citizens agreed, could miss a man that close with a shotgun. The break was over when Fallon was pulled from under a D & RG freight on the siding. The survivors were stripped, placed in a cell, and hosed for three days until they were ready to tell where the rest of the explosives were hidden.

Fisher and Fallon soon had enough of water constantly streaming in their faces from the guard's hose. They talked. Kuykendall and Armstrong, both ex-miners, admitted that they had secured the necessary ingredients to manufacture a variety of deadly explosives, secreting them in their cells and in the shop. The inept break could have turned into a catastrophe.

In 1904, the Santa Fe changed the sign on its depot on South Fourth Street from Cañon to Canyon City. The post office followed suit. This caused such a furor from County and State that the original name was soon restored. However, the tilde, long lost in common usage didn't return to the masthead of the *Daily Record* until 1969.

President Theodore Roosevelt made a whistle stop at Canon City on May 8, 1905, and regaled the citizens with a five minute address. Of course he had his picture taken at the Hanging Bridge.[6]

When Billie Sunday, the popular evangelist, arrived in Canon City for two weeks of meetings, he must have generated a great deal of news. Then Hardy decided to make his paper a daily. However, he had to use much boiler plate, pre-cast lead serials and features, to fill up his paper. In a fifty page special edition of his four column tabloid, he extolled the virtues of Canon City as a health resort, the climate and bright sunshine as ideal, then claimed that "sunstrokes are unknown and the plasmodium malaria has never found us out." There was no doubt then that the consumption cure vied with fruit raising as the leading industries.

Sunday evidently didn't lure all to the straight and narrow. The county built the present capacious jailhouse the following year. Probably the only time it was ever completely full was when eighty some men were held there after the Chandler March.

Another new building, the high school, built at Ninth and College at a cost of $45,000, had two bowling alleys for girls and an armory for boys. The military program, compulsory for all male students, turned out well-drilled, uniformed cadets.

161

The Canon City & Cripple Creek Railroad suffered a blow when a fire which started from a short circuit spread rapidly in waste and oil and destroyed its shop. Two engines were pulled out but everything burnable was destroyed on another engine. The shop was promptly rebuilt and the engine overhauled but by that time the tail had begun to wag the dog. Traffic continued between Cripple Creek and Canon City but only stub service from Oro Junta served Florence.

The tracks to Canon City crossed J. F. MacKenzie's ranch which extended from the little adobe Fourmile schoolhouse on the Arkansas about eight miles to the east to the Tong place. Although MacKenzie, living in Canon City, had a foreman and hands to care for his cattle, he came to a grisly end on the high trestle that carried the CC & CC across the arroyo on his ranch. His son came home from college to take over the operation. Some years later he sold some of the lower acreage to the pre-parole Release Center.

Although the Canon Savings Bank failed in 1905, the new Citizens State Bank opened on the corner of Sixth and Main. Raynold's Fremont County Bank survived the financial vicissitudes over the years.

The Canon City Mills on Mill Ditch at Second and Main modernized to produce the popular "On Time" and "Hard to Beat" brands of flour. The U. S. Smelting Company and the Empire Zinc Company greatly enlarged their capacities. On March 25, 1903, the U. S. smelter on South Fourth Street burned with a crippling loss of over $300,000. D. C. Jackling, who later made a name and multimillion dollar fortune for himself with Utah Copper Company, was superintendent of U. S. Smelting and of the Union Mill in Florence about this time.

Thriving Canon City had fourteen churches, including a Colored Baptist that met for regular services at the southwest corner of Fifth and Macon in the 1877 structure vacated by the congregation of Christ Episcopal when its new building at Eighth and Harrison was completed. When the old building was sold, the Colored Baptist congregation changed its name to Mount Olive Baptist and moved to South Fifth Street below River.

Late in 1905, C. J. Frederickson joined Dr. Pitt A. Wade and other partners in forming the Canon City Hot Springs Sanitarium Association to reopen the resort that had been closed for several years. Dr. Wade, a Seventh Day Adventist, had a wide practice among those afflicted with cancer and expected to renew interest in the Hot Springs by capitalizing on their curative qualities. However, despite Dr. Wade's reputation, this venture failed to flourish. Although the Hot Springs Hotel had boomed for a decade, its popularity had diminished with the decline of mining wealth. Lack of adequate transportation to town was put forth as one of the reasons the place wasn't as popular as had been hoped. Although the footbridge crossed the Arkansas there, cars and carriages had to use the

First Street bridge and the still unpaved lane along the south side of the river. Religious prejudice may also have played a part in Dr. Wade's lack of success.

Frederickson still believed that the region east of the Royal Gorge was underlain by oil even when he found himself more hot water. He leased oil rights from Josiah T. Hazard for land on East Central near Dozier Avenue and struck hot springs again. The 15,000 gallon per hour flow of 99½° sparkling lithia water was cooled in a storage reservoir before being used for irrigation. Hazard and others subsequently formed The Canon City Natatorium Company to develop a pleasure resort to include swimming pools, sanitariums, recreational gardens, and a fine restaurant at the spot. The Natatorium pool opened in 1907. A decade later the facility was finally enclosed. Little else but bathhouses materialized of the proposed plans.

The Natatorium remained a popular swimming place until about 1962 when the Health Department closed the pool because the water had become stagnant. The nature of the water caused it to cloud after exposure to air preventing the detection of a possible drowning. The owner balked at the expense of reactivating the spring and installing a filtering system.

Early in the century Canon City began to show signs of self-satisfaction and complacency. The population diminished as the mining frenzy subsided. The go-getters went elsewhere. Those who remained seemed content with their quiet county seat.

A visitor at that time remarked that the Booster Club was busy "hustling and howling about" Canon City where people were unconcerned about such things as the Panama Canal project or corruption in the big cities and lived "as if there were no outside world." The hustling was evidently to no avail. Although as late as 1912 some effort was made to refinance and continue the electric line to the Gorge, no rails were ever laid. Highway 50 west of Canon City now follows part of the old right of way. Some of the remaining grade can be seen to the left by those traveling west.

The general assembly of the 114 Presbyterians of the Cumberland Presbyterian Church of the U. S. in a rare ecumenical move voted to overlook their doctrinal differences and restore union with the Presbyterian Church of the U. S. of A. Following this the Canon City Cumberland Church (it had dropped the Mt. Horab name by 1879 at a meeting in Currant Creek) united with the First Presbyterian Church of Canon City and donated its real estate to the YMCA. The Y remodeled the church building and were to use it until 1912 when a building campaign permitted construction of a new $40,000 facility. Demolition of the church and manse obliterated an early landmark.

Another church merger occurred when Canon City's recently organized black Methodist congregation found going difficult and joined the Mount Olive Baptist Church. Although the town's black community shrank with the shift in Canon City's economy, the Baptist congregation continued to hold services until the mid 1950's.

Canon City's reputation as a resort had greatly diminished by 1909. No longer did the fashionable patronize her hotels. The McClure House became the Strathmore Hotel when C. R. C. Dye took it over. He ran it until World War I when he sold out to Mr. and Mrs. E. W. Eddy. They sold when their only son, Wilbur, was electrocuted while working on water pipes in the basement. The St. Cloud was idle briefly before it reopened as the Denton Hotel in 1910. It bore that name until 1915. Closed again, it reopened after World War I as Hotel Canon.

Although the hotels suffered, education advanced when St. Michael's School opened, staffed by sisters from St. Scholastica's Academy. However, funds for the long proposed $25,000 building were not forthcoming and a schoolhouse of much lesser value was built on Macon for the children of forty families. This was funded largely through the efforts of the Royal Gorge Council of the Knights of Columbus.

A new industry came to town the following year when Selig-Polyscope Company of Chicago moved in to film some wild and woolly westerns. Woody Higgins, then a partner of Charley Reeves in Reeves and Higgins Livery, and Charlie Canterbury were delighted to provide horses and to round up extras. Then, as now, the sunny days and variety of spectacular scenery for backdrops appealed to movie makers. Delighted with the climate, the ample housing, and ready availibility of horses and cowboys, the company came back again the next year to make more of those high budget pictures that allowed $3000 for five days shooting of one or two complete pictures a week.

The residents were charmed to feel that Canon City was on the way to becoming the movie capital of the world. Besides, being an extra was a glamorous way to earn five dollars a day.

Tom Mix was acting, directing, and authoring his own scripts by the time Selig joined other film companies heading for the hills around Hollywood, California. Although Mix remained partial to Colorado locations, he worked from Hollywood studios.

Canon City wasn't entirely deserted by cinema artists. The Colorado Motion Picture Company, backed by Denver money, then formed to continue filming in Cañon City. This company hired some of the Selig crew, some technicians, a few actors, and the producer, O. P. Thayer. The studios were in the AOUW Hall on the southwest corner of Third and Main, a building long since razed.

Thayer made a number of two reel films, mostly westerns, although a sudden snow was likely to inspire an impromptu script for an Alaskan adventure complete with dogsleds and mushing huskies. Unfortunately, tragedy struck before this studio had the chance to burgeon into another Inceville.

Grace McCue, one of the leading ladies of the time, panicked when her horse stumbled while she was fording the Arkansas near the Hot Springs Hotel. She was swept off and carried downstream by the current. Cameraman Owen Carter dropped his hand cranked camera, raced forty yards, and dove to her rescue. He got Grace safely onto a sandbar but when they attempted to reach the riverbank, the star stepped off a ledge into deep water, panicked again, and hysterically pulled Carter down with her. Both drowned. Miss McCue's mother sued and secured a court judgment that shoved the corporation into bankruptcy. Canon City's celluloid dream faded for awhile.

During these years, many Colorado towns had been vying for the State Odd Fellows Home. Spurred by the gift of $20,000 from H. A. W. Tabor, the mining magnate, the organization announced that Canon City was its choice and built a place that was a model of its kind in the West.

T. M. Harding[7] was in ill health when his son Ted got the urge to go to Old Mexico. T. M. couldn't see carrying on alone to provide for his wife, still an active clubwoman. He committed suicide in 1913. Ted, married, and the father of Margaret and T. M. the third, known as Buster, stayed to run the business and to become an energetic civic leader.

William McClure died the following year at seventy-six, one of the oldest surviving settlers dating from the time of the Resurrectionists. His heirs long continued to own Canon City property.

World War I brought more than personal tragedy to the residents. A raging fire destroyed the prosperous Canon City Mills, then owned by the Sidebottoms. Because wartime prices prohibited rebuilding, the owners consolidated their operation at their Kansas mill.

In 1916, Company K of the National Guard mobilized for duty on the Mexican border. The City Cornet Band, the High School Cadet Corps, the GAR and hundreds of citizens were on hand to give the men a rousing sendoff when they left to hunt down Pancho Villa.

P. H. Troutman, general manager of the Round Crest Canning Company (which later became the Prison Canning Company), bought the one-time Howe hospital building. Financial trouble soon forced him to sell it. Mrs. Thomas Balman later bought it and remodeled it for apartments. The well-kept lawn and garden indicated that this rancher's widow put the old house to profitable use.

Although the 1921 flood which pummeled Pueblo did little direct damage to Canon City, the town suffered a lasting effect from it. The washed-out Santa Fe grade above the steel city stopped passenger service. It wasn't renewed when the tracks were rebuilt. Canon City had its own share of floods. Nearly every spring the fire whistle alerted citizens to the threat. At the sound the kids hurried to the river to watch dead cattle and other interesting items float by. Dams upstream now serve to control this danger.

The Ku Klux Klan was late in coming to Colorado. Although Denver was a regional headquarters in 1921, Colorado remained one of three states not organized as Klan Realms. Then Dr. John Galen Locke moved from medicine to politics and became the Grand Dragon of the Klan in Colorado.

Within a year there were tens of thousands of members who succumbed to whatever appeal best suited the situation. The Klan soon infiltrated the Republican Party, but got nowhere with the opposition since there were too many Jewish and Catholic Democrats.

Canon City gained the dubious distinction of being a headquarters for the Klan. A local minister, the Rev. Mr. G. Arnold, was the Grand Dragon. The Klan soon controlled most of the county and city offices, the school board, and some civic organizations. The local headquarters, housed in the Canon Hotel, gave the Klan's handpicked candidate, Governor Clarence J. Morley, orders concerning appointments to be made.

The Klavern meeting hall upstairs at Fifth and Main was evidently not large enough for all gatherings. Contemporary pictures show hooded and robed Klansmen crowded into the Natatorium, possibly for initiation ceremonies. When state conventions were held in Canon City, hundreds marched in regalia and held cross-burning ceremonies on the old high school grounds at Ninth and College. In addition to coloring the news in Canon City's new daily, the pro-Klan *Daily American,* the Klan also published the monthly *Kolorado Klan Kourier* in Canon City.

With the Klan active, Benedictine monks had to work quietly to make a deal to buy eighty-nine acres of land for $40,000 from B. F. Rockafellow for their proposed $200,000 school and abbey. The Benedictines of St. Leander's became independent of St. Vincent Archabbey, then changed their name to Holy Cross Priory of Canon City. This was soon raised by indult from Rome to the dignity of Abbey.

Although the KKK was actively anti-Catholic, the Roman Catholics along the Arkansas enjoyed a special privilege beyond its control, dating from the days when the area south of the river was a Spanish colony. Pope Pius V was so delighted when King Philip II of Spain shattered the Turkish fleet in the name of Christianity that he issued a *bulla cruciabulis* permitting Philip the privilege of eating meat on Friday. Later he extended the indult to include all Philip's subjects in Spain. The Spanish colonists were quick to include themselves and claimed the privilege as immemorial custom. Thus, until recent times when the privilege was granted all Catholics, those not fond of fish could indulge innocently in steak on fast days by simply crossing the river to consume it on the south side.[8]

A small band of monks from Pennsylvania[9] arrived in 1924 to live in a rather airy old apple shed on onetime Fruitmere orchard land. By the time Abbey School opened there in September, 1926, the school building, containing some one hundred rooms, had cost $450,000. An unforeseen expense was incurred when underground water threatened the building. It cost $50,000 to sink 2100 piles to anchor the foundation. The order ran out of funds before the tower was built. It was added later by skilled stone masons from Brookside.

The onetime apple shed, converted into living quarters, chapel, and library, was accidently destroyed by fire in 1930 during a football game. Fans fought the flames but took time out to check the progress of the Abbey Bears against Walsenburg.

The Abbey later acquired adjoining land once belonging to the penitentiary. Stone buildings still standing show cornerstones dated 1936 as prison property.

Meantime, the Klan-controlled Colorado State Bank and newspaper failed after the *Daily American* lost a libel suit. The Rev. Mr. Arnold became disillusioned. Perhaps the one lasting reminder of that bigotted period is his tombstone with its symbol of a flaming cross.

Ella Gumaer, returning to Fremont County as a widow, bought the Coleman house at 921 Greenwood. She didn't mingle much in the life of the town. The local ladies felt that she was "society," although she was active as a member of the Episcopal church and gave a curtain and rail for the sanctuary. After Mrs. Gumaer died, Leb Harding, son of Leb Harding, junior, bought the house from A. H. Danforth who had often been seen there with her. Harding paid less that $10,000, a bargain even in 1926. Later Harding sold it to Don Hardy, son of the enterprising newspaper publisher, Guy Hardy.

The Hot Springs Hotel had been vacant for some time by the mid-twenties when Dr. William E. Justice, a Canon City chiropractor, bought it for $40,000, some $2,000 more than it had cost to build years earlier. He enlarged the original twenty foot square swimming pool at the west end of the hotel grounds, but he was unsuccessful in reviving the resort and health center.

The hotel itself was saved when the Hot Springs Plunge burned a couple of decades later. Dr. Justice auctioned off the furnishings in 1944 and sold the property in 1947 for a mere $10,000. The Oklahoma man who bought it offered it to the Church of God as an orphanage. The Church accepted and spent several hundred dollars in cleanup and improvement. However, the State of Colorado refused to approve its use for an orphanage because of the danger to children from the Arkansas River flowing in front of it.

Leo Garrett bought the property in 1950 and wrecked the longtime landmark for salvage. Today the hot springs are buried below a modern private home while the once inviting grounds under the majestic old cottonwoods are weedy and unkempt.

Having been successful in acquiring the Royal Gorge and Temple Canyon Parks, Canon City worked toward gaining Red Canyon Park. This large tract was granted to the city by Act of Congress on March 2, 1923, with the provision that a patent would be issued on payment of $1.25 an acre. Congressman Guy Hardy spent much of his fourteen years in Washington trying to have these three parks plus other natural wonders in the area declared a national park.

The colorful Red Canyon was once the home of Utes as evidenced by potsherds, grinding stones, ornaments, and other relics. A giant monolith, some one hundred feet high, the largest of its kind, towers above the red rocks. Otto Morganstein early homesteaded among the picturesque formations. More than once he was grateful that Colorow, one of the Ute chiefs, was a friendly neighbor. When the Morganstein horses wandered off, Otto had only to send word to Colorow and a young brave would help him round them up. And when Morganstein lost his good crop during the grasshopper plague, Colorow saved the family from starving.[10]

When the Morgansteins sought better prospects in Coal Creek, they left behind the graves of two of their children who had died of disease. The authorities asked the family if they wanted the graves moved when the place became a park, but the family decided to leave them undisturbed, peaceful in a park planned for the public's pleasure.

While the city was quick to grasp, she wasn't so ready to pay. A letter from the U. S. Land Office in 1935 showed that Canon City had not paid for nor received title to the tract. The Land Office was willing to accept $750 and to issue a patent on receipt of that amount.[11] Although the park is accessible from the Garden Park road and a primitive camp and picnic area provides a base for exploring the rock formations, much development work remains to be done.

Local clubs once tried to promote the use of a natural bowl-shaped space near the foot of the descending Skyline Drive for outdoor assemblies. Unpredictable rains spoiled the programs at this Skyline Bowl. Later, Easter sunrise services were held there. Such services now take place near the Angel's Walk at the Royal Gorge.

In 1926, The Chandler, Rockvale and Coal Creek Stage sported a splendid new glassed-in Reo bus with leather seats for twenty. This replaced the open 1914 Buick which for twenty-five cents hauled a passenger on the hour long trip from Coal Creek to Canon City via Rockvale, Williamsburg, Fremont, and Chandler or vice versa.

As Dall DeWeese approached the end of his life, he had long been known as the developer of Lincoln Park, a dam builder, a self-taught geologist, and a big game hunter. He had been a crack shot since childhood and his collection of mounted wild animals was known far and wide. Although he referred to his thirteen room log house as his shack, it housed an impressive collection of trophies, including all five varieties of Big Horn sheep and a moose head with a sixty-nine inch spread of horns, for many years a national record.

DeWeese had entertained many notables there, including Theodore Roosevelt who had been his host on a big game hunt in Africa. His guests amused themselves by boating on his lake or driving around his half-mile track, or sitting in the den before a crackling fire admiring the heads of game animals. They were the trophies of DeWeese's hunting trips to Alaska, Newfoundland, Canada, Old Mexico, Japan, Korea, Manchuria, China, Java, Straits Settlements, and India, as well as Africa. DeWeese hunted not only for his own satisfaction, but also for the government, being sent on such missions as an extended hunt in the Alaskan wilds to collect specimens for the Smithsonian Institution.

Shortly after his return from this Alaska trip, DeWeese conceived the idea of forming the Pike and Carson Club dedicated to protecting and preserving game animals of North America. For a number of years he was president of this organization, which was limited to members who had taken specimens of at least three species of large American game animals in a sportsmanlike manner.[12]

Like Frederickson, DeWeese was convinced that oil lay beneath the area. He persuaded W. F. McCormick, a Texaco official, to drill on the north side of his tract in Lincoln Park. DeWeese was almost ready to quit after eight dry holes. McCormick convinced him that he should continue. Luckier than Frederickson, he eventually had ten producers on the south side. Subsequent royalties from the oil companies added to his fortune.

He could well afford to offer his collection of trophies to the city. It contained some gastroliths, as well as sixteen unique blue flint points, five to ten inches in length, found in a single cache on Grape Creek.[13] His only condition was that the city furnish suitable exhibition space. Mayor A. J. Turner, realizing the need for a city hall, saw the possibility of making it a memorial building to house the collection.

Canon City voted sixty thousand dollars to build a municipal building with one room to be devoted to the DeWeese collection. This was erected near the Rudd homestead, complete with the cabin allegedly built in 1860, and the stone house Rudd had built in 1880 among his fruit trees and fields of fine clover. This homestead was given to the city about 1920 by James McClure.

As early as 1923, Rockafellow had suggested that the city use the stone house as a museum. The American Legion requested permission to use the building and proposed that the museum be set up on the second floor. That building is now used as a storehouse but plans are for it to be restored. The Rudd cabin has long since been refurbished and refurnished. Many thousands visit it each year as part of the museum.

DeWeese received $150 a month to locate and supervise construction of the new municipal building and to plan the landscaping. The completed structure opened in 1928 during one of T. Lee Witcher's three terms as mayor. The museum is upstairs, the Women's Club room downstairs, and city offices between the two.

Although the museum contains what are considered to be the last wild buffalo killed in Colorado, DeWeese was not responsible for those specimens. They were shot after the ban on bison slaughter. The corpses had been confiscated by the government and later were sold mounted to Pete Mulock of Leadville. Canon City residents raised a fund to buy the group for the amount Pete had paid for them. Robert Wesley Amick, a Western painter of note, provided the background for the group, a scene of the Indians' Signal Mountain, now known as Mount Pisgah.

Amick was born in Cañon City in 1879. He had practiced law for two years after obtaining a law degree at Yale. He gave up law to devote full time to painting in New York City although he usually chose Western subjects. In May, 1928, he filled a request from the museum for an example of his work by sending a set of seven prints with the requested photograph of himself. When his mother died in June he returned to his native city. People at once began to hint that he should paint the backdrop. When he saw the new museum he was enthusiastic enough to undertake the job which he completed in thirteen working days.

Amick died in 1969 at his home in Old Greenwich, Connecticut, at the age of ninety, after having produced many paintings of Western subjects. Amick's paintings were avidly collected by such admirers as Roy Coffee, Jr., a Texas lawyer who owns fifty of them. Perhaps more of Amick's works have been lithographed than those of any other Western artist. According to some critics, his paintings rank with those of Remington and Russell. Since his widow's health wouldn't permit the trip, his daughter, Cathryn Bigelow, accompanied his ashes to Canon City where he had requested that they be buried in Greenwood Cemetery close to the graves of his parents near the mountains he loved.

DeWeese died in Pueblo at the age of seventy-one, scarcely six months after the Amick mural was ready. He is remembered as a colorful and often opinionated person who didn't hesitate to indicate his strong likes and dislikes. Local legend claims that he once chased Guy Hardy out of the *Record* building with a buggy whip because he was annoyed at something Hardy had printed about him. He is remembered too as one who played a significant part in the development of Canon City.

The Municipal Museum also houses fine exhibits of the Canon City Geology Club. This club was the outgrowth of the interest a visiting high school student displayed in the geology of the Royal Gorge area. A paper he wrote on the subject was so good that the teachers fostered the start of the club. The group was responsible for rediscovering the site of the dinosaur excavations of Cope and Marsh. It found more bones of *Stegosaurus,* which are now in the Denver Museum of Natural History.

Although Canon City gained the Municipal Building, it lost a structure at the Penitentiary. On October 3, 1929, Danny Daniels with five fellow inmates killed Guard Elmer G. Erwin and set up their headquarters in Cellblock Number 3. There they held ten guards hostage to force compliance with their demands for safe passage from the pen. When Warden F. E. Crawford refused to capitulate to these demands on the grounds that such action would only lead to further insurrection, the gang put pressure on him by shooting six of the ten hostages at intervals, throwing their bodies into the prison yard.

National guardsmen and police fired teargas into the cellblock and set off charges of dynamite under the prisoners' headquarters. The battle raged for eighteen hours without ending until the thousand men on the side of the law had fired seven thousand rounds of ammunition. One of these shots is believed to have killed one of the mutineers. When the firing ceased at dawn, all of Danny's gang were dead. Four had been shot once each with Danny's pistol. Danny, too, was dead, the gun in his own hand. Fire had so badly damaged the central building that it had to be torn down. Another, pockmarked with bullet holes, was torn down a few years later.

Canon City, like many a small town, suffered the effects of the Great Depression. The YMCA was forced to close. It had been used as a government relief headquarters, then had been vacant for two or three years before the Benedictine Sisters of the Sacred Heart convent in Yankton, South Dakota, bought it on December 1, 1938, to augment the adjoining Fremont County Doctor's Hospital they had purchased three months earlier. They remodeled the old Y into a modern fifty bed hospital and named it for Thomas More, the English martyr. Through misunderstanding Saint was added to the name. As the Saint Thomas More Hospital the old building served until a new hospital was built in the 1960's.

While Catholic institutions flourished in Canon City, St. Michael's parish was anything but wealthy. Not until 1943 were the outmoded outdoor toilets at the parochial school replaced by modern facilities and long lacking playground equipment installed in the school yard.

The 1930's brought depression to the Harding home, too. Young T. M. III ended his short life as a gambler and drinker by a tragic fall from a window during a wild party at the Cosmopolitan Hotel in Denver. Three years later, his grandmother, Minnie Harding, died at the age of eighty, mourned by most of Canon City. The previous year, the *Colorado Club Woman* published a tribute to her that read in part.

. . . a life well spent, radiating goodwill to all, and what a beautiful life it was, untiring and willing, ever uplifting those in need, no problem too big, no request too great, rich and poor alike were greeted with the sunshine of a dear, lovable countenance that enkindled the friendships she had made, which are legion.

Minnie Harding had perhaps been too close to the big problems in her own family to realize that the solutions required more than mere uplifting with the sunshine of her countenance.

Another early resident was remembered when the Jaycees bought Maupin's plush carriage which had been stored in a livery barn since he had bought his first automobile. They paid $75 for it to use in the Old Timer parade and as a tourist booth. Some years later they gave it to the Canon City Municipal Museum where it grew shoddier each season while on outdoor display near the Rudd cabin. It's now under cover in the park near the prison grounds.

Canon City was a sleepy little town when World War II ended but a new surge of tourists soon rediscovered the Royal Gorge area and other scenic spots in Fremont County. Retirees recognized the happy combination of low costs with fine climate.

The Canon City Fine Arts Association was born in 1947 after Max Bernd-Cohen arrived in town to teach painting. His sparkling personality aroused enthusiasm for various aspects of a real program in the arts. A change in the city charter permitted the Fine Arts board to be included in the framework of the Canon City Library and Museum Association, making this city-sponsored organization unique in Colorado. The association sponsors a Blossom Festival Art Exhibit each year in May in addition to other art exhibits, lectures, musical programs, educational movies, and other cultural events. The Fine Arts Center now boasts a permanent collection as well.

More recently, a quite different sort of art group evolved. The Walled-In Artists Guild has become a key factor in returning artists in residence at the Colorado State Penitentiary to society as responsible citizens. The annual shows and sales point up the contrast between today's penal methods and those of the old dungeon days when the prison was first erected.

A morning or afternoon tour of the penitentiary gives the visitor greater insight into life behind the bars of a modern maximum security facility. In one hundred years, the original twenty-five acres have become eleven thousand, also accommodating a medium security institution, a women's correctional institution, a pre-parole release center, as well as honor farms and camps.

172

The pen was responsible for the return of another art form to Canon City. A dozen or so inmates broke out, all to be recaptured or killed within three days. It was an episode dramatic enough for a movie and did result in the filming of *Canon City* in 1948. The then warden, Roy Best, played himself, drawing favorable reviews.[14]

Warden Best, perhaps influenced by that break, proposed expansion of the parking lot near the prison and a realignment of the highway. As a result, Soda Point, adjacent to the prison walls, was wrecked in January, 1949, when the three stone pavilions constructed two generations earlier by talented convict stone masons were demolished. Historic Soda Spring was covered over to accommodate the wider State Highway 50. Although this was done in the name of progress, the public soon deplored the destruction and made donations to recover the spring. It was too late. Only a slight trickle was found and it wasn't of the strength of the old soda and iron water. The Soda and Iron Springs were dead beyond recall.

When the highway took the extra land for a right-of-way, the springs were found to be on land which J. A. Draper had sold to Colorado Territory in 1868. It was deeded back to Draper when Colorado became a state in 1876. It subsequently saw several owners including CCI, CC & I, and CF & I. In 1900, George W. Bowen acquired the springs and sold them the same year to Pueblo Realty Trust Company. The city had donated the solid stone pavilions protecting the springs to replace the earlier rustic shelters.

About 1905, a company tried to commercialize the springs by charging one cent a glass for either the iron or the soda water but the city halted this practice in the belief that this was state property. However, since 1888 Ferdinand Stockder had been adding flavoring and coloring to water from the iron spring, bottling it in snap-top bottles with rubber stoppers. He had two teams with wagons to deliver his product to all the towns and coal camps, making a two day round trip to reach his Wet Mountain Valley customers.

Stockder soon found that the spring water didn't hold its fizz very long and invested in an artificial carbonation machine. His widow carried on the business for a decade after his death in 1908.

Not until 1932 did the fact come to light that the springs were on private property. It was then owned by the Colorado Realty Holding Company of Denver which had obtained the property in a blanket deed from the Pueblo Company in 1920.

Once Ted Harding had settled down to run the family hardware business after his father's death, he became active in civic affairs and was a great home town booster, promoting everything he felt worthwhile, from school athletics to wildlife conservation. When he died in 1955, six years after retiring from business, he was rightly considered to be Mr. Canon City. He had often said, "There's no finer place in the world than right here." Many of today's residents would agree.

FOOTNOTES

1. See "Canon City," *Facts,* 11:9-11, June 10, 1899, for a description of the town in 1899.
2. See *Canon City Illustrated.*
3. Ibid.
4. LeRoy Hafen claims this first for Dr. Bartlett in "The Coming of the Automobile and Improved Roads to Colorado," *The Colorado Magazine,* 8:1-16, January, 1931.
5. *Canon City Illustrated,* 1905, presents an enthusiastic promotional view of the city and its surroundings.
6. President Roosevelt may also have taken a side trip to Cripple Creek since he is often credited with the statement attributed to Mr. Dooly, the humorist, by *Canon City Illustrated.* According to this source, the statement, "It's the one day's outing that bankrupts the English language," refers to the trip from Canon City to Colorado Springs via the CC & CC, the F & CC, and the Short Line railroads.
7. Marie Rogers Altpeter's unpublished paper on Minnie Harding and interviews with Mrs. Altpeter of Colorado Springs furnished many details in addition to items gleaned from local papers and biographical sources. Mrs. Altpeter is a niece of L. L. Harding, Jr.
8. Clyde Brion Davis, *The Arkansas,* p. 158-159.
9. Father Justin McKernan, who now serves as chaplain at St. Thomas More Hospital, was one of this group.
10. Interview with John R. McFall, November 14, 1969. McFall is related by marriage to the Morgansteins.
11. *The Royal Gorge Country: Presentation to the National Park Service,* November 9, 1940, gives the history of the lands proposed for inclusion in a National Park.
12. *Canon City Illustrated* gives details about DeWeese not found elsewhere.
13. Julia Newell Chappell, "The Canon City Museum," *The Colorado Magazine,* 8:74-77, March, 1931, describes the collection at that time.
14. Movies continued to be made in Fremont County, including such well known ones as: *Vengeance Valley, The Outcast, Big House, U. S. A., Saddle the Wind, The Ballad of Cat Ballou, Stagecoach to Seven, In Cold Blood.*

PART III

ROYAL GORGE AND WESTWARD

GRAPE CREEK CAÑON.

CHAPTER XIV

WAGON ROADS WEST

Petroglyphs and small rock shelters showing tool grooves indicate that there had long been an Indian trail along the north bank of Currant Creek. The first wagon road west from Canon City, and for many years the only one, generally followed the Indians' path, circling north around the impassable gorge, then along Currant Creek and beyond to the diggings.

The small community of Currant Creek, established in 1868 about twenty-one miles northwest of Cañon City near the Park County line, became the center for the farms and ranches along the creek. Selina McCanles lies buried near two others at a now unmarked spot on the abandoned Asher place. Long ignored by her affluent son, James, she died there, old and frail, in her daughter's arms.

School District #9 was established in 1871 to educate the children of the twenty-five to fifty families there. Currant Creek probably reached its peak in the 1880's when O. P. Allen had the general store supplying the neighboring ranchers who included the Mulocks and the Witchers.

Although John Witcher had traded land near Phantom Canyon for the place about five miles east of present Guffey on West Four Mile in Park County about 1871, his history ties in with that of Fremont County. T. Witcher who had a one-third interest in their partnership lived alone on the West Four Mile Ranch when Currant Creek was the nearest town. Their cattle ranged in both counties and later in Pueblo and Chaffee Counties as well.

John Witcher was among the incorporators of the Upper Arkansas, San Juan and Pacific Railroad in 1878 to build from Cañon City to Leadville when it appeared that the D & RG would run into difficulties in the Royal Gorge. T. Witcher went to Texas that year with his associates for four thousand head of four dollar cattle. They made a second trip for five thousand more, and in 1879 drove three thousand more back to stock their share, and perhaps more, of the open range.

The cattle industry was in full bloom when the Fremont County Cattle-growers Protective Association was formed late in December, 1897, at a meeting at the Currant Creek school house. Robert W. Pope was elected President, Don C. Crampton, secretary, and Jesse Rader, treasurer. The executive committee included W. A. Stump and T. Witcher. In addition to controlling cattle rustlers and horse thieves, the Association soon found it necessary to appoint a committee to meet with the sheepmen to establish a permanent boundary between the cattle and sheep ranges.

That year also saw the platting of twelve hundred lots in Bare Hills City near a placer approximately three miles west of Marigold City. Marigold

City was earlier established on the old toll road in the slice of Fremont County carved away when Teller County was formed in 1899. Marigold City petitioned for a school district in May, 1896, on stationery of the Marigold Hotel. This district was short-lived for in 1900 the same district number was assigned to Whitehorn. The school district set up for the few families in Bare Hills City in August, 1896, was annulled in 1901, evidently without ever having held school. Although the 1898 *Colorado State Mining Directory* lists fourteen mining companies in Bare Hills, there is little to show a permanent population. These promoters' dreams are now part of a cattle spread. No roads at all now exist to take one to the sites.

Currant Creek declined after Guffey began to grow in the 1900's. Even the Cattlegrowers met elsewhere.

Fremont County and private contributors raised $1400 in 1871 to construct a single span bridge over McCandless Ford at Twelve Mile. The bridge had hardly been put to use when a drove of Texas cattle crowded over it causing the green lumber to spring away from the abutments. It remained impassable for more than a year while the County tried to raise the four hundred dollars needed to rebuild it.

Since there was no direct route to the western counties and to the San Luis Valley, in the fall of 1872 the Fremont County Commissioners appropriated three thousand dollars for a road up the Arkansas. They wanted it completed in the sixty days before winter set in. The route was to be over the old Wet Mountain Valley road that circled north of the river and branched off the Currant Creek road, crossed the McCandless Ford bridge, then continued up Copper Gulch to Texas Creek. The new road would continue south along Texas Creek, west to Oak Grove Creek, and then westerly and northwesterly along Pleasant Valley where a 120 foot bridge would span the Arkansas. It would then continue on the north side for eighteen miles to another 120 foot bridge and on for a few more miles to the county line. This would cut the distance from eighty-two miles to only sixty-four. Six-horse stagecoaches and heavy ore wagons from Leadville soon rutted the road hub deep while short tempered drivers fought to pass on the narrow trace.

Activity in the San Juans inspired more activity in roadbuilding in the western part of Fremont County. B. F. Rockafellow, James Clelland, W. R. Fowler, Thomas Macon, and Lyman Hayden were among those who organized the Canon City and San Luis Wagon Road Company in 1874 to build a road from the west end of Main Street in Cañon City, up Grape Creek along the route then being improved to Webster Park. The hardest part of building the creekside section was cutting the thickets of wild grape vines which had overgrown the old Ute trail first followed by whites when Pike's party went that way in 1807. The road, constructed under contract by William and John McClure, then veered along Soda Creek to join the

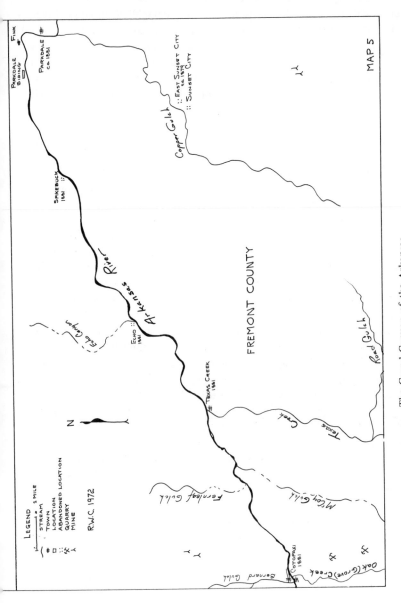

The Grand Canyon of the Arkansas

Once better known than the now famous Grand Canyon of the Colorado, the canyon
carved by the Arkansas west of the impressive Royal Gorge provides a scenic route to
the Continental Divide.

Copper Gulch Road. Capitalized at $25,000, the company proposed crossing the Sangre de Cristos at Hayden Pass. The McClure brothers suffered a setback when the toll road they had completed up Grape Creek was demolished by flood before it could be inspected and accepted.

A couple of months later very much the same group of men formed The Canon City and South Arkansas Wagon Road Company, capitalized at $20,000, to seek a shorter route through Webster Park to Pleasant Valley. This was a bid for the traffic from the railroad to the San Juan mines via Cañon City and Poncha Pass. This shorter toll road proved popular when completed.

The activities of these road companies evidently slowed progress of the Currant Creek Wagon Road. Originally dated January, the corporation didn't actually get organized until March, 1874, and then it could raise only $8,000 to build a better and shorter road along the existing route to Fairplay in an effort to facilitate trade between Park, Lake, and Fremont Counties.

Nor was there yet much of a road to the river canyon that was considered a pleasant ride above town, "a noted place for lovers of the beautiful, grand, and sublime in nature." Tourists who came to Cañon City on the narrow gauge were impressed with the wild scenery where the Arkansas emerged from the mountains through perpendicular granite walls. One wrote, "The scene here is wild, weird and romatic, it is superlatively grand, and incomparably awful." Rose Kingsley, daughter of the famous Canon Charles Kingsley of Westminster, spent some time in Colorado, and wrote in 1874 that the great canyon of the Arkansas was the finest canyon north of the Big Canyon of the Colorado. That now famous Grand Canyon was scarcely known and little visited until the late 1880's.

The Grand Canyon of the Arkansas was, however, a prime tourist attraction although the gorge itself was then nearly a day's excursion from Cañon City. One of the first picnic parties to make the trip crowded ten people into two wagon seats and stowed the lunches where they could. After they rounded the point of rocks at Soda Spring, they followed the valley of Red Sand Creek, detouring well away from the river and entered Eightmile Park through the rugged Devil's Gate. They left the main road to Fairplay for a faint, rough trail to the left. They counted the ten mile trip worth the time and effort when they suddenly came upon the terrifyingly deep chasm hidden from them until they were nearly upon it. They gazed in awe at the silver thread of a river some twelve hundred feet below. This, and later, parties laboriously chipped a half mile of steps in the rocks to reach the bottom of the gorge which was considered impassable by boat or on foot although the river had been ascended in winter on ice.

Although all who saw it were impressed, this spectacular stretch through the narrowest part of the canyon seems to have had no special name until the Rev. Mr. Richard Wheatly referred to it as the Royal Gorge in September, 1875. The following April, the newspaper reported that a new road connecting with the Grape Creek Road would be open to the south side of the chasm where the view was considered to be superior. Wheatly's name caught on and has been used ever since.

A little narrow gauge D & RG puffer pulled the first excursion train with two hundred people through the gorge on May 7, 1879. The train stopped to let them gaze upward to marvel at the slight slit of sky high above them. They marveled too at the Hanging Bridge which carried the track in the narrowest part of the gorge, a novel engineering feat accomplished by lowering men, tools, mules, and carts down the canyon walls by ropes. The Hanging Bridge, a popular spot for picnickers, was considered a pleasant walk along the tracks from the Hot Springs Hotel.

By the turn of the century, the residents of Canon City realized what an attraction the gorge was for visitors in the area. Guy U. Hardy, publisher of the *Record,* spent much time in Washington, D. C., at his own expense in an effort to secure the two thousand acre Royal Gorge Park for Canon City. It was granted to the town in June, 1906, by Congressional action. Convicts from the penitentiary built a road to it but Canon City had no further funds for development.

However, on the strength of the grant, men formed the Canon City, Florence and Royal Gorge Interurban Railway Company. In 1907, the Canon City and Royal Gorge Railroad took over its franchise and began grading a twenty-two mile scenic route. Frank Heath of the Great Western Coal Company was president and former Governor James H. Peabody was vice-president. Directors included Warden John Cleghorn and other local men with the town's interest at heart, as well as bankers from Kansas City and Philadelphia.

Billie White, under contract, had nearly completed the grade, several miles of ties were in place, two electric locomotives and cars to seat seventy-five had been ordered, and a handsome stone power substation had been completed by the time the company issued a prospectus to interest possible investors. This indicated possible extensions to East Canon, South Canon, and Lincoln Park, and spurs to limestone and livestock shipping points in Eightmile Park. In addition to freight business, the company hoped to carry 100,000 passengers a year from Canon City to the top of the Royal Gorge for a dollar a round trip.

Unfortunately, the Panic of 1907 sent the entire country into a financial crisis before the $1,500,000 worth of stock could be sold. Although the officers and directors spent substantial sums of their own money, they were unable to keep the company afloat. It sank into obscurity, leaving behind a stack of handsome unsold stock certificates at the company office at 404 Main Street. Although no rails were laid before the money ran out, traces of the grade may still be seen by westbound motorists along the hillside to the left of Highway 50.

Failure of the company left Billie White unpaid. Broke, he and Mary Jane went to ranch on Vic McCandless's Hardscrabble property. White, a man of unusual conscience, spent several years paying off the debts he incurred in the grading project, although he himself was never reimbursed. He was content to serve as a sub-contractor during construction of Schaeffer Dam.

Royal Gorge Park remained fairly inaccessible until 1911 when a new road was built up Priest Canyon. School was dismissed to celebrate the opening of this road named after James Priest, an early prominent livestock dealer. Alas, despite scenic switchbacks the road proved to be little improvement. It was too steep. Few autos of the day could make the grade. The railroad in the canyon still provided the easiest way to approach the scenic sight. Those who could use the road enjoyed the hospitality of the Reel California Girls who had a lodge, restaurant, and dance hall. It burned down and the road washed out in the mid-twenties.

The D & RG maintained guards at the Hanging Bridge during World War I to prevent sabotage of that critical stretch of track. Other railroad bridges were also guarded because many of the German residents of the Wet Mountain Valley were still sympathetic to *der Vaterland*. The only reported trouble occurred when someone shot a highpowered rifle from the upper walls of the canyon, grazing one of the guards on the cheek. The sheriff dispatched men at daybreak to search for the assailant but no trace of one was found.

The Colorado legislature established the Royal Gorge State Game Refuge of several thousand acres in 1923 to protect the animals and birds in that area. Sometime after that, Lon P. Piper, a Texan, saw the Royal Gorge and dreamed of building the world's highest suspension bridge across it. A new boulevard to the top of the north side of the gorge permitted drivers to reach the Bungalow Hotel and campground in high gear. The old Priest Canyon road was made one-way downgrade to provide a spectacular circle tour no longer open to the public.

Although Lorin Forgy had a concession lease from the city dated August 29, 1925, Piper soon had approval of the city fathers for his fantastic plan. In 1927, they leased him a portion of the park for an annual rent of one thousand dollars. Piper formed the Royal Gorge Bridge and Amusement Company, assigned his contract with the city to the company, and hired George F. Cole to build the bridge.

The south rim was practically inaccessible until the bridge company financed an access road to allow delivery of construction materials. The county, short of funds, had long neglected the earlier road. After the bridge was completed in December, 1929, visitors could peer directly down to the silver wisp of a stream below and could see the Hanging Bridge and the thirty-inch wooden stave pipeline which carries water to Canon City. This quaint, leaking arrangement disappears into tunnels in some places and is pinned to the granite walls in others. It was even then overdue for updating.

The bridge company soon made plans for an incline railway, the steepest in the world, to take visitors to the bottom of the gorge. This new facility, constructed in a natural fissure in the rock, was formally opened June 14, 1931. The passenger loading platform at the top is decorated with animal horns from the famed Dall DeWeese collection.

With the county suffering from depression and drought, the company was forced to make a new contract with Canon City in 1936 reducing payments to compensate for the county's failure to maintain the roads. When World War II with its traffic restrictions followed hard on the heels of the depression, Piper found his tourist temptation no longer a money-making proposition. He was glad to sell his interest in it to the wealthy Texas Murchison brothers in 1947. Ralph J. Wann, Jeff Tong's son-in-law became the new manager.

Piper's plight inspired a group to seek National Park status for the Royal Gorge Park. The Royal Gorge Park Association was organized in Pueblo in September, 1939, for the purpose of attaining national recognition of the Royal Gorge area and advancing development of the recreational resources there. The association compiled an impressive memorial in its bid for acceptance. The proposal included exhibits of additional attractions, such as the Skyline Drive, The Temple in Temple Canyon, and Red Canyon, pointing out that all these public areas, outside of the small leased portion near the bridge, were neglected but much too valuable to be allowed to deteriorate. A U. S. Weather Bureau report showed that the facility could be a year round proposition since the mean temperature there is fifty-four degrees and it is protected from excessive cold by the natural flow of air.

Stockmen, of course, showed up at the hearing to express concern that they might lose their Taylor Grazing Act rights or leases if the area became a park, and a number of leased land representatives also indicated opposition. Although the sponsors of the memorial were unsuccessful in their attempts to make the Royal Gorge part of a national park, they did draw attention to the area. The Royal Gorge Scenic Railway Company was formed in 1950 to operate attractions for tourists in an area along the gorge just west of the city's holding. But six years later, the city was still unable to meet the recognized need for drives, trails, and picnic places in its two mile wide and four mile long park.

In 1957, Don Tyner was at last able to fulfill his dream of using the model train he had constructed with a simulated diesel engine to haul passengers through a delightfully scenic area to the rim of the Royal Gorge.

The tickets are free — but passengers are expected to pay what they feel the trip is worth. The management is seldom disappointed.

Karol W. Smith also fulfilled a dream. A Colorado native with an interest in history, he had long wanted to restore the 1859 mining town of Buckskin Joe but he had met no one with the same desire to halt the disappearance of such reminders of the early days until he, Don Tyner, and Malcolm F. Brown, art director for MGM Studios, met one day. As they talked they revealed their interest in relics of the past and the others were soon enthusiastic supporters of Smith's plan.

Since it was then too late to restore the original Buckskin Joe on the site, the three men planned a reconstitution of the original on land adjoining the Royal Gorge Park. They searched Colorado for buildings that would match particular structures that had stood in the original Buckskin Joe. The logs were taken down and numbered to insure accurate rebuilding when they were put in place on a plat sketched from the memories of old timers who recalled the original town near Fairplay and Alma.

A building from Uncle Billy Barker's 1884 homestead on Adobe Creek, later part of Gumaer's ranch, was chosen to represent the glass and china shop in Buckskin Joe. The photo gallery was once Barker's barn. The newspaper office came from the adjoining William Draper ranch which also later had belonged to Gumaer. The trading post once served as the Tallahassee School on a ridge above Cottonwood Creek. Built between 1888 and 1900, it was abandoned as a school when the district consolidated.

The saddle shop had been Samuel Y. Lancaster's homestead on the mesa where Highway 115 now crosses Beaver Creek. This was the home of David Hollifield when his wife served as postmistress at Glendale. The Wells Fargo office was one of the first permanent homes built in Garden Park and the store furnishing miners' supplies was once the home of George Griffin on pre-empted land near the short-lived Yorkville. The bricks in the chimney were made at the Catlin kiln. One building, the general store, is actually a Buckskin Joe original. It was built about 1861 by H. A. W. Tabor and used as a store and postoffice.

Because Karol Smith had been associated with the motion picture industry ever since his high school days when he worked in the local theater, it was natural that he had in mind more than the mere preservation of the relics. He figured that he'd not only have a tourist attraction but an authentic setting for western movies. And indeed Buckskin Joe has been just that. Parts of several movies have been filmed there including *Cat Ballou* and *Barquero*. Even without the aura of glamor from its film connections, the authentic approximation of old Buckskin is well worth a visit.

With these added attractions and the Bridge Company's addition of an aerial tramway across the Royal Gorge, that awesome chasm, so long cussed as an obstacle, has become a magnet that attracts the welcome tourist.

The arrival of the railroad had less impact on the western part of Fremont County than on the eastern. The land west of the Gorge remained a ranching and mining area. However, there are even fewer living there today than when the railroad cared about passengers.

Grizzly bears long continued to be a menace despite the settlement of ranches and towns. One alone, known to all as Old Mose, was estimated to have killed some eight hundred cattle and horses between 1870 and 1904. He headquartered near Black Mountain, ranging from Tarryall to Cochetopa Pass about once every thirty days according to a representative of the U. S. Biological Survey. He was credited with killing three men and may have killed eight or nine more. One of his victims was Jake Radcliff, an experienced hunter. Old Mose charged him in 1883, crunched his right leg in his powerful jaws, and tossed the mangled man into the air. Radcliff's companions carefully carried him to the Mulock Ranch but he died of his wounds despite their care.

Old Mose was shot many times and trapped once but suffered only the loss of two toes. He continued to terrorize the neighborhood until James W. Anthony arrived in Canon City with thirty dogs he had used to kill sixteen bears in Idaho. When the dogs found Old Mose, Anthony, after several shots, finally managed to lodge a bullet in the beast's brain on April 30, 1904. The great grizzly weighed between one thousand and fifteen hundred pounds and measured nine feet from nose to tail. It took seven men to haul him to W. H. Pigg's Stirrup Ranch. Anthony eventually willed his trophy skin to the Zoology Department of the University of California.

Once the wagon road was improved, considerable traffic crossed the bridge near where James McCandless' Big Spring Ranch had been. Known as McCandless Ford, Twelve Mile Ford, and, after the bridge was built, as Bridge, it became Parkdale when a community was established there in 1879. It is situated about twelve miles west of Canon City on the edge of beautiful Webster Park which provides summer pasture for ranchers across the river. Good farms once flourished on the north bank where the soil was not too gravelly for cultivation. Parkdale had a postoffice but it closed two years later leaving the population of ten without mail service. By 1884 the population had risen to fifty as shipment of railroad ties and copper ore began. The postoffice was reactivated in 1888 and served a small population until 1970.

During the Cripple Creek excitement, men from Parkdale and Canon City joined Easterners in incorporating the Rio Grande, Cripple Creek and Northern Railroad. Their ambitious plan of reaching Cripple Creek via the Freshwater Mining Company's property and extending branches to Como and Black Mountain died aborning.

Old Mose

J. W. Anthony, shown here, killed this grizzly bear in 1904 with the help of his trained bear dogs and other hunters. *Canon City Illustrated, 1905.*

Fink, just beyond the second of two right angle bends of the Arkansas, became the railroad stop for a cement works. About a mile above Fink the flat at Parkdale Siding accommodated cars needed for shipping a variety of commodities. Consolidated Feldspar built a plant there in 1948. Although this company was absorbed by the International Minerals and Chemical Corporation, the plant was idle in the 1950's.

Spikebuck, six miles beyond Parkdale, was one of the other little stops that sprang up along the railroad. Although it never seems to have had a postoffice, there was a population of twenty-five in 1883, possibly section hands, and it was listed as a D & RG stop as late as 1906. There is little sign now that it ever existed. Two miles above Spikebuck, near the mouth of Five Points Gulch, the Five Points picnic area was newly furbished in 1968. Across the river Echo was once a whistle stop which gave access to a picnic spot popular for the echoing quality of a small canyon. For years there was a side track and water tower there but the only inhabitants were a rancher or two and the railroad's telegrapher.

These stops could never become towns for beyond Webster Park, the Grand Canyon of the Arkansas is narrow and the river flows between steep walls for about twelve miles. There wasn't even a road along this stretch until 1914 when convict and county crews completed a road from Parkdale to Texas Creek. Narrow, rough, and dusty though it was, it marked a big step forward and was properly inaugurated with a picnic and ceremony near Echo.

The postoffice known as Ford, serving fifteen souls where the canyon is a bit wider, became Texas Creek after the railroad arrived. This new Texas Creek was never a metropolis. It enjoyed a flurry of activity when the D & RG built a relatively floodproof standard gauge branch up Texas Creek to tap the revived Westcliffe market, lifting the tracks out of the valley on a long, spectacular trestle to loop around around a thumb of land east of the mouth of the creek.

W. P. Noble took advantage of what trade there was. He built a general store there in 1906 and in addition ran a saloon. His wife kept a boarding house until a fire put them out of business about 1918. The one room school averaged a dozen or so pupils.

The community earlier known as Texas Creek was slightly south of where the stage road along Road Gulch came into the Texas Creek Road. The creek itself was named about 1862 by Nat Rich and Joseph Lamb.[1] The two young men had been hired to drive fifty head of Texas steers to California Gulch. The old trail went right by the junction of the later roads. The men camped there one night and no sooner had the cattle quiet than a mountain lion screeched. The southern steers had never heard such a sound and promptly stampeded. It took Rich and Lamb several days to round them up and get them on the trail again. Lamb ever after called the stream where they had so much trouble with the cattle, Texas Creek, and the name stuck.

Despite that difficult trip, Joseph Lamb decided he liked that spot and later homesteaded nearby. When Colorow told him he couldn't build a cabin there, only a tepee, Joe explained that a white couldn't live in a tepee in the winter and that he'd be going to the mines in the summer. Colorow consented. He had considered Lamb a *wano hombre* ever since Joe had alerted the Chief to two renegade Indians who had made off with a couple of Colorow's horses when he was camped near Three Mile Spring. Lamb's homestead is now part of the Leftwich Ranch which sports a $40,000 log house built by an Easterner in the 1950's. The original house, remodeled, is still on the property.

When Joe Lamb was there, stages and freight traffic passed his door. A long line of white wagon covers moved slowly toward Gunnison, Ruby, Gothic, and Leadville. Those coming up the Copper Gulch Road passed through the short-lived Sunset City and East Sunset City.

Twenty-three year old Joseph Milton Lamb had arrived in Denver in 1859 and was one of the first to get to California Gulch. After the placers played out, he ran a pack train of ten burros to carry goods from Cañon City to the mines. There was no road in 1863. He made his own trail. The undergrowth was so thick in Copper Gulch that his burros had to follow the old Indian Trail on the side of the hill.

That spring he joined the posse to hunt the bloody Espinosas. In the fall, he volunteered in the Colorado cavalry under Colonel Chivington. He was at Sand Creek to see the Colonel pocket a dispatch which he failed to read until it was too late to prevent the controversial encounter.

Joe was thirty-six when he married Sarah and brought her to his homestead. Their son Frank was born in 1881. Some of Frank's three brothers and three sisters were also born at the homestead. After the D & RG was completed in Leadville, Lamb found it hard to make a living when the market for his produce no longer passed his door. The Lambs were painfully poor in 1885 when they moved to Hillside where a postoffice had been established the year before, close to the Custer County line.

The small house Joe managed to build in between raising crops soon burned and left them with nothing at all. He moved a log cabin on to the place, using it to house ten people for eight years. By 1890, Joe was running a shingle mill to serve the Hillside population which swelled to one hundred. The boom didn't last. He had to mortgage his home place. In January, 1893, he couldn't repay two promissory notes for $150 each secured by his deed of trust for $1500. The interest was long past due and the place was foreclosed. The sheriff's sale was postponed until March, then the Lambs had to get out and start from scratch again.

Joe Lamb got a job hauling old ties from the abandoned Grape Creek railroad grade to the Bull Domingo mine, northeast of Blackburn. He bought the old section house to be paid for by his hauling and moved it to eighty acres next to his old place at Hillside and rented the farm land he had once owned. The Lamb children walked one and a half miles to attend school four months each year. The district was too poor to pay teachers any longer. Joe Lamb was enough of a pioneer to cope successfully with a series of adversities before he died at eighty-three in 1919. His Sarah died six months later.

His son Frank passed his eighth grade examination at seventeen and in 1899 taught the Texas Creek school near his father's earlier homestead. He later married Maude Conover who also taught there one year. Frank went on to become a surveyor and a successful mining engineer.

Like his father before him, Frank felt the lure of gold and went to Goldfield, Nevada, during the rush there to work and to acquire interests in many claims. He would have been well off if he'd cashed in on his claims before the Panic of 1907 sent the prices tumbling to realistic levels. He returned to Colorado to ranch and was content to be County Agent for some years. He retired from ranching in 1950 and surveyed again during the uranium boom until his legs dictated a more leisurely life. He spent the remaining years of his long life putting his recollections and legends of local history into form for publication.

Hillside's population, depleted since the depression of 1893, remained at a fairly constant twelve. There was a bit of a boom in the 1920's but Beach's Store seldom supplied more than forty people.

The Cloverdale Mines and the Peerless Consolidated Copper Company operation livened things up for awhile in the 1930's as did the neighboring Rainbow Lake Club resort, but after the D & RG branch was abandoned in 1938, Hillside all but became a ghost. Ranches absorbed the smaller places and autos took the ranchers to larger centers to trade. The cemetery holds those whose lives ended there, among them Joseph and Sarah Lamb and three of their daughters and a son. Today it's easy to drive right through town without realizing that you've reached it as you admire the unspoiled scenery along Texas Creek on the way south to Westcliffe.

FOOTNOTES

1. Interview with Frank Lamb, son of Joseph, April 10, 1968, augmented by Smith's article on the life of Joseph Milton Lamb.

CHAPTER XV

COTOPAXI AND CATTLE THIEVES

William Docke, who arrived in Cañon City in 1860, went West on the wagon road to take up a ranch on Oak Creek, south of the Arkansas. He heard shrill screams one day as he rode in search of stray stock near Cottonwood Springs. Investigation revealed that Plains Indians had killed the mates of four Ute squaws. They were expressing their grief by beating their own bodies with brush, tearing their hair, and wailing in tones wild enough to scare off anyone's stock. Docke soon had other unhappy neighbors.

Emmanuel H. Saltiel, a Portuguese Jew and successful mining man, numbered among his investments two mines north of the Arkansas near Bernard Creek about thirty-two miles west of Cañon City. Henry (Gold Tom) Thomas had first filed claim to the Cotopaxi Lode, naming it after the Andean volcano.

In December, 1880, Saltiel and his partners incorporated the Cotopaxi Placer Mining Company to placer gold and other precious metals along Bernard Creek and to lease and rent lands. The following year the *Colorado Business Directory* listed him as a mine operator there dealing in gold, silver, zinc-blende and carbonate ores; mica, crude, sheet, and pulverized; feldspar; and rose and crystal quartz in any quantity.

Saltiel[1] balked at paying the high wages wanted by miners during the height of the early Leadville boom and conceived a novel way of solving his problem. He offered to settle a colony of Jewish farmers on his lands.

Pogroms in Russia had caused many Jews to seek asylum in this country. Saltiel represented himself to the newly formed Hebrew Immigrant Aid Society as being interested in developing agricultural land near a platted townsite named for himself. He promised houses, barns, sheds, furniture, household equipment, tools, seed, cattle, horses, wagons, and a year's supply of feed – all for $8,750. The colonists were to raise $1,250 to provide transportation. Julius Schwartz, a young Hungarian, visited Cotopaxi, named for the lode rather than the man after all, and wrote a glowing report of a mining headquarters in a beautiful valley served by the railroad. The HIAS voted ten thousand dollars to set up an agrarian colony.

The T. Witchers were living at their Lower Ranch when Saltiel reigned over the new community as president of the Cotopaxi Town Company. Witcher had lived alone on West Four Mile until he married Mary Bell Harden who lived with her mother on a small ranch on Cottonwood Creek. Mary then shared T.'s bachelor quarters until February, 1881, when she went to Cañon City to stay with her mother for the birth of their son, Otis.

Witcher built a house on farm land which he hoped to homestead about two miles north of the Arkansas on Bernard Creek some nine miles below his Bernard Ranch. While T. called this thirty-two foot square house commodious, Mary was not enthusiastic about the four room, one-story box house made of lumber salvaged from old buildings near a saw mill.

Mary wasn't impressed with her new neighbors either. Most of the twenty families who agreed to come were headed by bearded Chassidim, members of a pious mystic sect from Russia, knowing not a word of English. Saltiel's cousin, E. Samuel Hart, met them in New York and escorted them to Cotopaxi. His own wife and family followed on the next train. Hart became the proprietor of the Cotopaxi Hotel and a general store.

The immigrants marveled at the awesome Royal Gorge as they came through it — and also at their accommodations when they arrived on May 8, 1882, to swell the town's population to two hundred. They could scarcely believe their eyes when they saw twelve poor cabins without chimneys, doors, windows, or stoves. The 160 acre farms were eight miles south on a narrow strip of land along Oak Creek and were only partly suited to cultivation. The property had water rights but there were no irrigation rights left on the stream which was dry in summer and flooded in spring. The colonists could only conclude that there had been some horrible misunderstanding.

Hopefully, prayer would alleviate their predicament. They decided that their first need was a synagogue. When the HIAS sent a Sefer Torah, the Biblical Scroll, they housed it in an abandoned cabin behind the general store. Two weddings were performed there in the first and only synagogue in Cotopaxi.

Even prayers failed to improve the situation. One man harvested only fifteen bags of inferior potatoes from the fourteen bags of good seed potatoes he had sown. The very severe winter was nearly unendurable. The penniless people had no fuel, no adequate clothing, and no ammunition for hunting with their European guns. They were plagued by marauding bears and begging Indians. There was nothing to do but work for Saltiel at his mines four miles away.

There they earned $1.50 on the day shift or $2.50 on the night shift and were paid in vouchers good only at Hart's store. They soon realized that they'd been victimized and left the mines to dig trenches in Salida for the D & RG. They sent a delegate to Denver for aid. The HIAS investigated, and Denver's Jewish community agreed to help them. By this time Saltiel was the president and general manager of the Bee-line Milling and Mining Company working the lode of magnetic iron ore north of Cotopaxi, and was agent for the Enterprising and Cotopaxi lodes of zinc blende and copper.

Cattle was the leading industry along the Arkansas by 1883 when T.

Witcher's second son, T. Lee, was born in the little house north of Cotopaxi. The Witchers found themselves involved in the first of several sensational situations. Their widespread cattlemen neighbors who also rawhided on the open range didn't like to see the western part of the county building up. But while settlers were an annoyance, other cowmen caused real trouble. Although rustling was a major crime, there was hardly a cowman in the county who didn't believe that any maverick found on the range belonged to the man with the longest rope.

Ira Mulock, his three sons, and brother Joshua had followed the usual procedure of homesteading 160 acres at some favored spot for each adult member of the family. Homesteads could be enclosed and, with drift fences and natural boundaries at strategic intervals, could effectively contain cattle on a technically fenceless public domain.

Suave, good-looking L. Edwin Watkins,[2] who had recently married Mrs. Mary Green, headed a group to the west of the Mulocks. This college educated young man, once a Kansas schoolteacher, had established his home ranch on Badger Creek in 1877. Later, he had another ranch, complete with slaughter house and cattle pens, in a secluded valley near Bald Mountain at the head of Cottonwood Creek.

Watkins supplied meat to the Salida markets, mines, sawmill crews, tie hacks, and section gangs. His cowboy piñon busters would circle a bunch of wild cattle, ambush and shoot them. After bleeding out and butchering them, they would pack out the meat and hides. Their reeking butcher ground gave names to Bloody Mountain and Bloody Gulch on Badger Creek.

Mulock was suspicious of this tall, dark, and handsome non-smoking teetotaler and his associates, Ernest Christenson, Ben Jameson, Frank Reed, Bruce Cameron, Will and John Taylor, and others. When Mulock missed some cattle, he was more than ready to point the finger at Ed Watkins. He was sure his **IM** brand had been changed to Watkins' Ⓜ. Watkins, in turn, seems to have suspected Dick McCoy. According to one account, he or his friends enlisted the help of Gold Tom, who worked a small placer about a mile below Cotopaxi, to gather evidence against the McCoys.

Richard McCoy[3] had come in when the D & RG was being built. With him was his wife, Susan, four sons, Charley "Nibs," Joe, Tom "Kid," Streeter, and two daughters, Minnie and Fannie. Six-foot, stocky Dick McCoy, with a fine head of hair and a full set of whiskers, made a reasonably respectable appearance not matched by his later reputation.

The McCoys established a claim on Sand Gulch between Cotopaxi and Texas Creek running cattle on both sides of the river, crossing at a ford to a flat of natural river gravel on the north side. The neighbors complained when the McCoys attempted to file on several 160 acre homesteads located so that they controlled a border around a hollow square of government land. The Land Office disallowed the McCoys' claims after an investigation. This resulted in hard feelings.

Others beside the Mulocks were leary of Watkins' operations. Twelve-year-old Tom McQuaid made friends with a race horse owner named Fisher and went with him one day to the Watkins ranch to look for a lost cow of McQuaid's. They found a stockade-like corral there with twelve rifles pointed through the ports. When Fisher and the boy turned away, Watkins rode up to ask what they wanted. Fisher explained. Watkins introduced them to his wife and sister, gave them lunch, and helped them look for the cow. He gave them another when they failed to find the one they were seeking but when young Tom innocently asked why it was freshly branded with a splotched brand, Watkins became angrily venomous. He told Tom that if he ever said he had seen such a thing he'd be hanged or shot as a liar. A year later Tom learned, when Fisher's body was found in the mountains, that he had, in truth, been a cattle detective hired by the large ranchers who suspected Watkins of wholesale slaughter of their cattle.

In April, 1883, J. W. Eddy offered to furnish grub and bedding to encourage distant members of the Cattlemen's Association to attend a meeting. The members agreed to send Johnny Hyssong and Delos Sampson, both seventeen, on the spring roundup to see what they could learn about Watkins' business. The boys stayed several weeks without arousing suspicion, then reported that they saw plenty of thievery going on apparently unnoticed or ignored by Watkins. There were a couple of hundred head on both Watkins' and Christenson's ranches with changed brands and about sixty head of fine dappled grey draft horses from Leadville hidden in Watkins' mountain pastures.

When Mulock and his friends heard the report, some wanted to take immediate drastic action but cooler heads decided a committee should wait on Watkins. It went into action after the July 14th *Fremont County Record* reported that forty head belonging to Mulock and Company had been driven up Chalk Creek to have the brands changed.

Watkins met the men with rifle in hand and refused to let them look over his cattle. The repulsed ranchers, annoyed, called a meeting at Mulock's ranch. After the meeting twenty men, armed and supplied, moved on the Watkins' property and drove off the forty head with changed brands which they thought had belonged to them. They met up with Watkins and eight of his armed men at the Christenson ranch. When Watkins saw that he was outnumbered, he spurred his horse and raced to Salida to get papers to repossess the contested stock by due process.

The following day, the sheriff from Salida arrested the three Mulock sons, William Gribble, Gregory Gross, T. Witcher, and J. T. Sampson to hold them on three hundred dollars bail each for cattle stealing. Almost at the same time, Watkins was arrested and charged with rustling with his bond set at four thousand dollars. He had three thousand but begged permission to go to Salida to raise the rest. When he failed to get it he returned to the Cañon City calaboose. In mid-August, Sheriff Jones escorted him on another trip to try to obtain the needed cash.

The two indulged in a restaurant meal in Cañon City before returning to the jail about midnight. On the way a masked group jumped them and bound Jones. Watkins fled. Shots rang out: In the morning, Watkins' body dangled from the upper bridge across the Arkansas, a bullet wound evident. The August 18th *Record* headlined it.

LYNCHED!
A COWARDLY, DASTARDLY MURDER
FRIDAY NIGHT

The masked men were never identified despite offers of reward for information. When Mulock and some twenty friends had gone to Salida on August 13 for their preliminary hearing, several hundred armed men crowded them off the station platform. When a train came along, Mulock's men left on it, at the urging of Baxter Stingley, Salida's marshal, before anyone was hurt. Watkins' friends threatened to lynch T. Witcher who deemed it wise to walk home through the mountains instead of hopping the train with the rest.

When the Mulock men arrived at the Monte Cristo Hotel two days later for the criminal trial, they saw Watkins' bunch armed with rifles and six-shooters on the balcony overlooking the lobby. Witcher men commandeered handcars and headed back down the track, returning with reinforcements. Marshal Stingley swore in fifteen armed constables to protect them. All surrendered their arms and proceeded to the Opera House for the trial. Watkins' attorney, after examining the brands on the evidence, decided his departed client had no case for replevin.

Although general opinion considered twenty-nine-year-old Watkins and his bunch guilty, he had many friends who were sure he'd hurt no one, perhaps because he was generous with drinks for the thirsty. At this late date it's impossible to know whether he was the innocent dupe of his hands and neighbors. Maybe he was.

Changed brands turned up at roundups for the next several years. Christenson was later sent to the pen. When he turned State's evidence in 1888, he admitted that as many as three thousand cattle were stolen in one year. Others of that bunch disappeared from the scene after Frank Reed shot and killed Marshal Stingley.

The cattle stealing continued. T. Witcher and others formed The United Rocky Mountain Stock Grower's Association to try to combat it. Witcher was treasurer when all stockmen in the area were urged to attend a

February, 1884, meeting in Salida. Even the organization, however, failed to foil the rustlers then or to prevent other violence.

There are several versions of how Gold Tom met his end. Charley McCoy said he was shot and killed on the steps of the Cotopaxi Hotel by A. Hart. Young Josiah C. Hart said he saw a man by the name of McCoy leave the Hart store and shoot Thomas on the porch of the store across the street.

A completely different version[4] credits George Meyers with the killing after ill feeling was initiated because Meyers threw a bucket of water over Gold Tom. Tom's oily clothes had caught fire while the men warmed themselves before the pot-bellied stove in the Cotopaxi railroad station in the presence of Charley McCoy. Sometime later, George and Charley sicked the Meyers' dog on Gold Tom as he passed their house. Thomas warned them not to do that again. They not only did it again, but began to pack guns and talk big about getting Gold Tom.

There seems to be no written evidence of Gold Tom's arrival in the area, although he evidently was a friend of Lyman Hayden, a character in his own right, who had met him in a mining town before becoming an early pioneer of the later Hillside. Henry Thomas had earned his nickname from his habit of always carrying gold dust and nuggets in his money belt.

Unless Gold Tom, a quiet, generally solitary man, had informed on the McCoys, there seems little reason for twenty-four-year-old Charley McCoy's continued harrassment of the older man with the help of his friend Meyers. Whatever the cause, Thomas had had enough of it by June 6, 1884. He rode in to Cotopaxi by the back way, prepared to deal with his tormentors.

He tied his horse behind the building across from Hart's store. As he rounded the corner of the building, he saw Meyers on the bench by the door. He drew but fired too soon. The bullet hit the corner and ricocheted to announce the beginning of a real Western shoot 'em up hardly equalled in a modern TV show. In brief, Meyers sprang through the door. Gold Tom followed. Meyers found himself at a dead end in the back room, cornered. He turned and fired when Thomas incautiously opened the door. Gold Tom dropped, fatally shot.

An inquest cleared Meyers on the ground that it was justifiable homicide. Thomas had 121 cartridges, two Colt revolvers with extra cylinders, a Bowie knife and $121.60 in cash but no gold on him when he died. Lyman Hayden saw that his friend had a decent burial in Canon City. The undertaker noted scars left by leg irons. This led to speculation that he might have been a prisoner during the Civil War.

The land around Gold Tom's cabin was well cultivated after his death when hopefuls dug for the gold they were sure he had buried. No one ever admitted finding any. Today, Gold Tom Rock keeps alive the legend of

Cotopaxi's only victim of a wild west shootout. A rock, with mossgrown letters five inches high reading GOLD and an arrow pointing beneath a crevice, probably was carved by a long-ago prankster.

The Cotopaxi colonists' problems were resolved about the time of Gold Tom's demise. Denver's small group of Jews undertook the task of resettling the misguided farmers and, although it was a heavy burden on them, did it well. Nearly all elected to stay in Colorado despite their miserable start. Many went to Denver and in time founded famous families.

The Witcher brothers dissolved their partnership. Despite the trouble, they had several profitable years. T.'s share was over one thousand head of cattle and twenty horses. He bought several well improved hay and farm ranches southeast of Cotopaxi, largely in Custer County.

By this time, the CCI Company had an interest in the Cotopaxi mines. Saltiel promoted his Mica and Porcelain Company there. V. J. Banta ran the general store to serve the hundred or so who remained in town.

John Witcher went to Texas to buy three thousand more longhorn steers and five hundred heifers near Lampassas. The following year, his young son, John Taliaferro, known as Tol, helped him move the cattle. By that time eight to ten thousand head in four counties carried their 76 brand. John started a meat market in Canon City to help dispose of the beef. In 1885, he sold two beeves a day by contract to the Penitentiary for four cents a pound, dressed.

He sold most of his cattle to Denver stockyard brokers. After the cattle were gathered north of the river, they were forded at Cotopaxi, driven up Oak Creek, down Copper Gulch to Canon City and on to Teller Pasture, acquired through a deal by the politician, and now part of the Fort Carson Reservation. In those days, open range cowmen waited until the steers were three years old before gathering them for sale. Many became pretty wild in that length of time in such rough country.

Although Cotopaxi had a schoolhouse even before District #23 was formed in July, 1882, the school evidently left something to be desired although T. Witcher himself was on the board. In 1887, the year T. got title to the homeplace of 140 acres, Mary Witcher moved to Canon City for the ostensible purpose of sending Otis to school. She took rooms in the building that housed Merit's market and furnished them comfortably.

The next year T. had a contract with the D & RG to furnish seven dressed beeves a week for the contractor's crew. These men, including some fifty Indians, were putting in a third rail so that standard and narrow gauge trains could use the same roadbed. T. butchered this beef on the range and packed it on mules to Echo and Cotopaxi.

In June, Mary Witcher left her six and four year old sons in Canon City and eloped to Eagle County with a lover. She didn't return until her brother went to fetch her a month later. She refused to return to T.

although he offered to build her a bigger and better house at the Wet Mountain Valley ranch and to buy her a team and carriage. Or, if she didn't want to live with him, he'd build her a house in Canon City and pay her bills if she'd remain single and take care of the boys. She refused, claiming T. was "avaricious, penurious and morose" and went instead to live with her uncle, J. D. Hylton, at Cotopaxi. She earned a bit of money helping him run the post office for four months and then she went back to stay with her mother in Canon City.

T. prevailed upon his niece, Nannie Gambill, to move to the Wet Mountain Valley ranch to take care of the youngsters. By September, 1889, since he realized that reconciliation was impossible, he sued for divorce and custody of the children. That began proceedings which lasted three and a half years while Mary tried to prove that she had not deserted him, the richest rancher in the county, and he tried to prove that she had committed adultery and that he was nearly destitute because he had had to convey most of his stock and property to friends in exchange for borrowed money.

On top of this, T. was having more cattle trouble too. Elton T. Beckwith with his brother, Edwin F., who had ranched in the Wet Mountain Valley since 1869, owned 2,300 acres and ran over 7,000 head of cattle and 200 horses in the Arkansas Hills south of the river across from T.'s large range. Dick McCoy ran cattle on the same range. When he filed a brand that closely resembled the Beckwiths', Elton soon suspected him of changing brands on Beckwith cattle. McCoy, like others, sold dressed beef to section gangs, the many placer miners then in the area, and anyone else who would buy.

Witcher and Senator Beckwith both wondered where McCoy, who was thought to be an ex-Quantrell raider from Missouri, got all the meat he sold. They hired an educated half-breed Pinkerton detective, William J. Arnold,[5] said to be a two-term convict himself, to find out. Witcher and other ranchers had built a corral on the flat across the river from McCoy's house. On December 18, 1888, the McCoys saw Arnold put some cattle in that corral and rightly guessed that he was trying to get some information about their operations. Dick McCoy took Charley's shot gun loaded with whittled-down spikes, slugs, and #2 buckshot, and Joe McCoy carried a rifle when they crossed the river to investigate.

The post mortem revealed that Arnold had been shot once by a shotgun and once by a rifle. Dick and Joe McCoy were arrested, then released on bond until the long and bitter court battle began the following October. Augustus Macon was the McCoys' attorney. He found twenty-six citizens who swore that they had no prejudice against Joe McCoy and didn't want to see him convicted.

Jasper Duckett testified that T. Witcher had stated that he and Beckwith had employed Arnold to drive McCoy from the neighborhood. They had promised him a decent burial if he should be killed in the attempt and that they'd prosecute those connected with the killing to the fullest extent of the law.

The McCoys claimed that Arnold had drawn his revolver first on the fatal day and that he had threatened to kill McCoy on various occasions. Knowing Arnold's reputation as a crack shot, they had wasted no time when they saw his gun, but had shot to protect themselves.

Beckwith brought in John M. Waldron, a famous Denver lawyer, and for local color, Maupin, by then well-known as a brilliant criminal lawyer. Despite the number of witnesses for the McCoys and the lack of any for Arnold, who had been engaged to be married when he was shot, the jury found Dick and Joe guilty of second degree murder.

One juror came down with typhoid fever during the trial but the District Attorney and Macon agreed to continue anyway. That, however, led to a new trial on the grounds that there were only eleven jurors. The next jury found Joe guilty of first degree murder.

Charley McCoy, considered the good one in the family, then kept a saloon in Cotopaxi and was thought to be too lazy to get into trouble. His wife, Ruby, may have had something to do with his keeping straight. Tom, the Kid, wasn't too bad, but Streeter was the meanest of all. Both he and Joe tended bar for Charley on occasions when carousers crowded the place.

Their mother, Susan, was a coarse-looking, weatherbeaten, witchy bitch who put them up to all the deviltry. After the trial she was alleged to have said that she was "raising a son to kill Elton Beckwith and T. Witcher." The trial didn't end the trouble with the McCoys. Joe managed to break out of jail on January 26, 1890. Susan later expressed her opinion of Maupin by trying to carve him up when he was invited to deliver the speech at the Fourth of July celebration at Sell's Island Fruit Farm and Pleasure Resort in Canon City.[6]

Oscar B. Carroll's store in Cotopaxi was robbed on August 30, 1891. The following night an eastbound D & RG passenger train was held up near Fernleaf Gulch across the river not far above the McCoy place. As the express neared the deep and lonely canyon, the engineer was startled by the explosion of a torpedo, soon followed by two more, the signal of danger. He applied the air brakes as soon as he saw a swinging red lantern.

Seven masked men approached when the train stopped. One came over the tender and told the fireman to take a coal pick and break open the car door. He obeyed at gun point but insisted that there was nothing of value in that car. The holdup man then handed the pick to the engineer and ordered him to break into the next one. He was annoyed to discover that it was the mail car and wanted to know why the engineer hadn't told him so. He then went to the express car and forced the express messenger to open the box. It contained only two small packages. The messenger had hidden the cash. Angered, the robber grabbed the messenger's Winchester and poked around between the trunks and boxes until he found nine hundred dollars and two boxes of gold nuggets. Most of the passengers slept through the excitement while the conductor carefully lay low in a car near the end of the train.

Doc Shores, Sheriff of Gunnison County, was soon on the scene at the request of the general manager of the Rio Grande Express Company. He found the countryside swarming with U. S. Marshals, Pinkerton men, and armed posses when he checked into the hotel at Cotopaxi. He met Tom Horn, an ex-Indian fighter and a deputy for the Pinkerton Detective Agency, riding a horse rented from T. Witcher.

Shores and Horn learned from local law men that the house across the river from the site of the robbery was that of Dick McCoy, then on parole, and that his son, Joe McCoy, who had broken jail the year before, was still at large. Gossip at the general store revealed that hardly a term of court passed without Dick McCoy's being up for cattle rustling or horse stealing. The storekeeper also remarked that he hadn't seen Burt Curtis or Peg-Leg Watson, two recently released convicts, since the robbery. The McCoys, wearing six-shooters, often drunk and looking for trouble, usually checked the smoking cars whenever a train stopped at Cotopaxi to see if any law men were on board.

Horn and Shores watched the house near Sand Gulch and saw young Kid McCoy leave with a pack outfit heading toward the Sangre de Cristos. The pair had a variety of adventures before they caught up with Burt Curtis at Washita Station in Indian Territory forty-three days later. Shores took Curtis to Denver while Horn, who later came to a bad end himself, waited to apprehend Thomas Watson.

The bandits claimed that Joe McCoy, who escaped jail in Canon City with William Parry and William Boyd, had nothing to do with the train robbery although its purpose had been to obtain funds to carry Dick McCoy's battle for another offense to the Supreme Court. Nevertheless, the detectives tracked Joe to Utah and returned him to Denver.

The trial that started January 13, 1892, in Judge Hallett's court in Denver was of great interest to the public since the train robbery had been the most audacious and the best executed of any on the local lines. Kid and Dick McCoy, Frank Hallock, and John and Frank Price stood with the defendants Curtis and Watson, two notorious and fearless criminals wanted in several states for a variety of crimes. Augustus Macon and four other lawyers appeared for the defense while the U. S. District Attorney, John D. Fleming, opened the case for the government.

William Parry turned State's evidence to tell of dividing the money and burying the nuggets and of the agreement to meet again at the World's Fair

200

in 1893. He also testified that Watson and Curtis had discussed killing T. Witcher since Mary Witcher, still fighting for alimony, had promised them half of her legacy if the plan succeeded. Curtis went so far as to procure strychnine from Mrs. McCoy. He poisoned a calf's liver with it, soaked split bullets in it, and went gunning for Witcher. Fortunately for T., he was unsuccessful.

Surprisingly, Charley McCoy was a witness for the prosecution while witnesses for the defense swore that Curtis and Watson had been in Salida the night of the robbery. Mrs. Witcher claimed that she was not at the McCoy ranch the night that the three excapees arrived as Parry had testified.

Watson and Curtis were found guilty of mail robbery and sent to the House of Correction in Detroit for life. A month later, Kid McCoy, Hallock, and the Prices were tried as accessories to the robbery. The first two were discharged for lack of evidence and the others found not guilty. Joe McCoy was also released for lack of evidence. He was returned to Fremont County in April to serve out his sentence for the Arnold murder but was paroled in October, 1893.

Although they had little love for the McCoys, many of the ranchers and other residents were more in sympathy with the robbers than with the railroad. The trains too often killed cattle rightfully grazing on the public domain and then the railroad refused to pay damages. The railroad in turn insisted that ranchers often drove their cattle onto the tracks and then insisted on being paid more than the market value for the victims.

The railroad suffered a greater loss near Fernleaf Gulch when a wreck shattered the quiet Sunday air in August, 1893. It was too late to stop the train by the time the engineer saw the sand washed over the tracks by heavy rain. He jumped but the train turned over on him and killed him.

The McCoys obtained funds in devious ways. Their ranch, a hangout for local boys and unsavory characters, was the scene of many a high stake poker game. These often ended in trouble. About 1895, an old prospector with a string of burros stopped there for awhile and won a considerable amount. He then moved down to camp at a grassy spot below Echo.

With no road on the south side of the river then, his nearest neighbors were the section men working on the railroad tracks across the river. They reported one day that they hadn't seen the Burro Man for several days and that his animals were wandering around. No one knew what ever became of him. Thirty years later a road grader fashioning a barrow pit along the new road near his old camp unearthed an old skeleton. Old timers allowed that this could well have been that of the missing Burro Man.

In April, 1894, A. R. Gumaer and partners formed The Cotopaxi Mining and Milling Company, capitalized for a million dollars, to acquire by discovery, location, and purchase, mines, mining properties, mills, and reduction works. However, the ore, much of it practically pure lead from the mines north of Cotopaxi, proved hard to treat. The zinc ore found there had to be shipped to Kansas since it differed from the kind handled in Canon City. Later, when leasers from Leadville worked Saltiel's mine, they greedily took out the supporting tiers to get the lead in them, leaving a dangerous situation underground.

O. B. Carroll, who ran the Cotopaxi store, finally got a patent on forty acres south of the river. He was accustomed to let his land taxes lapse only to redeem the land at the last moment. It was his son-in-law, Earl Hendricks, operating as Hendricks and Company, who coughed up the necessary consideration of $5.83 in 1903.

Two of Fremont County's leading cattle families merged when Tol Witcher married Minnie Stump in 1896. Minnie's father, William, once worked with Tol's father, John, then settled on Fourmile next to Jesse and Elizabeth Rader. He admired Rader's little girl, Mary Jane, and married her when she grew up. Their daughter Minnie was born in 1876 in Rader's log cabin on Fourmile. By the time Minnie married, Stump had prospered raising cattle in the 7UP brand and had built a fine stone house on the ranch.

T. Witcher's son, Otis, completed his schooling at Beaver Creek and Canon City, then attended the Colorado State Agricultural College at Fort Collins. T. was distressed when Otis came home in 1901 because an epidemic of smallpox closed the school. The huge herds on the rawhiding ranches continued to attract trouble. The entire county was in a turmoil. Another cattle detective had been murdered. Revenge and lynching were on everyone's mind. Killings were expected at any moment. T. had a right to be worried but Otis was not harmed. He married Bertha Medearis in 1902 and subsequently had seven children.

John Witcher remarried in Cripple Creek in 1905. Two years later, Tol, his youngest son, and Walter (called Boss) sold off 3700 head, keeping a herd of 1200. Tol and Dave Walker went to Old Mexico and Arizona in 1912 to buy several thousand head to drive back what was perhaps the last of the big herds in Fremont County. Tol with his older brother, William, ran the 76 Ranch on shares after their father's death. By the time one of Tol's sons, John Stump, grew up, he decided that there was more money in courts than in cattle. Both he and T.'s son, T. Lee, became prominent Canon City lawyers.

In addition to his ranches, T. Witcher owned a quarry near his Cotopaxi place to provide flux for the Pueblo iron furnaces. Later Judge Joseph D. Blunt leased it and sent limestone by rail to Concrete where his brother, Roland, had been foreman. The Portland Cement Company eventually bought the quarry.

With the decline of the cattle industry and only a modest interest in mines, Cotopaxi was a quiet country crossroads when the Rainbow Route highway was completed south of the river in the 1920's. There wasn't much to talk about except the weather. That was sometimes well worth a mention such as when a fifty-four inch snow fell in November, 1931, after ranchers had prayed for moisture. They certainly hated to see it in a form that brought as much hardship as the drought had.

Cora Stout McCrory, who came to Cotopaxi after her marriage in 1896, continued to live there to a great old age, keeping house for herself far into her nineties in the substantial brick home once surrounded by their farm land.

The well kept road along Oak Creek south past the store now run by Grandma McCrory's grandson and his wife, joins the Texas Creek road a short distance above Hillside, making a pleasant circle side trip for today's visitors exploring the beautiful unspoiled ranch country.

FOOTNOTES

1. See Ida Libert Uchill, *Pioneers, Peddlers, and Tsadikim,* pp. 173-189, and Allen D. Breck, *A Centennial History of the Jews in Colorado, 1859-1959,* pp. 74-80.
2. Harry A. Epperson's pamphlet *Colorado As I Saw It* seems to be the most reliable account of this affair. Raymond G. Colwell's "South Park: Colorado History in Miniature" is a repetition of Epperson's story. George G. Everett and Wendell F. Hutchison in *Under the Angel of Shavano,* and Everett's *Cattle Cavalcade of Central Colorado* include added details not always accurate. The interview with T. Lee Witcher, July 30, 1968, reveals his father's version. The interview with Cora Stout McCrory, October 13, 1966, indicates that the published accounts may be prejudiced in favor of one group of ranchers. An unidentified clipping in the Canon City Municipal Museum also states that *The Record* condemned the hangers for their action.
3. The story of the McCoys has been told by Victor Miller in "The McCoy Gang," *Old West,* Summer 1970, pp. 22-25[+], and other articles. Everett's books, Cyrus Wells Shores, *Memoirs of a Lawman,* pp. 277-323, and the interview with T. Lee Witcher filled in additional details. James D. Horan in *The Pinkertons* connects Ed Watkins with the McCoys and "an old miner," p. 378.
4. Letter from Victor Miller, a long-time resident of Cotopaxi, to Riley M. Simrall, [January 1970], and Miller's "The McCoy Gang."
5. There are many slight variations of this story. This version is distilled from those that most generally agree.
6. Horan gives 1884 for this incident. Persons interviewed recall the anecdote but can't date it. Most think it was when Maupin was running for office.

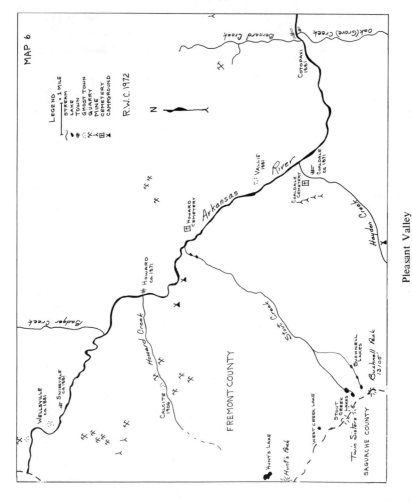

Pleasant Valley

The open valley of the Arkansas in western Fremont County appealed to settlers seeking a respite from the rigors of the mountain mining towns on the upper reaches of the river.

CHAPTER XVI

COALDALE

The Grand Canyon of the Arkansas narrows west of Cotopaxi for a couple of miles and then opens onto the twelve to fifteen mile picturesque Pleasant Valley. Prospectors who came down Badger Creek from wintery Tarryall named the valley when they found it free from snow and ice. Although only the lower end was inhabited as late as October, 1872, when the road survey crew came through, hundreds of acres were fenced and under cultivation producing six foot high wheat or crops of potatoes, corn, turnips, tomatoes, and melons. Many horses and cattle thrived on the range beyond the fields. Camblin and Brothers claimed to have the best spring in the Territory and milked twenty-five cows. When the new road was ready, a stage station served each end of the valley.

The Hayden family was among those who settled there about that time. Lewis Hayden[1] had come from Iowa in 1859 to pioneer on Plum Creek in what became Douglas County. He was flooded out there and moved down to Colorado City to run cattle on what was later known as Broadmoor. He settled in Bijou Basin in later El Paso County about 1863, then sent his eldest son, Frank, back to Indiana to fetch the part of his family he had left there.

Bijou Basin proved an unhappy home for the Haydens. Two of their children died there. Young daughter Mabel's husband of a few months froze to death there. Chauncey grew up with a great fear of Indians after a bunch of red and white renegades stampeding a herd of more than a hundred horses came whooping and hollering around the Hayden cabin, presenting a scene as wild as a Grade B western. The fourteen-year-old saw them coming and galloped to warn the women of the family who were alone at the time. Lewis Hayden, wanting to do his share to rid the country of the red menace, was later one of Chivington's one hundred day volunteers at the time of the Sand Creek slaughter.

When the Haydens forsook the Basin in 1867 to try mining, their daughter, Isabel, stayed with her husband to ranch and raise a family there. Settling near Granite, Lewis Hayden built and operated the first stamp mill there and later extended his mining operation to Washington Gulch. As a Lake County commissioner he felt the ire of the Committee of Safety during the unpleasant "Lake County War"[2] of 1874-1875. It may have been the strong suggestion of that vigilante group that caused him to move his family and settle in Fox Canyon near Hayden Creek.

According to family legend, the Hayden men sometimes hosted the James boys and their less well-known outlaw cousins, the Daltons, at the

205

ranch without revealing their guests' true identity to their wives. A Dalton, possibly "Kid", a cousin of the better known Bob and Frank Dalton, is said to have had a cabin south of the river east of Texas Creek. This may have been after he gave up outlawry to become a peace officer in Pueblo under another name.

Bears were a continuing danger as one unusual tragedy shows. A Cañon City gunsmith sold a gun in 1872 to a stranger who was never seen again.[3] His fate wasn't known until a cowboy happened on the skeletons of a man and a grizzly tangled in mortal embrace, the gun beneath the bones. Experienced bear hunters surmised that the man had wounded the bear and had nearly finished reloading before the bear charged, engaging him in a hand to hand fight to the death.

A bear gave Chauncey his next fright. He was hunting with Dr. J. F. Lewis of Cañon City and Jasper Duckett and his sons. They found a cinnamon mother near her cub which had been caught in a trap. One of the party shot the cub while Duckett aimed at the mother bear. The bullet glanced down her spine. She staggered, then sat up. One young Duckett climbed a quaking aspen so limber that it came over with him. Chaucey fled. As he tried to jump a swampy spot, he landed mid-leg in muck. Dr. Lewis followed him into the mire. The bear grabbed Jasper Duckett's leg and gnawed it, leaving him lame for life. John Duckett beat the bear's head to jelly with his empty gun, saving his father from further damage.

There was some interest in mining as well as agriculture in Pleasant Valley by 1879. Lewis and Lyman Hayden, like others, prospected in their spare time. The growing community in the new mining district of Hayden Creek, which was also known as Pleasant Valley, soon boasted the third largest school district in the county with seventy-two students. Felix Toupain, a French Canadian who had come to farm in 1874, after working as a carpenter in Cañon City for seven years, opened a hotel.

James Polson[4] was another who came to farm. He settled on Fox Creek next to the Haydens. With him was his teenage daughter, Mary, a young son, his second wife, Ragnhild, her teenage daughter, Sarah, and their daughter, Kittie, born in 1874.

Jim Polson had little to say about himself beyond the fact that he had been raised by his Norwegian grandfather and that he had been an assayer at the Denver Mint. It was obvious that he was well educated for he was literate in seven languages. He built a sturdy cabin of large logs which cost thirty-five cents each, a factor limiting its size. The crowding was relieved when Mary and Sarah found work in Nathrop. Enlarged now, the house is still occupied by Kittie's daughter, Stella Denek.

Lewis Hayden quit farming after he was stricken with paralysis in 1880. He bought and developed several pieces of real estate in the valley, then homesteaded near his son Lyman in later Hillside. Lyman had settled there with his bride, Georgia Meyer. Georgia was an accomplished musician. Her parlor boasted a great square piano brought out by wagon.

Joe Stock, the orphaned son of a Methodist minister, lived with the young couple. When Joe grew up, Lyman educated him for the ministry as he had promised the dying father. Joe became like a brother to Stella Hayden, the survivor of twins born at the Hillside ranch in 1875. Stella had a real brother when Louis was born in 1886 at the McClure House in Cañon City where the family had gone to ensure good care for the event.

Although Lyman Hayden long served as treasurer of the Texas Creek School District, he headed a group to petition for a separate district for Hillside. He became president of the new board when the Hillside District was set up in February, 1892. J. O. Mow took on the treasurer's chores. The Texas Creek and Cotopaxi Districts consolidated in 1917 but Hillside maintained its independence for twenty more years before it sought to take advantage of Cotopaxi's better school.

Stella's grandfather, Lewis Hayden, died January 26, 1893. He was buried in the cemetery on the hill across the road from the Hayden ranch. His wife, Margaret, lived in robust health to the age of ninety-one before she was buried beside him. Stella, depressed by the view of the cemetery from her front door, vowed she'd be buried elsewhere when her time came.

Chauncey Hayden married his neighbor, Mary Polson, then teaching school. They raised a family of five at their ranch on the wide flat where Hayden Creek meets the Arkansas. A grove of trees marks the spot where the original two-story log house stood before it burned. The white house that replaced it is still nearby.

Although there was plenty of water for all at first, and so many fish in Hayden and Hamilton Creeks that they could be speared with pitchforks, trouble developed over water rights as more people came in. Feuding over rights kept the community churned up for years.

Charcoal burning was one of the area's early industries. The Harps brothers built seven kilns along Hayden Creek near the Hayden Ranch. They also built the brick store that still stands. Men got a dollar fifty a cord for cutting and a like fee for hauling the wood to the kilns. If they didn't stack it tightly enough in the cordwood piles, the supervisor came along with a twelve pound hammer to tighten the stack before giving credit for it.

Each kiln, from twenty-five to thirty-feet in diameter at the bottom and twenty to twenty-five feet high, held many cords. Turning out a proper load of charcoal required a certain amount of skill and attention.[5] First of all the burner had to build a fire nest of big chunks from the center to the bottom of the door, cover these with small dry pieces of cedar, and put chips on top of that to make a quick fire. He stacked the green wood, preferably piñon, on top of that through the upper doors. He started the fire with an old gunny sack soaked in coal oil. When the fire was under way, he closed the bottom doors and left the green wood to bake like biscuits for three to five days and nights. The resulting charcoal was shipped to smelters at Leadville, Pueblo, and later to Cripple Creek. The charcoal kilns were shut down when the smelters began to use coke.

By 1881, Hayden Creek boasted a post office by the name of Palmer and became the center for mining camps. As usual, the railroad ignored the existing communities by setting up a station called Pleasant Valley five miles to the west. Later the station near Hayden Creek was called Pleasanton. Although there was no regular conveyance serving the settlement, traffic passed through when the Hayden Pass Road was completed by Toupain and his partners. O. B. Carroll, the Cotopaxi storekeeper, opened a second shop in the store building. He served as the Palmer postmaster for the population of fifty. The 1885 brand book lists Lewis Hayden and his son Chauncey as stock breeders with the 4H brand (long coveted by the 4 H Club). Among others, J. A. Cramlet, W. A. Hendricks, and Albert Philipp had also entered the thriving cattle business.

The population doubled in the next five years. Carroll's daughter married I. Earl Hendricks, son of his partner, W. A. Hendricks. This no doubt accounts for the fact that the postoffice became Hendricks instead of Palmer. W. A. ran the store and Earl was the postmaster. The community acquired its present name of Coaldale when it became a busy coal town about three years later. The Portland Cement Company still later developed a large open pit gypsum operation which continues to supply the company.

In addition to ranching, Albert Philipp made a tidy living for his family from saloons and sawmills. He was often suspected of getting prospects to put up money for sawmills, then using the cash for schemes of his own. Perhaps prejudice against this Jewish family sharpened the criticism of their ill-kept ranch adjoining the Polsons' place and inspired the local youngsters to call Albert Philipp, "Old Swiney."

Philipp was responsible for one of the many feuds over water rights. He tried to appropriate Polson's right after he let his own right revert to the government. Tempers flared. There were threats to kill before a date for a hearing in Cañon City was set. Polson's neighbor at Stout Creek, William Stout, came down to accompany Jim Polson to the hearing. He found Polson suffering so severely from a rupture that Jim decided not to contest Philipp's claim. As a result, the Polson property has since had less water than it might have.

Two other early ranch families were united when Lyman Hayden's daughter, Stella, married Thomas G. Balman in 1896 at the Hayden Ranch near Hillside. Young Tom Balman seemed destined to know the sting of untimely death as had his mother. He and Stella lost their first baby and, later, their other son, Douglas. A born rancher, Douglas at twenty-two was riding for cattle on the Price ranch when his horse threw him, then dragged him until his handsome features were nearly beyond recognition.

Tom and Stella's daughter, Evelyn, grew up to marry Leon Hook. Today, the combined and augmented Balman-Hook ranch, ranging in both Fremont and Custer Counties, is one of the more notable ranches in all Colorado, fulfilling the vision Thomas Drake Balman had of the area as a great cattle country.

But when Tom and Stella were newlyweds, ranchers north and south of the Arkansas continued to have trouble with cattle rustlers. The McCoys were under suspicion again by 1897. Late that year, the Fremont County Cattlegrowers Protective Association hired Charles Withers, a noted cowboy and Pinkerton detective, to find out whose meat it was that the McCoys sold, after O. B. Carroll complained that he was missing some cattle. The stories the old timers tell agree on little of what happened next.

Evidently Whitey Withers set up a cow camp on McCoy Park and returned there one day to find it torn up and the groceries scattered. He at once suspected the McCoys. Another source claims that McCoy had a corral there for holding and butchering Carroll's cattle and that Withers tore it down. Withers moved into a room behind the Coaldale store, then run by young Earl Hendricks, after the camp was wrecked.

On Christmas night, 1901, he asked Earl if he wanted to ride down to Cotopaxi on horseback with him. When they got there, Withers said he wanted to go north of town on business and that Earl should wait for a half hour for him. Whitey ostensibly started north but circled back down the trail along the river to the McCoys' house. He fired three shots from the hill behind the house into McCoy's bedroom. He hit the bed but no body. By mere chance, McCoy was in another room and escaped harm. The McCoys soon tracked Withers across the river and accused him of the shooting. Charley Gilray, then twenty, had made friends with Withers, with whom he often rode. He always claimed that the McCoys shot up their own place as an excuse to get Withers.

Charley planned to go to a dance at Barnes City with Whitey after riding the range with him on the twenty-eighth. He cleaned up, had supper, and put on his glad rags but when he went to meet Withers, Whitey claimed he'd forgotten the dance and had turned out his horse. Gilray offered to catch the animal while Whitey washed up, but he declined. Perhaps he felt that a dance would be an unhealthy place for a man accused of shooting at a McCoy.

He might have been safer there. Gilray had barely reached Barnes City when a rider came in with the news that Withers had been shot. Gilray galloped back to Coaldale to his friend's side. He was too late to help. The store was locked.

Charley could see Whitey through the window. He lay on the floor, dead. The crowd outside was saying that Street McCoy and George Mow, who were proprietors of a house of ill-repute across the present highway from the Texas Creek trading post, had lost at freezeout and had thus been elected to silence Withers because he had caught the McCoys butchering beef that didn't belong to them. Mrs. McCoy had proposed that the best way to keep him quiet was to shoot him dead.

Street and George had tied their horses to the hitching rack and entered the store. Earl Hendricks was behind the counter, Chauncey Hayden and Withers were standing near the stove. Withers had his thumbs hooked under his broad suspenders in a characteristic pose when Street fired. The bullet cut off one of Whitey's thumbs and entered his chest. He ran to his bachelor quarters at the rear of the store for his six-shooter and came back shooting. One bullet passed through Mow's hat and cut a part in his hair. Withers fell as he fired his second shot. That bullet went through the counter where Earl had ducked. Only a notebook he had slipped into his shirt pocket saved his life.

The two assassins were arrested, released on bond, but rearrested when they were caught carrying firearms. The Fremont County Cattlemen's Protective Association, at a special meeting in February, 1902, agreed to raise an assessment of five hundred dollars to prosecute the pair. They were sentenced to fifteen to twenty-five years and sent to the pen in June. Neither sentence was carried out. Street died in prison of disease contracted by frequently patronizing his own business. The very day he died, Governor Peabody signed a pardon to allow him to go home for Christmas. Mow, the renegade son of a good Wet Mountain Valley family, was paroled in December, 1904, then was granted a full pardon in 1916 by which time the gang had scattered.

At the time of the shooting, Barnes City[6] was a popular mountain resort offering a large hall for dancing, fine food and liquor. Summer picnics were a specialty. Fourth of July celebrations provided many athletic and drilling contests, horse racing, and high stake wagering. The site, about three miles up Hayden Creek from Coaldale, was promoted by two men who arranged high grade ore from Cripple Creek at strategic spots easily seen by men with more money than brains. When the ore was assayed with astonishing results, the suckers, backed by an English syndicate, spent thousands of dollars driving a tunnel which produced nothing. The two original promoters also built several good houses and the resort. They made more money from them than the miners derived from the mine.

There were as many as three hundred homes in Barnes City at one time but when work on the mine stopped and the resort closed, the town became a ghost. Many of the houses were carted off to other locations. Later, those that remained were used as summer homes. Now the spot is popular for camping and summer cabins are being built.

Things had quieted down around Coaldale by the time Chauncey Hayden's daughter, Laurel (always known as Girlie), married Walter Runyan whose family homesteaded on neighboring Hamilton Creek about 1904. Girlie graduated from Salida Academy and taught school at Hillside for awhile. Descendants of the various Haydens and their in-laws still live in that part of the county. Others turned to the cities to engage in the professions.

The Philipp ranch was quite a show place by the time middle-aged Martha, the only heir, inherited it. She disappeared under mysterious circumstances many months later. Although the river was dragged and the fields were searched no trace of her was found until spring when her body turned up in the river. Suspicious neighbors felt that it hadn't been thrown into the water until after the search had eased for they had frequently seen her dog sniffing about her field as though she might be there.

Only occasionally has crime marred the placidity of life here in recent years. The small store building yet stands, the gypsum operation continues, and Stella Denek still runs the landmark ranch virtually single-handed. Change comes slowly to Coaldale.

FOOTNOTES

1. The Hayden family information is derived from interviews with Dr. Harold C. Runyan of Colorado Springs, great grandson of Lewis Hayden, and with Stella Denek of Coaldale, granddaughter of James Polson. Everett's books and John Ophus, "The Lake County War, 1874-75," *The Colorado Magazine*, 47: 119-135, Spring 1970, help establish dates.
2. Ophus, *op. cit.*, gives a full account of this fighting and feuding over water rights.
3. Julia Newell Chappell, "The Canon City Museum," *The Colorado Magazine*, 8:74-77, March, 1931.
4. Interview with Stella Denek, May 10, 1970.
5. Interview with Clyde Mitchell, October 13, 1966, who burned charcoal at the Howard kilns 1910-1912, furnished the description of this process. See also Everett and Hutchison's *Under the Angel of Shavano*, p. 187.
6. While Fremont County families recall something of Barnes City, Everett gives a detailed account in his *Cattle Cavalcade in Central Colorado*, p. 193. However, none of the recollections can be counted on for total accuracy.

William Stout

Elvira Stout

William Stout brought his wife, Elvira, and their children by wagon through roadless territory to early settle near Stout Creek. *Courtesy Ella Stout Dunlap.*

CHAPTER XVII

HOWARD AND BEYOND

A man named Wasson once homesteaded where the river road crossed to the north side of the flat now known as Vallie. He built a fine two story log house before he realized that there was no water available and had to abandon his investment. For years the deserted house a couple of miles west of Hayden Creek, with legends of hauntings, stood to tell of his folly.

When the tracks reached the spot, Vallie became a lively railroad town with several families, a section house and a depot. A signpost alone now marks it.

Forty-year-old William Stout[1] and his twenty-eight-year-old wife, Elvira, were among those who headed West after the Civil War. They left Tennessee and stopped to raise two crops in Indian Territory before continuing. Because of Indian trouble, they were compelled to wait until others joined them and the government supplied an escort.

After the sixty-family train disbanded in eastern Colorado Territory, Stout invested his last nine dollars in a sack of flour and, with only thirty-five cents in shinplasters left in his pocket, headed for Fairplay. There he dug ditches while his wife cooked and washed for the miners to earn cash.

Duckett, who had prospected in the Wet Mountain Valley and along the Arkansas, told the Stouts about the fertile stretch along the river. Stout packed up his family as soon as he could, went down Ute Pass to Colorado City, and followed the tortuous route to Texas Creek. He set off cross country from there since there was not yet a road along the river. The party had to lower the wagons with block and tackle to cross the deepest gulches.

When they reached the creek now named for Stout, they stopped near where Jonah Paregrine, a Welshman, had already settled. Stout immediately built a log shanty at the edge of a huge virgin forest to house his family for the winter. He left a cut for a fireplace, but while he was gathering rocks for it, he saw the tracks of a large elk, grabbed his gun, and went after it. He was gone five days with little more than a couple of biscuits to live on, leaving his wife and three little ones in the unprotected cabin. His eldest daughter, Florence, born in Tennessee on the day of Lincoln's Gettysburg address, had just turned nine. Belle and Foster were younger. Stout, a true hunter, brought home the elk, the only one seen in those parts that winter.

Stout turned to choosing a permanent location once his family was sheltered and fed. He selected a spot near the mouth of the creek and

213

Stout Homestead
William Stout named the Twin Sisters that form the backdrop for his unfulfilled
dream of a dwelling. *Photo by the author.*

Stout Creek School
Built about 1906, this sturdy building was in use for fifty years until the District
reluctantly consolidated with Cotopaxi, Coaldale and Hillside. *Photo by the author.*

214

built a more substantial cabin, roofed with handhewn shingles. He pre-empted a homestead, secured water rights, put in an orchard, and brought in wellbred Devon cattle to thrive on the lush hay. He gave the name Twin Sisters to the two peaks that embrace Stout Lakes above his place. In those days, the mountains were covered with snow from October to midsummer and the creeks ran full.

Traffic from the mines along the new road brought additional settlers to the west end of Pleasant Valley which was ringed by high hills of white volcanic tuff capped with lava. Newt West settled on the creek east of Stout and gave his name to that stream. Rube Hargis, who had traveled to Fairplay with the Stouts, took up the place where Stout had built his first cabin.

Five-year-old Foster Stout died a month before his sister, Cora, was born in the hilltop cabin in 1875. Harvey, Ella, and Irwin were born there in succeeding years. Stout, who had taught school in Tennessee, wanted his children to be educated. Florence and Belle boarded at Hayden Creek the first summer for the three months that school was held. Stout helped organize School District #13 for Stout Creek and built the first school-house in later Howard across the river from his home, opposite where the Howard Cemetery now is. There Mrs. Adams taught three Grays, two Stouts, and two Wests remote from supervision of the County Superintend-ent. His required visits took five days round trip by horseback or buggy from Cañon City via the Copper Gulch Road.

As more families took up small farms, this part of Pleasant Valley took the name of Howard for the pioneer, John Howard, who had settled on Howard Creek. Many irrigated twenty-acre farms flourished around Howard as the farmers found a profitable market in the mining towns. The kilns, a few still in good condition, produced a good supply of piñon charcoal. Fortunately for the forests, coke replaced charcoal when large corporations replaced the small smelter operators.

Howard was soon aware of the handsome, college educated young man who took up a ranch on Badger Creek. Ed Watkins made many loyal friends in the town. Although he was the star performer in the literary society and could recite "The Charge of the Light Brigade" in a way to thrill his audience, he was equally admired as a crack shot who could shoot the eye of a rabbit as far as he could see the rabbit.

Stout, an honest and educated man himself, always thought that Watkins would never steal and that he had been framed. Many in Howard agreed and were staunchly on his side during the Mulock-Watkins feud. They believed that he was the victim of his associates and paid the penalty for them when he was strung up in Cañon City.

The Stouts felt differently about John Davis who came about the same time, after a short stay at Hayden Creek. They mistrusted him as soon as

215

he moved in to settle above them on Stout Creek. He had been with Sherman's march to the sea and let everybody know it. The Stouts considered him a killer which he was. He shot a boy in the Howard railroad station after a drunken brawl in Vallie. He threatened the people at the depot until they promised not to talk and then lit out for New Mexico. Neighbors took care of his family until he dared return several years later.

The advent of the railroad caused a great deal of excitement. Stout and his neighbors got out ties from the big timber. He was with the crew on the tie drive which guided the ties down the river with prods. Howard was as lively as any end of track town while the railroad was building. The cars were soon bringing people from Cotopaxi to Howard for parties and dances. Of course, like other towns on the D & RG, Howard was some distance from the station named Pleasant Valley by the railroad.

After the grading began, the children could hardly wait to see the wonder that their elders said would travel on the tracks. Cora Stout remembered into her nineties how disappointed she was when the first train arrived. It was a work train bearing the track crew and was far from her expectations. If that was what "riding the cars" would be like, she didn't think much of it.

Many more settlers came when the railroad was completed. Soon there was need for another school. This log structure south of the river above the present day motel was used for church services too. One evening two young ladies on their way to service attempted to cross the bridge under construction just below Stout Creek. They laughed and joked as they clambered across the unfloored bridge until one slipped and fell. The other screamed but no one was near enough to help. Her friend drowned as she struggled to return safely to the river bank. An iron bridge replaced this one in 1904. It in turn was recently replaced after a Texas couple established a trailer resort on an old farm north of the river.

Now and then there was a camp meeting under canvas. William Stout would do his share by killing a beef to help feed the crowd gathered to get religion. He was prosperous enough to consider building a fine stone house for his family. Arch, Tim, and John Allen laid up the stone in a big grove of cottonwoods. Jonah Paregrine, a good carpenter, had the roof on and was starting to finish the interior when he fell and could no longer work. While the house was as he'd left it, a flood came roaring down the gully, poured through the deep windows on one side and on out the door on the other. The well built foundation held but the premises were a mess. Although Stout dug a ditch to divert any future flood the house remained unfinished when he moved his family into it in 1887. The handsome structure, looking like a bit of old New England from the highway, isn't finished yet and probably never will be.

Charcoal Kilns at Howard

These kilns produced charcoal until 1904, then were modified in 1909 for use as coke ovens and so used until 1919. *Photo by the author.*

By 1883, the IM ranch established by Ira Mulock and his three sons at the head of Badger Creek was running eight thousand head on range extending from Cañon City to Buena Vista. After Gumaer acquired it to run it as the Boston Land and Cattle Company, Fremont County cattlemen thought his move was morally wrong even if it might be legally right. For that and other reasons, they didn't enjoy working with him. Gumaer in turn complained that his men did all the work for the roundups and that he was the only one who had to furnish pastures. He probably had that impression because he attended only the roundups on his own range.

Gumaer decided he'd be ahead rounding up his own cattle. He bought a large yellow paneled circus wagon and had The Boston Land and Cattle Company lettered on it in white.[2] It carried all the comforts of home for use in a tent so huge it took eleven cowboys to set it up.

Since Gumaer would't cooperate with the other cattlemen, they didn't give him any help. He soon discovered how vast the open range really was. Running his own roundup cost more in cash and loss of calves than his contribution to the community roundup. It cost him something in horses, too. He shipped his hands a carload of mares, something no respectable cowboy cared to ride. The boys managed to ditch those mounts in a washout on the IM range.

Gumaer reported only a thousand head for assessment purposes to the Fremont County Cattlemen's Association, although most members thought that The Boston Land and Cattle Company ran six times that many. It was probably common practice to shave the figure for Tol Witcher reported three thousand, T. Witcher one thousand, and Stump only five hundred when their neighbors' informal estimates were higher than that. It was considered poor manners to ask or answer direct questions concerning the number of cattle a man owned. The quality of the cattle varied. Most were Mexican dogies and Texas longhorns crossed with Shorthorn, Durham type bulls.

The cattle that grazed on Cameron Mountain were displaced for awhile. In 1897, Derius Patro, a tie hack working on the wooded eastern slope, noted some float and had it assayed. That led to the staking of the Independence, Cameron, Golden Eagle, and other claims. A village grew up and soon the *Whitehorn News* was being published.

Two mines shipped to the smelter while six others hauled ore to the Whitehorn Mill. In January, 1899, The Cameron Mines, Land and Tunnel Company platted a proper town which formally became Whitehorn, named after a civil engineer, assayer, and always accomodating grubstaker, Arthur L. Whitehorn. This led to a surge in building of all sorts including the grading of streets and laying of sidewalks.

When the District Court ordered the local children to attend school in Fremont County instead of convenient Chaffee, a group in 1900 wrote a

View up Howard Creek

Calcite, a limestone quarry town, abandoned about 1930, lay three miles up this valley from Howard. *Photo by the author.*

petition on stationery of the Miner's Hotel for a thirty-seven square mile district around Whitehorn. This was granted, only to be abolished in 1909 when there were no longer any school age children in the area.

A 1902 fire razed twenty buildings before the bucket bridade could be effective. But the place was soon rebuilt. A stage from Salida brought passengers, freight, and mail. The post office was discontinued in 1918 when mining had all but ceased. There was nothing left of the place but a vestige of rotting sidewalks when Cecil R. Miller of Cincinnati bought the townsite of 332 acres for $1550 at a tax sale.

In May, 1899, two of Gumaer's cowboys drove thirty-two purebred Hereford bulls from Haver Station of the Colorado Midland to the IM ranch, a two-day trip. The rest of the range then was covered with longhorned, longlegged, longbodied, and longwinded wild old steers that were hard to round up and dangerous to rope. Five-year-olds and older running in bunches used all their guile to outwit the cowboys.

Gumaer, always willing to grubstake homesteaders and to foreclose when they couldn't make it, once acquired a bunch of dairy cows. It took his cowboys four days to drive them from Florence to the IM spread, until then never burdened with milch cows except for one gentle Jersey which gave them cream for their coffee.

The Boston Land and Cattle Company owned about seven different brands by the time Johnny Hyssong, who had earlier spied on Watkins for the ranchers, became foreman. The first uniform bunch of whitefaces to appear on the western Fremont County range carried Mrs. Gumaer's ELG.

A severe winter followed by a dry summer compounded by a money panic spelled the end of the county's range cattle industry. Edward Levitt, then Gumaer's foreman, drove some twelve hundred head of IM cattle suffering from the cold to Adobe Park where he fed them hay. The Boston Land and Cattle Company was the last big company to operate in the western end of the county.

After Gumaer's death, Cox and Smith bought the cattle and land from the estate. Hyssong again became foreman. The outfit became a steer operation for which the range was not suited. Times had changed. It was no longer practical to operate a ranch on scattered 160 acre claims taken up around the best water when homesteaders broke up the previously open range with desert, timber, and stone claims. The Forest Service acquired title to much of the summer range and then, finally, the Taylor Grazing Act, with its provision for fencing, put the final strokes on the old cattle picture. Today the IM ranch headquarters house stands vacant and the little remaining land carries a small herd of cattle in the summer.

The quiet little farm community of Howard,[3] where four families out of five worked twenty acres or less, had a small mining boom during the first decade of this century. The CF & I, the Colorado Cement Company, and other companies took coal and limestone from nearby claims. Howard's charcoal kilns, busy until 1904, were used as coke ovens from 1909 until 1919.

About 1906, the residents of Howard clamored for a new school on Howard Creek. Those near Stout Creek wanted the new building there. When William Stout heard the hassle going on at the village store, he offered to give land for a new schoolhouse. Howard then cut off from the Stout Creek District and built its own school. Directors of the Stout Creek District built the brick building which still stands near Ella Stout Dunlap's quonset where she lived after 1947 when her husband had to quit working. They had to sell the home place with its stately unfinished stone house.

Twenty pupils attended the brick school when the Dunlaps' four went there. Later, for twenty five years, the settlement around Stout Creek fought consolidation with Cotopaxi. The parents felt that the small school was like having a private tutor for their children. They couldn't see the advantage of sending them as far as Cotopaxi to attend a slightly larger school. District #13 had always been one of the wealthier ones and could afford fine teachers. In the end, Stout Creek gave in to consolidation with Cotopaxi, Coaldale, and Hillside to become part of West Fremont District #51. About 1960, Howard and Wellsville joined the Salida School District in Chaffee County.

There were many freights and eight passenger trains a day through Howard in the early days of this century. Some were express trains which didn't stop. One evening, Bert Kelso, a dairyman, was bringing in a bunch of dogies from Texas. He and some others were in the caboose of the train which carried the cattle. He had worked hard and was played out. The others left the train. When he didn't follow, they called. He roused himself and sleepily climbed down on the wrong side right in front of a fast train. The engineer recognized him but couldn't stop in time to avoid killing him.

There was another round of ranch trouble in 1913. Watson J. Tunnison, an unsuccessful New York produce dealer, homesteaded in Gribble Park and started a cow ranch. He was a hard worker who also had an interest in a mine above Badger Creek. His nearest neighbor was George C. Ansty who once studied for the ministry. He had a home west of Howard as well as the homestead adjoining Tunnison's.

Ansty wasn't popular with the cowmen. As early as 1909, the Fremont County Cattlegrower's Protective Association advised him that he wouldn't be allowed to take part in the local roundup because of his unfriendly conduct toward members during the previous winter.

However, in 1913, Ansty agreed to serve as Tunnison's rep at the roundup while Tunnison worked at his mine. Tunnison's discovery that one of Ansty's cowboys had put his boss's earmark on Tunnison's cattle led to a dispute about fencing— and probably other matters. As a result, Tunnison shot and killed Ansty.

T. Lee Witcher, by then a lawyer, represented Ansty's interests. The many witnesses revealed that both sides showed pure cussedness in their relations with one another. Nevertheless, since one witness had actually seen Ansty defiling Tunnison's well and because the shooting occurred on Tunnison's property, he was acquitted. He took the precaution of moving to South America.

Howard's small farms began to follow the wider trend. They were gradually absorbed by larger ones which in turn reverted to ranch land. Now, as the pressure of population is felt in other parts, this scenic stretch along the Arkansas is sought for vacation homes where the 6700 foot altitude provides pleasant summer temperatures. Some holiday homes have appeared along the highway but more are tucked away along the creeks. So many Kansans come to the new summer colony up Stout Creek that the natives refer to it as little Wichita. Howard itself was bypassed when the highway was moved south of the river.

During Howard's brief mining boom, the CF & I opened a large limestone quarry about three miles up Howard Creek to provide flux for its blast furnaces in Pueblo. Before long, the community of two hundred became Calcite, complete with a railroad, school, post office, and the inevitable company store. There the kids from Howard enjoyed the first picture shows they had ever seen.

Many millions of tons of limestone at fifty cents a ton were shipped from Calcite before the company shut down the quarry about 1930. The houses were moved to other locations and the railroad branch was abandoned in 1936. The quarry was worked briefly by a private contractor but Calcite became a ghost town.

The Grand Canyon of the Arkansas narrows for a couple of miles northwest of Howard. Beyond this highwalled, winding stretch hot springs emerge on a broad gravel flat on the north side. Here Max Zeise took up land and ran his JOZ cattle. He was perhaps one of the Swiss tie hacks who settled there when the D & RG had a sidetrack and section house at the lower end of the flat. Or he may have been farming at the lower hot springs before the railroad arrived. At any rate, he had a dairy there on the old county road when the place was known as Swissvale. It was a railroad stop from 1880 to 1889 although there was no community as such.

By the time the highway was moved south of the river, Swissvale was marked only by a small railroad signal house, some old foundations, and traces of the old wagon road. It had almost lost its name too by the time Reece and June Johnson bought a little café, a small filling station, and four tumbledown cabins near the highway in 1960. The highway department remarked the location at their request and put it back on the map.

At Swissvale

A modern chalet perches high on the south bank of the Arkansas River. *Photo by the author.*

The Arkansas was considered one of the finest fishing streams in the State until mud and minerals which washed into the stream at Leadville drove the fish out. Not until the mining activity lessened did the fishing improve. Stocked by the State, it now provides pleasure for anglers the year around.

Game fared little better than the fish. As early as 1905, when Fremont County was home to fewer than 20,000 persons, thoughtful citizens deplored the situation. "Destructive in his instincts, the white man began a war of extermination on coming into the valley and most of the game was in a few years either killed off or driven into more inaccessible regions." Today each hunting season sees an endless stream of pickup campers pulling four wheel drive vehicles to carry in- and out-of-state hunters ever closer to their quarry in the name of sport.

A short distance above Swissvale, Wellsville Springs carry so much lime in solution that they mark the river bank where they emerge. These hot springs deposit lime in the form of calcareous tufa that builds up in domes around the springs. Old masses of tufa, nearly pure carbonate of lime, were quarried near here for use in refining beet sugar and as flux for iron furnaces. Opened by the American Smelting and Refining Company, this quarry operated long before the one at Calcite. Arrowheads found in the area indicate that Ute and Blackfoot Indians made use of the springs and hunted nearby.

George Wells was the first to settle at Wellsville, twenty-nine miles from Cañon City. There was a post office as early as 1881, although there was never a large permanent population. A pleasure resort centered around a large hot spring used as a bathing pool attracted crowds of visitors for several decades. The old stage road passed above the pool and the tall house near it. Nearby, the Captain claim, located in 1881, showed an interesting mix of magnetic iron, copper, gold, and silver ores.

During the mining boom, V. C. Davenport developed the resort into a popular place for picnics and outings. There was a hotel, a dance hall, and a baseball field. Lodges and other such organizations could rent the place for special occasions. Fourth of July might see as many as a thousand people enjoying the facilities and foot and horse races.

Around 1920, Frank Negri bought the 160 acre Knapp placer there for about $6000 and operated the quarry until he accidently blew himself up. He set a bomb to punish thieves who persisted in stealing gasoline from the tank at his quarry. He inadvertently tripped the trap himself and died as a result. Bid in at auction by the Holly Sugar Corporation in 1932, it is now operated by the U. S. Soil Conditioning Corporation.

Travertine marble was once also quarried in the area. There is still a large quantity of black, blue and green mottled Serpentine marble awaiting a profitable demand.

There is little activity and no real community along the western edge of Fremont County. But while the western third of the county is poor in population, it is rich in other ways. The Sangre de Cristos forming the western boundary provide beauty to be explored within the San Isabel National Forest where pack and foot trails lead to gem-like high lakes. For the less intrepid, old ranch roads wind through mountain ranch country.

FOOTNOTES

1. Interviews with Ella Stout Dunlap, October 12, 1966, and Cora Stout McCrory, October 13, 1966.
2. Epperson, *op. cit,* p. 45, attributes this gaucherie to Gumaer, McConnell, *op. cit.,* p. 242, to Mulock.
3. Interview with Roland Willoughby, October 12, 1966. Clyde Mitchell and Denzel and Marcheta Goodwin, October 13, 1966, furnished further information about the area.

CHAPTER XVIII

FREMONT COUNTY'S FUTURE

The jealous territorialism, all too typical of small towns everywhere, plus a stubborn resistance to change, long made it difficult for Fremont County residents to look to the future with imagination. Their enthusiasm for the status quo didn't diminish until high powered developers in nearby areas began to wreak havoc in the name of progress.

A subtle shift in attitude encouraged cooperation to replace antagonism. Communities began as never before to exhibit a willingness to work together to preserve their favored scenic and climatic location and to treasure their long legacy of history, taking pride in being the longest settled area in the entire State of Colorado.

Regardless of what picture present day puffery presents of the area, the vast chasm of the Royal Gorge remains the magnet that most often first draws visitors to the region. Once the barrier that deterred exploration and settlement then later offered a challenge to engineers and engines, the Grand Canyon of the Arkansas continues to serve as an inspiration for all who visit or reside round about it.

The time is ripe for a new generation of Resurrectionists whose concern is much the same as those of over a hundred years ago—sound growth of the region and a good life for their families—to lead the Gate City and all of Fremont County to complete realization of its early recognized potential.

* * *

BIBLIOGRAPHY

Anderson, George L.: "The Canon City or Arkansas Valley Claim Club, 1860-1862," *The Colorado Magazine,* 16:201-210, November, 1939.

Athearn, Robert G.: *Rebel of the Rockies, a History of the Denver & Rio Grande Western Railroad.* New Haven, Yale University Press, c1962. 395 pp.

Black, Robert C. III: *Island in the Rockies; the History of Grand County, Colorado, to 1930.* Boulder, Colorado, Pruett Publishing Company for the Grand County Pioneer Society, c1969. 435 pp.

Block, Ben A., comp.: *Colorado, Its Resources, Its Men . . . a Lesson in Prosperity.* Published by authority of James B. Orman, Governor, for free distribution at the Pan-American Exposition, Buffalo, N.Y., June 3, 1901.

Bradley, Glenn Danford: *The Story of the Santa Fe.* Boston, The Gorham Press, c1920. 288 pp.

Breck, Allen D.: *A Centennial History of the Jews of Colorado, 1859-1959.* Denver, Colorado, The Hirschfeld Press, c1961. 360 pp.

Byers, William N., ed.: *Encyclopedia of Biography of Colorado.* Chicago, The Century Publishing and Engraving Company, 1901. 477 pp.

Cafky, Morris: "The Railroad That Couldn't Make Up Its Mind," *Trains, the Magazine of Railroading,* 26:38-46, August, 1966.

Cafky, Morris: *Rails Around Gold Hill.* Denver, Colorado, Rocky Mountain Railroad Club, c1955. 463 pp.

Campbell, Marius R.: *Guidebook of the Western U.S.; Part E, the Denver & Rio Grande Western Route.* (U. S. Geological Survey Bulletin 707) Washington, D.C., Government Printing Office, 1922. 266 pp.

"Canon City", *Facts,* 4:9-11, June 10, 1899.

Canon City, Colorado. Canon City Chamber of Commerce, n.d. n.p.

"Canon City Illustrated," supplement to *The Canon City Record,* November 23, 1905. n.p.

Carter, Harvey Lewis: *'Dear Old Kit,' the Historical Christopher Carson; with a New Edition of the Carson Memoirs.* Norman, University of Oklahoma Press, c1968. 250 pp.

Carter, Harvey Lewis: "Tom Tobin," *The American West,* 2:91-94, Fall 1965.

Chalfont, Harry: "The Life and Times of Roland and Elizabeth Blunt," *The Colorado Magazine,* 40:81-91, April, 1963.

Chapman, Arthur: *The Story of Colorado, Out Where the West Begins.* Chicago, Rand McNally and Company., c1924. 270 pp.

Chapman, Joe and Dinah Jo Chapman, eds.: *The Royal Gorge.* Canon City, Colorado, Royal Gorge Company, c1965. 36 pp.

Chappell, Julia Newell: "The Canon City Museum," *The Colorado Magazine,* 8:74-77, March, 1931.

Colorado. Mineral Resources Board: *Mineral Resources of Colorado.* Denver, Colorado, 1947. 547 pp.

Colorado State Business Directory and Annual Register for 1878. Denver, Colorado, J. A. Blake, [1878]. (Also subsequent state and local directories.)

Colwell, Raymond G.: "South Park: Colorado History in Miniature," *Denver Westerners Monthly Roundup,* 12:5-16, September, 1956.

Conard, Howard Louis: *"Uncle Dick" Wootton, the Pioneer Frontiersman of the Rocky Mountain Region: an Account of the Adventures and Thrilling Experiences of the Most Noted American Hunter, Trapper, Guide, Scout, and Indian Fighter Now Living.* Chicago, W. E. Dibble and Company, c1890. 472 pp.

Cook, D. J.: *Hands Up; or, Twenty Years of Detective Life in the Mountains and on the Plains.* Norman, University of Oklahoma Press, c1958. 319 pp.

Cruzen, Bob: "Florence Prepares for Future with New Filtration Plant," *Colorado Municipalities,* 9:244-245[+], September, 1963.

Davis, Clyde Brion: *The Arkansas.* New York, Farrar and Rinehart, c1940. 340 pp.

Dunham, Harold H.: "Coloradans and the Maxwell Grant," *The Colorado Magazine,* 32:131-145, April, 1955.

Epperson, Harry A.: *Colorado as I Saw It.* [Privately printed? 1943?] 137 pp.

Everett, George G.: *Cattle Cavalcade in Central Colorado.* Denver, Colorado, Golden Bell Press, c1966. 446 pp.

Everett, George G.: *The Cavalcade of Railroads in Central Colorado.* Denver, Golden Bell Press, c1966. 235 pp.

Everett, George G. and Wendell F. Hutchison: *Under the Angel of Shavano.* Denver, Colorado, Golden Bell Press, c1963. 526 pp.

Fossett, Frank: *Colorado, Its Gold and Silver Mines, Farms and Stock Ranges, and Health and Pleasure Resorts; Tourist's Guide to the Rocky Mountains.* 2nd. ed. New York, C. G. Crawford, 1880. 592 pp.

Gannett, Henry: *A Gazetteer of Colorado.* (Bulletin 291, Series F, Geography 51, Department of the Interior, U. S. Geological Survey) Washington, D. C., Government Printing Office, 1906. 185 pp.

Goetzmann, William H.: *Exploration and Empire; the Explorer and the Scientist in the Winning of the American West.* New York. Alfred A. Knopf, 1966. 656 pp.

Grant, Blanche C.: *When Old Trails Were New, the Story of Taos.* New York, The Press of the Pioneers, Inc., c1934. 344 pp.

Griswold, Don and Jean Griswold: *Colorado's Century of "Cities."* Privately printed, c1958. 307 pp.

Hafen, LeRoy R.: *Colorado, The Story of a Western Commonwealth.* Denver, Colorado, The Peerless Publishing Company, c1933. 328 pp.

Hafen, LeRoy R.: "The Coming of the Automobile and Improved Roads to Colorado," *The Colorado Magazine,* 8:1-16, January, 1931.

Hafen, LeRoy R.: "The Counties of Colorado: a History of Their Creation and the Origin of Their Names," *The Colorado Magazine,* 8:48-60, March, 1931.

Hafen, LeRoy R., ed.: *The Mountain Men and the Fur Trade of the Far West; Biographical Sketches of the Participants by Scholars of the Subject and with Introductions by the Editor.* Glendale, California, The Arthur H. Clark Company, c1965. 10 vols.

Hafen, LeRoy.: "When Was Bent's Fort Built?" *The Colorado Magazine,* 31:105-119, April, 1954.

Hall, Mabel: *Stella Hayden Balman: a "Rush to the Rockies" Centennial Story.* Privately printed, c1959. 27 pp.

Hall, Mabel: *Story of Phantom Canyon.* Privately printed, c1963. 46 pp.

The Hardscrabble Irrigation District in Fremont and Custer Counties, Colorado: *Prospectus, a Proposition to Bond Investors.* The company, November, 1912. n.p.

Henderson, Junius and others: *Colorado: Short Studies of Its Past and Present.* Boulder, Colorado, University of Colorado, c1927. 202 pp.

Hill, Alice Polk: *Tales of the Colorado Pioneers.* Denver, Colorado, Pierson and Gardner, 1884. 319 pp.

History of the Arkansas Valley, Colorado. Chicago, O. L. Baskin and Company, 1881. 889 pp.

Horan, James D.: *The Pinkertons: the Detective Dynasty That Made History.* New York, Crown Publishers, Inc., c1967. 564 pp.

Horgan, Paul: *Great River; the Rio Grande in North American History.* New York, Holt, Rinehart and Winston, c1954. 1020 pp.

Hurd, C. W.: *Bent's Stockade, Hidden in the Hills.* Las Animas, Colorado, Bent County Democrat, c1960. 92 pp.

Jackson, Donald: "Zebulon M. Pike 'Tours' Mexico," *The American West,* 3:67-71[+], Spring 1966.

Jones, Charles Irving: "William Krönig, New Mexico Pioneer, from His Memories of 1849-1860," *New Mexico Historical Review,* 19:185-224, July, 1944; 19:271-311, October, 1944.

Keith, Adam: "KKK... Klose Kall in Kolorado," *Denver,* August, 1965, pp 24-27.

Kessler, F. C.: *The Royal Gorge of the Arkansas River in Colorado; Its History and Geology with Maps and Illustrations.* Canon City, Colorado, Canon City Daily Record, c1941. 32 pp.

[Kingsley, Rose Georgina]: *South by West; or, Winter in the Rocky Mountains and Spring in Mexico;* ed. by Rev. Charles Kingsley. London, W. Isbister and Company, 1874. 411 pp.

Lamar, Howard Roberts: *The Far Southwest 1846-1912, a Territorial History.* New Haven, Yale University Press, c1966. 560 pp.

Lavender, David: *The American Heritage History of the Great West.* New York, American Heritage Publishing Company, Inc., c1965. 416 pp.

Lavender, David: *Bent's Fort.* Garden City, New York, Doubleday and Company, c1954. 450 pp.

Lavender, David: "How to Salt a Gold Mine," *American Heritage,* 19:65-70, April, 1968.

LeCompte, Janet: "Gantt's Fort and Bent's Picket Post," *The Colorado Magazine,* 41:111-125, Spring 1964.

LeCompte, Janet: "The Hardscrabble Settlement, 1844-1848," *The Colorado Magazine,* 31:81-98, April, 1954.

Lee, Mabel Barbee: *Cripple Creek Days.* Garden City, New York, Doubleday and Company, Inc., c1958. 270 pp.

Little, W. T.: *Roundup.* Fremont Cattlemen's Association, [1966]. 36 pp.

Lloyd, Bob: "John R. McFall Recalls Experience as U. S. Treasury Department Agent," *Colorado Law,* May, 1956, p. 2.

McCandless, James A. vs. Sarah McCandless, Bill of Complaint, September 29, 1874. District Court, Fremont County.

McCandless, Julius: "Florence, a Tale of a Town," *Mountain Sunshine,* 2:37-39, June, July, August, 1900.

McConnell, Virginia: *Bayou Salado, the Story of South Park.* Denver, Sage Books, c1966. 275 pp.

McFall, J. R.: *A. B. (Ben) McFall, Pioneer Civil Engineer, Florence, Colorado.* Florence, Colorado, Privately printed, n.d. n.p.

McKernan, Justin, ed.: *Historical Review of St. Michael's Church, Canon City, Colorado, 1880-1945.* No imprint. n.p.

McMurtrie, Douglas C. and Albert H. Allen: *Early Printing in Colorado.* Denver, The A. B. Hirschfeld Press, c1935. 305 pp.

Miller, Victor W.: "The McCoy Gang," *Old West,* Summer 1970, pp. 22-25[+].

Nebraska History Magazine, 10:67-146, April-June, 1927. Entire issue devoted to the Rock Creek Ranch fight.

The Occasional Leaflet of the Colorado Library Association, 2:126, November, 1919.

Ophus, John: "The Lake County War, 1874-75," *The Colorado Magazine,* 47:119-135, Spring 1970.

Ormes, Robert M.: *Railroads and the Rockies; a Record of Lines In and Near Colorado.* Denver, Colorado, Sage Books, c1963. 406 pp.

Osborn, Henry Fairfield: *Cope: Master Naturalist.* Princeton, New Jersey, Princeton University Press, c1931. 740 pp.

Parsons, Eugene: *A Guidebook to Colorado.* Boston, Little, Brown, and Company, c1911. 390 pp.

Pictorial Tourist Review. Florence Chamber of Commerce, n.d. (Various annual editions.)

Plate, Robert: *The Dinosaur Hunters, Othniel C. Marsh and Edward D. Cope.* New York, David McKay Company, Inc., c1964. 281 pp.

Poole Brothers Mining Directory. Chicago, Poole Brothers, 1898. 926 pp.

Portrait and Biographical Record of the State of Colorado Containing Portraits and Biographies of Many Well-known Citizens of the Past and Present. Chicago, Chapman Publishing Company, 1899. 1492 pp.

Priest, Henry: "The Story of Dead Man's Canon and of the Espinosas, as Told by Henry Priest to Elsie Keeton," *The Colorado Magazine,* 8:34-38, January, 1931.

Rock, Robert L.: Mineral Survey of the Canon City, Colorado, Area. Canon City Chamber of Commerce, [1955?] 24 pp.

Rockafellow, B. F.: "Fremont County, Colorado," *Mountain Sunshine,* 2:34-37, June, July, August, 1900.

Rudd, Anson S.: "Early Days in Canon City, an Interview with Anson S. Rudd in 1884, [obtained by H. H. Bancroft]," *The Colorado Magazine,* 7:109-113, May, 1930.

Semi-centennial History of the State of Colorado. Chicago, The Lewis Publishing Company, 1913. 2 vols.

[Shores, Cyrus Wells]: *Memoirs of a Lawman,* ed. by Wilson Rockwell. Denver, Colorado, Sage Books, c1962. 378 pp.

Smith, J. Andrew: *Buckskin Joe.* Cañon City, Colorado, Master Printers, c1961. n.p.

Southern Colorado, Historical and Descriptive of Fremont and Custer Counties with Their Principal Towns, Cañon City and Other Towns, Fremont County, etc. Cañon City, Binckley and Hartwell, 1879. 136 pp.

Spencer, Elma Dill Russell: *Green Russell and Gold.* Austin, University of Texas Press, c1966. 239 pp.

Sterling, Janet: *Legends of the Royal Gorge Region.* Canon City, Colorado, The Canon City Daily Record, c1943. 59 pp.

Stiff, Cary: "The Do-It-Yourself Hanging Machine," *Empire Magazine,* The Denver Post, June 13, 1971, pp. 45, 47.

Stone, Wilbur Fisk, ed.: *History of Colorado.* Chicago, The S. J. Clarke Publishing Company, 1918. 4 vols.

Summering in Colorado. Denver, Colorado, Richards and Company, 1874. 158 pp.

[Sykes, C. P.]: *Petroleum in Colorado Territory.* New York, W. H. Arthur, 1865. 15 pp.

Tarbell, Ida: "An Unholy Alliance," *McClure's Magazine,* 20:398, February, 1903.

Taylor, Bayard: *Colorado: a Summer Trip.* New York, G. P. Putnam and Son, 1867. 185 pp.

Taylor, Donna: *Memories from the Foot of the Gorge.* Canon City, Colorado, Canon City High School Printing Classes, 1969. 111 pp.

Taylor, Jackson, Jr.: "Early Days at Wetmore and on the Hardscrabble," *The Colorado Magazine,* 8:115-117, May, 1931.

Taylor, Morris F.: "Capt. William Craig and the Vigil and St. Vrain Grant, 1855-1870," *The Colorado Magazine,* 45:301-321, Fall 1968.

Taylor, Morris F.: *First Mail West; Stagecoach Lines on the Santa Fe Trail.* Albuquerque, New Mexico, University of New Mexico Press, c1971. 253 pp.

Taylor, Morris F.: *Trinidad, Colorado Territory.* Trinidad, Colorado, Trinidad State Junior College, c1966. 214 pp.

Taylor, Ralph C.: *Colorado, South of the Border.* Denver, Colorado, Sage Books, c1963. 561 pp.

Tonge, Thomas: *All About Colorado.* Denver, Colorado, Thomas Tonge, c1913. 112 pp.

Ubbelohde, Carl: *A Colorado History.* Boulder, Colorado, Pruett Press, Inc., c1965. 339 pp.

Uchill, Ida Libert: *Pioneers, Peddlers, and Tsadikim.* Denver, Colorado, Sage Books, c1957. 327 pp.

The Welcome Mat. Canon City, Colorado, Master Printers, August 12, 1966. n.p.

Welcome to Fremont County— Where the Sun Spends Four Seasons. Canon City, The Daily Record, n.d. 37 pp.

Wilmot, Luther Perry: "A Pleasant Winter for Lew Wilmot," *The Colorado Magazine.* 47:1-15, Winter 1970.

"Wolfe Londoner," *The Trail,* 5:30-31, December, 1912.

Woodson, Hunter: *Canon City, Colorado.* No imprint. 24 pp.

UNPUBLISHED SOURCES

Altpeter, Marie Rogers: *Minnie Harding*

Briscoe, Judith A.: *Early Fremont County*

Cragin, F. W.: *Papers, Notebooks I-X.* Pioneers' Museum, Colorado Springs, Colorado.

Fremont County Grantees Book 1, January 1862-June 1880. Fremont County Courthouse, Canon City, Colorado.

McCandless, Carol: *Rock Creek Ranch Fight.*

Potter, Genevieve A. Carlin: *McCandless Family.* Manuscript in Penrose Public Library, Colorado Springs, Colorado.

The Royal Gorge Country: Presentation to National Park Service, November 9, 1940, Canon City, Colorado.

Shadford, Ada B. W.: *Miscellaneous Papers on Early Days in Penrose.*

Wilson, A. V.: *One Hundred Years of Fremont County History of Education.*

INTERVIEWS

Altpeter, Marie Rogers – Colorado Springs
Ashlock, Chick and Monie – Coaldale
Corley, Mrs. W. D. – Colorado Springs
Denek, Stella – Coaldale
Draper, J. Louis – Wetmore
Dunlap, Ella Stout – Howard
Frederickson, Mr. and Mrs. C. Arthur – Canon City
Goodwin, Mr. and Mrs. Denzel – Howard
Hamilton, Alex – Colorado Springs
Harding, Alice Campbell – Canon City
Hook, Evelyn Balman – Canon City and Hillside
Johnson, Mr. and Mrs. Reece – Swissvale
Lamb, Frank R. – Canon City
McCandless, Charles Grover – Florence
McCrory, Cora Stout – Cotopaxi
McFall, Mr. and Mrs. John R. – Florence
Malone, Katherine Howe – Colorado Springs
Mitchell, Clyde – Howard
Price, Mr. and Mrs. Charles E. – Florence
Riede, Mr. and Mrs. Fred E. – Canon City
Runyan, Dr. and Mrs. Harold C. – Colorado Springs
Westwater, Edgeworth – Florence
White, Elwood G. – Canon City
Willoughby, Roland – Howard
Witcher, John Stump – Canon City
Witcher, Minnie Stump – Canon City
Witcher, T. Lee – Canon City
Woodford, Elton B. – Canon City

NEWSPAPERS

Various issues of the following:
Canon City *Daily Record*
Canon City *Sun*
Cañon City *Times*
Colorado City *Iris*
Colorado Springs *Out West*
Denver *Republican*
Florence *Citizen*
Pueblo *Chieftain*
Pueblo *Star*
Pueblo *Star-Journal and Sunday Chieftain*

INDEX

Illustrations are indicated by boldface numbers.

Adamic family 111-112
Adams, Governor Alva 158
Adams, Rev. Mr. M. B. 44, 46
Adelaide (station) 81, 88
Alling, Ebenezer T. 130, 136, 138
Alvord and Company 30
American Lead and Zinc Smelting Company 138, 149
American Mining and Smelting Company 124
American Nauheim Baths 92
American Smelting and Refining Company 224
American Zinc Lead Company 146, 152, 157
Amick, Robert Wesley 170
Ammons, Governor Elias M. 110
Ansty, George C. 221-222
Anthony, James W. 185
Arkansas River 3-5, 8, 11, 19, 20, 22fn, 29, 32, 42, 62, 178, 180, 224
Arkansas Valley Electric Light and Power Company 80
Arkansas Valley Oil and Land Company 75
Arnold, Rev. Mr. G. 166, 167
Arnold, William J. 198-199
Ash, William 69
Autobees, Charles 8, 10, 18, 27-28, 37

Baca, Marcelino 16, 19, 27-28
Balman family 116-117, 120, 165, 208-209
Banks
  Bank of Florence 79, 83
  Canon City Bank 117
  Canon Savings Bank 162
  Citizens State Bank 162
  Colorado State Bank 167
  Exchange Bank 136
  First National Bank (Canon City) 142, 158
  Fremont County Bank 117, 135, 139, 162
  Mulock Brothers and Company 136
Banta, V. J. 197
Barclay, Alexander 11, 13, 14, 15, 16, 17, 18, 19
Barclay, Teresita (see Suaso, Maria Teresa Sandoval)
Bare Hills City 177, 178
Barker, William 184
Barnes City 209, 210

Bartlett, Dr. Frank L. 157
Beam Milling Company 86
Bear Gulch (community) 101-102, 103, 142
Beaubien, Charles 13-14, 27
Beaver Creek (Community) 36, 41, 57, 59, 60, 61, 119
Beaver Creek Land and Irrigation Company 61
Beaver Park (community) 61-62, 66
Beaver Park Land and Water Company 61, 62
Beckwith, Edwin F. 46, 198
Beckwith, Elton T. 46, 198-199
Bee-line Milling and Mining Company 192
Beecher, Henry N. 159
Bell, Dr. William A. 21, 127
Bell's Springs 5, 27
Bent, Charles 7, 13, 16, 27
Bent, William 7-8, 10, 20, 22fn, 28
Bent's Fort 10, 17 (see also Fort William)
Beral, Leandro 20
Bercaw, Albert F. 34
Bercaw, Robert 28
Bercaw, W. N. 32
Bernd-Cohen, Max 172
Best, Roy 173
Blackburn (community) 125, 127
Blossom Festival Art Exhibit 172
Blumeneau 47
Blunt, Joseph D. 202
Blunt, Roland 65, 98, 109, 202
Boettcher, Charles 65
Bolin, B. H. 29
Boone, Albert C. 16
Born, Harry E. 66
Boston Land and Cattle Company 78, 85, 91, 143, 218, 220
Bowen, Gabriel 29, 34, 38
Brewster, John K. 107
Brewster, W. R. 71
Brewster (town) 83, 107
Briggs, Calvin 11, 13, 18
Brookside 83, 107-108, 110
Bruce, William 21, 37
Brush Hollow Reservoir 62
Buckskin Joe (original town) 31, 59, 184
Buckskin Joe (reconstituted town) 184
Buffalo 3, 11, 12, 16, 20, 170
Burdette, Felix J. 37, 42
Burnett, Edson H. 90

235

242